The
SMALL PRESS
GUIDE
1999

*The complete guide to poetry &
small press magazines.*

- 4th Edition -

© Writers' Bookshop 1998
ISBN 0 9529119 8 1

First published by Writers' Bookshop
1-2 Wainman Road
Woodston Peterborough PE2 7BU

All rights reserved
Edited by Anne Sandys

Acknowledgements

Thanks to all who generously shared their information and ideas to make this book possible.

A note from the Publisher

This is the fourth edition of this small magazine guide, which we hope will help both magazine editors and writers wishing to submit work for publication.

The information used has been supplied by the magazine editors themselves.

The Small Press Guide is updated annually. If you feel we have omitted useful information or that the Guide could be developed further, we would like to hear from you.

Good Luck!

Introduction
Peter Finch

The first thing you notice about little magazines is their sheer variety. Everything from sonnets to poesie sonore and from romanticism to rebellion. The field is as wide as it can be. Anyone can take part. Thousands do.

The little magazine as a vehicle for self-expression, self-aggrandisement, self-congratulation, performance, perverseness, glory, wonder, delusion, magnificence, fun, fabulosity, fantasy and faith has been on the rise since the establishment of *The Germ* in 1850. Regarded by many as the first genuine little mag, this Pre-Raphaelite invention paid neither its editor nor its contributors. Five hundred copies were printed out of which forty were sold. It ran for four issues and then folded in a state of financial loss. As a model for small literary magazines it has been followed, to greater and lesser degrees, ever since.

> *let's start a magazine*
> *to hell with literature*
> *we want something red-blooded*
> *ee cummings*

Little magazines are so easy. Collect a few poems. Print them up and go. Estimates vary but by my calculations there are some five hundred or so little mags published in the British Isles. About half this number devote most of their pages to poetry. You'll find entries on the majority of them here. As institutions they change like the wind. Few last more than a dozen issues with most folding after far less. Their editors move house, give up, pass the project on. The names and addresses given here have all been checked when the directory was printed. I can't speak for the day after that.

Little magazines differ from their commercial counterparts in a number of significant ways. To begin with they lack the shiny slickness of the mass market journal. They do not have the advertisers. They need not conform to the standard, distributor-required shape. They don't have a large financial base. Commercial magazines come into being because entrepreneurs see a gap in the existing market and take steps to fill it. *Practical Boat Owner*, for example, started because people with boats as a hobby wanted something to read. The income from potential sales alone was enough to turn a profit. Literary magazines, on the other hand, start up because the writers need them, not because there are readers out there with time on their hands. This is art, not capitalism. The consumer is by no means king.

Little magazines are often at the cutting edge of literature. Unrestrained by taste, readership or potential advertisers, they are able to promote the unpromotable. They provide boltholes for the forgotten, the beginner, the neglected, the outsider, the specialist, the difficult, the hermetic, and the arcane. The unfashionable get published here as regularly as the new. There are no shareholders to please. Little magazines can do what they want.

Circulations are usually low. Run on shoestrings out of back bedrooms, lofts and basements, little mags often never print more than three hundred copies. Those with grants from their arts board or local authority manage a few more. Only the half a dozen or so national magazines have circulations into four figures. Sales are not achieved, as most of you will have noticed, from the shelves of local branches of WH Smith (who regard such poetic ephemera as unshiftable nuisances). They happen when individual buyers try their luck by post, through subscriptions (send £15 and get three issues annually, if you are lucky) or as a result of hand-to-hand pushing at poetry readings, writers' workshops and literary clubs. Selling is the toughest part. The contributors get free copies. Finding other individuals willing to buy copies for the genuine joy of reading their contents is a struggle.

At one time the well-heeled little mag could readily be told from the upstart by the look of the production. The hobbyists used hard-to-read, scruffy mimeo and set their poems on a typewriter. The grant recipient used professional typesetters and proper printing: letterpress, offset litho. But today with the advent of serious home word processors, desktop publishing packages and perfect plain paper photocopying it is much harder to spot the mag with resources. The new technology has a million advantages. Published poetry has no excuse anywhere for not looking good. At least half the poets in the business of publishing their work now own decent word processors and submit clear, crisply prepared manuscripts. It is the brave magazine that prints them looking less so.

British little magazines split into at least three main types. At the top of the pyramid comes the small group of magazines with some claim to providing a total overview of poetry in the UK. The best in the literary field appears here. These magazines are usually (but not always) in receipt of subsidy and run by teams rather than an individual editor. Circulations are in the low thousands. Copies are occasionally seen on the shelves of newsagents. Libraries hold them. This is serious territory. Probably the best known is the magazine of the London based Poetry Society *The Poetry Review*. This is a well-printed, spine-bound compilation of new verse, news, views and reviews. It was begun as long ago as 1909, has published everyone from Ezra Pound to Ted Hughes and sees itself as the centre of poetry in Britain. Others will disagree, no doubt. Fellow national magazines include the arty and often experimental *Ambit*, Michael Schmidt's solid Carcanet-produced *PN Review*, *Stand*, *The Rialto*, *Orbis*, *Outposts* and *Agenda* along with Forward Press's own high flyer *Poetry Now*. Other magazines may have aspirations - notably *Thumbscrew*, *Smiths Knoll*, *The North*, *Envoi* and *Acumen* - but few come into the circulation range of the leading batch.

After these UK nationals come the regional mags and the genre specialists. Regional magazines concentrate on work from specific parts of the British Isles and Ireland. Many of their names make this obvious. *Poetry Wales* is Welsh, *The Edinburgh Review* concentrates on Scotland, *Poetry Ireland* is the Irish national mag. The regional aspect of other magazines are often harder to discern. *HU* in earlier, less politically correct days was known as the *Honest Ulsterman*, *The Interpreter's House* is from Bedfordshire, *Northwords* looks in that direction, *Planet* is the Welsh internationalist, *Makinney* centres on Galloway, *Lines Review* and *Chapman* slug it out for the prize of being Scotland's best.

Genre specialists concentrate on the work of a specific form, type or style. *Haiku Quarterly* and *Blithe Spirit* specialise in haiku and other eastern forms, *Barfly* stays with the beat generation, *Psychopoetica* uses psychologically based material, *Fragmente*, *Angel Exhaust* and *First Offence* handle modernism and language-based texts. *Writing Women* sticks to that sex. *Modern Poetry in Translation* is just that.

Below these groupings are the places where risks are taken, ideas tried out and dogmas expounded. Small mags begun because the editor was interested in poetry, because a local writing group wanted an outlet, because it seemed a good idea at the time. Little magazines so varied in style, shape, size and content that the British library system fails to contain them all. Many live for an issue or two then fade. Their names can be wonderful. You want to subscribe just to get that title on the shelf. *A Doctor's Dilemma, Strange Faeces, Strength Before Bingo* and the much sought after *Bollocks To Uncle Jeffrey*, gone now, just yellow paper. But we do still have *Fatchance, Acid Angel, First Time* and *Smoke*. Plenty of idiosyncrasy there.

If you manage to appear in any of these magazines do not expect to get paid much. It is an illusion that money can be made from poetry. Maybe Roger McGough can make a bit when he writes for television and Ted Hughes when he sells his latest to a Sunday national. Here in the world of magazines most of the time the best you will get is a free copy of the magazine that carries your work. Occasionally generous editors offer a free subscription to contributors or even a small handful of copies but the small mag that pays has to be in receipt of subsidy. At the top end you may get £30 for a page, very occasionally more, but the real poetry is carried for what it is. You want to make cash? Sell double glazing.

Basic Submissions Rules

* Research your market. Do not submit your work to the first magazine name that takes your fancy. Have a look at it first. Send for a sample back copy. This will cost you a pound or so but it will not be that much. Study the market before you mail anything out. You can greatly increase your chances of acceptance by selecting magazines that will be sympathetic to your style. *Fragmente*, for example, will not be that keen on seeing your fundamentalist sonnets. On the other hand *Christian Poetry Review* will not want to view your agnostic concrete poems.

* Learn a bit about the shape of the contemporary poetry world. Read anthologies of new poetry. Read widely and look into areas that at first do not appeal to you. Visit your library and your local bookshop. Keep up to date.

* Word process, type or otherwise set your poems single-spaced, laid out exactly as you would like to see them printed. Hand written texts are ignored by most publishers. Use white A4 paper. Print on one side of the paper only. Include your name and address either at the beginning or the end. Give your poem a title, even if this is its first line, or title the work 'poem'. Staple multiple sheets together, top left.

* Keep a record of what you write, to where you submit it, when and the reaction you got. You may imagine you will be able to remember this kind of information. After a time, believe me, you will not.

* Enclose a stamped addressed envelope in sufficient size to carry your poems (if necessary) and the editor's reply back. Submissions without SAEs get binned.

* Expect to wait. Replies from some magazines come instantly. Others take weeks. It is not unusual to be kept waiting for a month or so. Longer than that write to enquire what is going on.

* Try to avoid submitting the same material to more than one magazine simultaneously. If the piece gets accepted by both you could be in embarrassing trouble.

There are enough magazines around of differing standards and different styles for everyone to get published. So long as you have a modicum of talent, persistence and an ability to follow both the rules and your nose you will get published. You may never become famous, nor rich, but you will get your name in print. The depression of constantly returning rejected poetry can be alleviated by always having some work out there being considered. Submit to groups of magazines rather than concentrating on a single one. Rejection does not necessarily mean that your work is bad. It could well be simply unsuited, submitted at the wrong time or sent to a magazine that is already full.

Short Fiction

More around than there used to be. More magazines testing the water and a positive boom in those using dark fiction - gothic fantasy, strange worlds. *Nasty Piece of Work, Kimota, Tales of the Grotesque & Arabesque, Saccade, The Third Alternative, Back Brain Recluse, Raw Nerve.* Don't expect payment here either. The rules are the same as for poetry.

There are so many writers around. Be inventive rather than imitative. Plot can beat style. Be new. Make sure you provide what the market requires. Read as much as you can.

Prose, of course, takes up much more space then poetry. It takes longer to read, costs more to send. Expect, perhaps, to wait a little longer for replies and don't inundate magazines with more than an example or two of your work each time. Expect a higher rejection rate. There are far fewer slots waiting to be filled. Expect to find it takes much longer if you choose to revise a piece following an editor's comments.

Prose fiction should be submitted double-spaced, single side on A4 sheets, stapled to left hand corner, clearly titled. Put your name and address on the final sheet. Show extent (ie 2500 words). Number pages (*1 of 8* being the best style).

And keep your eyes open. New magazines start all the time. Check the listings published in the back pages of most titles for news of new arrivals. Do it now.

100% BOY

The only UK club that appreciates Boy George. UK membership covers 4 newsletters. Each issue focuses on The Boy himself, ie the man behind the make-up, his words of wisdom, his thoughts and humour. The fanzine does not cover any of his careers specifically. Issues come out regularly and you'll receive each newsletter when full. So if you prefer to read a fanzine about George and only George, then 100% Boy is definitely for you. I welcome your submissions to print, handwritten contributions will be retyped.

Editor Name(s): Minnie
Address: 100% Boy, 42 Winter Grove, Parr, St Helens, Merseyside WA9 2JS
Mag Frequency: Membership covers 4 issues
Subscription: £4
Single Issue: £1 sample copy
Overseas: Europe £10 cash for 7 issues/RoW £10 cash for 5 issues
Payment in: Overseas please send registered post
Payable to: P Bayley
Inserts accepted: If relevant
Advertising Rates: Free
Circulation approx: Members only

10th MUSE

10th Muse publishes poetry instrumental in dissecting the 'unique' sound patterns of 'words', expanding these into 'a small number of phomenic components'. These reflect nothing of the objects for which they stand, they create a world of relations alien to the world of things. We reconfigure words in their aspect as 'preconscious force', an enablement that is both 'abstract' and 'representational'. 'Notoriously objective,' 10th Muse is made of paper, dried ink (black) and 2 staples. It has a cardboard cover.

Editor Name(s): Andrew Jordan
Address: 33 Hartington Road, Southampton, SO14 0EW
Mag Frequency: Yearly
Subscription: £5 for 2-issue sub/ £7.50 for 3-issue sub
Single Issue: £3
Back Issue: £1
Overseas: £5 or US$10 for 2 issues (cash)
Payment in: Cheque/Overseas cash only
Payable to: 10th Muse
Inserts accepted: Yes
Terms: Ask first
Circulation approx: 201
Payment terms to contributors: Free copy
Accept/rejection approx times: 1-3 months

AABYE (Formerly New Hope International)

A gathering of talented poets from around the globe; new and old together; traditionalists meet the avant-garde; haiku to long poems; translations; a collage of writing that consistently surprises. Submissions arriving without return postage are not considered.

Editor Name(s): Gerald England
Address: 20 Werneth Avenue, Gee Cross, Hyde, Cheshire SK14 5NL
Email: newhope@iname.com (no email submissions)
Mag Frequency: Irregular (2-3 per year)
Subscription: £10 for 3 issues
Single Issue: £3.75
Overseas: £5 singles/£13 for 3
Payment in: Overseas: cash or IRCs at exchange of (10 IRCs=£8); or International Giros (sterling). No foreign cheques.
Payable to: G England
Inserts accepted: No
Advertising Rates: No ads
Circulation approx: 600
Payment terms to contributors: Contributor's copy
Accept/rejection approx times: Usually quickly (2-3 weeks) but can be up to 3-4 months when busy.

ABRAXAS

Founded November 1991, Abraxas is an exciting quarterly magazine with a growing readership, incorporating The Colin Wilson Newsletter, bringing together poetry and fiction, philosophy and meaphysics. On the philosophy side, it has published essays by Colin Wilson on Jacques Derrida, Alfred North Whitehead and Edmund Husserl, while on the literary front it has featured translations of stories from Pablo Palacio, Jose de Cuadre and poems from DM Thomas and Zofia Ilinska. Articles have varied, from a penetrating study of criminal messiahs to an analysis of the angel craze sweeping America and probing, sceptical reflections on the UFO abductee syndrome. Furthermore there are book reviews, readers' comments and artwork. Abraxas includes a booklist of Colin Wilson titles, enabling readers to obtain personally-signed copies of his works.

Editor Name(s): Paul Newman/Pamela Smith-Rawnsley
Address: 57 Eastbourne Road, St Austell, Cornwall, PL25 4SU
Telephone: 01726-64975
Fax: As phone
Mag Frequency: Variably (intended quarterly)
Subscription: £12 UK/£15 Europe
Single Issue: £3 or £6
Back Issue: £3
Overseas: £15
Payment in: Sterling
Payable to: Paul Newman - ABX
Inserts accepted: Yes
Terms: If interesting or amusing
Advertising Rates: £50 full pg/£25 ½ pg
Circulation approx: Exclusive
Payment terms to contributors: Free copy of mag; booklets
Accept/rejection approx times: 8 weeks

ACE OF RODS

This is not a Gothic Horror Stories magazine but a contact magazine for those interested in paganism/wicca craft and is run as a non-profitmaking venture. Diary events are mentioned, advertising is free to subscribers but commercial ventures are advised to study the advertising rates. The magazine is run cheaply and therefore we cannot pay for contributions. The magazine aims to include extra features such as news, articles, reviews, letters (please specify if letter is for publication) where space permits. All material should be of interest to pagans and may include folklore, magic, nature, crafts, tradition as well as reviews of books, events and music. Illustrations may be seasonal, magical, mythological but in all cases enquiries should be accompanied by a stamp and manuscripts clearly marked with a return address and sufficient postage. Contributors are advised to see the magazine.

Address: Acca and Adda, BCM, Academia, London WC1N 3XX.
Website: http://www.corpex.com/users/akademia/ocreviw.htm
Mag Frequency: 8 times a year
Subscription: £7.50
Single Issue: £1 plus postage stamp
Payable to: Acca and Adda
Payment terms to contributors: N/A

ACID ANGEL

Acid Angel (previously Acid Rainbow Dada Dance) was launched in 1998 as a visionary, corrosive, ambrosial, pre-millennium feast to fill yr empty viscera with hallucinating stimulants that will peel open yr eyes as we sleepwalk and stumble into the 21st Century. Acid Angel is more than just a literary magazine. It is a caustic, vibrant celebration: a soul-centred hurricane that will blow the cobwebs out of your brain. Once tasted, it will be all you crave. More than diet cola. More than cocaine. For only five quid, it is the ultimate fix. Featuring only the best writers and artists, including Ivor Cutler, Edwin Morgan, Alasdair Gray, James Kelman, Alan Warner, Magi Gibson, Chris Kenny, Jay Ramsay, Yoshi Ooshi, Eve Lilith MacRae, Robert Mackenzie, Mario Petrucci, Rupert Loydell and a whole host of shining, sparkling others. Buy it and be happy.

Editor Name(s): Dee Rimbaud
Address: 35 Falkland Street (GFL), Glasgow G12 9QZ
Telephone: 0141-221-1223
Mobile: 040-333-2737
Email: acidangel@acidity.globalnet.co.uk
Mag Frequency: Whenever it's possible
Subscription: $20
Single Issue: £5
Overseas: Europe, add £1 per item; Overseas, add £2 per item
Payment in: Sterling only
Payable to: Dee Rimbaud
Inserts accepted: Yes
Terms: Large contributions to the magazine
Advertising Rates: By negotiation
Circulation approx: 500
Payment terms to contributors: 1 complimentary copy
Accept/rejection approx times: Anywhere between 1 week and 1 year depending on mood

ACUMEN

Acumen is a literary magazine with an emphasis on poetry. It seeks to please the intelligent reader with high-quality, well-written prose and poetry. In addition it has an extensive reviews section devoted mostly to poetry publications; and a recent innovation has been the issue of a free focus sheet and poster combined that provides a sampler of the poetry of an individual poet. Its overall aim is to emphasise the continuity of English poetry and literature into the present age.

Editor Name(s): Patricia Oxley
Address: 6 The Mount, Higher Furzeham, Brixham, Devon TQ5 8QY
Reviews to: Glen Pursglove, 25 St Albans Road, Brynmill, Swansea SA2 0BP
Email: pwoxley@aol.com.uk
Mag Frequency: 3 times per year
Subscription: £10
Single Issue: £4
Back Issue: Various
Overseas: $35-45
Payment in: Cheque/PO/IMO
Payable to: Acumen
Inserts accepted: Yes
Terms: £100 per 1000
Circulation approx: 750
Payment terms to contributors: Negotiable
Accept/rejection approx times: Rejections 2 weeks/Acceptances 3 months

ADVENTURE PROBE

Fanzine for players of computer adventure games (all machines) - specialize in older text adventures on 8-bit machines, but still cater for larger computers. Non-profitmaking no payment for contributions.

Address: 52 Burford Road, Liverpool L16 6AQ
Mag Frequency: Monthly
Subscription: £2 x copies(up to 12)
Single Issue: £2
Overseas: £2.50 Europe/£3 RoW(all airmail)
Payment in: Stamps for small amounts/Cheque/PO
Payable to: Adventure Probe
Inserts accepted: No
Circulation approx: 150
Payment terms to contributors: None

ADVERSE EFFECT

Magazine devoted to underground/experimental/electronic/avant-garde/psychedelic/ etc. Music and areas of similar interest. Coverage extends to features on film(s), book reviews, profiles on film-makers and authors, underground art and topics generally swept under the carpet of what's termed popular culture. Although music is the main focus, the underlying concern is towards anything eclectic, innovative, adventurous, exciting, challenging and demanding. With a salubrious approach that excels in taking no prisoners. Space sometimes also available for short stories of a similar, idiosyncratic nature.

Address: PO Box 63, Herne Bay, Kent CT6 6YU
Fax: 01227 369855
Email: N/A
Mag Frequency: Quarterly
Subscription: N/A (Yet)
Single Issue: £3.50
Payment in: Cheque/Cash/PO
Payable to: Fourth Dimension
Inserts accepted: No
Circulation approx: 1000+
Payment terms to contributors: Negotiated
Accept/rejection approx times: 21 days

THE AFFECTIONATE PUNCH

Now in its 4th year and part-funded by the National Lottery-A4E, The Affectionate Punch is a stylish compendium of new unpublished poetry and fiction from new and established writers. £10 is paid for the piece of work receiving the most accolades in a given issue. Well thought-out poetry and fiction by people who care is most welcome. We are an anorak-free zone. Poetry: 40 lines max. Fiction: up to 1200 words. Book reviews: 500 words. SAE essential with all submissions.

Editor Name(s): Andrew Tutty
Address: 35 Brundage Road, Manchester M22 0BY
Mag Frequency: Bi-annual (spring & autumn)
Subscription: £5
Single Issue: £2.50
Back Issue: £2
Overseas: £6 - sterling only
Payment in: Cheque/PO (sterling)
Payable to: The Affectionate Punch
Inserts accepted: Yes
Terms: By arrangement
Advertising Rates: £30 half page
Circulation approx: 300
Payment terms to contributors: Free copy (+£10 for vote winner)
Accept/rejection approx times: 1-4 months

AGENDA

My editorial criteria are personal - to print a poem I have to some degree to be moved by it. A great poem must remain a mystery. In every age it is a rare event. I look for poems that can be lived with over years rather than work of immediate impact. Agenda does not believe poetry should be affected by fashions. Lasting poems remain timeless - they do not date, unlike the ephemera - often the most popular in whatever era. Editing Agenda is for me rather like making a book which gradually takes shape throughout a lifetime. The magazine's growth is thus organic like a tree . . .

Editor Name(s): William Cookson/Asst Ed Anita Money
Address: 5 Cranbourne Court, Albert Bridge Road, London SW11 4PE
Telephone: 0171 2280700
Fax: 0171 2280700
Mag Frequency: Quarterly
Subscription: £24 (Individual)
Single Issue: Varies £5-£6
Back Issue: Varies but generally £5
Overseas: £26 Europe/£28 Overseas (for individuals)
Payment in: Cheque/Credit card
Payable to: Agenda
Inserts accepted: Yes
Terms: £80 per 1000
Advertising Rates: Varies: £250 full page
Circulation approx: 1,200
Payment terms to contributors: £15 p pg poetry/£10 p pg prose - but only when we can afford it
Accept/rejection approx times: 3 months

AH POOK IS HERE

Poetry/fiction/the usual . . . Pook is on hold for the moment, pending a few wins on the horses, so please no contributions/payments/etc. Come the millennium there may be more issues!

Editor Name(s): Jon Summers
Address: 158 Waltwood Park Drive, Llanmartin, Newport, Gwent, NP6 2HG
Mag Frequency: Irregularly
Subscription: N/A
Single Issue: Free
Inserts accepted: Yes
Circulation approx: 500+
Payment terms to contributors: None
Accept/rejection approx times: 1 month

AIREINGS

Poetry magazine - 40 pages. Begun in 1980. Run by a group of women. We lean towards women's work, but welcome work by men too. Twice yearly. Joint editors Jean Barker & Linda Marshall. We are rooted in Yorkshire but welcome and publish work from all over the world.

Editor Name(s): Jean Barker/Linda Marshall
Address: 24 Brudenell Road, Leeds, W Yorks LS6 1BD
Mag Frequency: Twice yearly
Subscription: £5.50
Single Issue: £2.50
Overseas: £7.50
Payment in: In sterling or the equivalent of £15 to cover bank charges
Payable to: Aireings Publication
Inserts accepted: No
Circulation approx: 300
Payment terms to contributors: 2 free copies
Accept/rejection approx times: Editorials in January/July - work returned after if not accepted

ALBEDO ONE

Albedo One is Ireland's only regular fiction magazine specialising in SF, horror and fantasy. It started life as an A5 digest sized magazine and changed to A4 in 1996. Published regularly since 1993, it has featured stories from Brian Stableford, Anne McCaffrey, Ian McDonald, Gill Alderman and the ubiquitous DF Lewis. Coming up will be stories by Norman Spinrad and Jeff Vandermeer as well as instantly recognisable small press names and new writers. Each issue carries an author interview, extensive book reviews, a comment piece (usually about 2000 words) and readers' letters. We are always looking for thoughtful, well written fiction. Our definition of what constitutes SF, horror and fantasy is extremely broad and we love to see material which pushes at the boundaries. We are also looking for interviews with high profile authors and book reviews. Our comment section is open to anyone who feels they have something to say (we don't need to agree with what they say but we do have to agree that it's worth saying) and the more keenly felt the emotion the better the chances are of publication. To get a real feel for what we are about, other than buying a copy of the magazine, you could visit our website at www.iol.ie/-bobn. It features a selection of stories from past issues plus interviews, book reviews and other wonderful stuff.

Address: Albedo One, 2 Post Road, Lusk, Co Dublin
Reviews to: Robert Neilson, 8 Commons Road, Loughlinstown Co Dublin
Email: bobn@iol.ie (BOBN) bhry@iol.ie (BHRY)
Website: www.iol.ie/-bobn
Mag Frequency: 3 times per year (4 monthly)
Subscription: £10 per 4 issues
Single Issue: £2.50
Back Issue: Cover price
Overseas: £16/$24 Europe; £20/$30 RoW (all airmail)
Payable to: Albedo One
Inserts accepted: No
Circulation approx: 400
Payment terms to contributors: Comp copy/best story in issue £25 prize
Accept/rejection approx times: 4-6 weeks

AMBIT

Ambit publishes a wide range of experimental new poetry, short fiction, fine art and illustration, plus a vigorous and stimulating reviews section. Established writers appear alongside up-and-coming new talent and hitherto unpublished writers. Ambit, now funded by the Arts Council of England, was started in 1959 and has been published quarterly without interruption since. Meticulously edited by Martin Bax, Carol Ann Duffy, Henry Graham, J G Ballard, Geoff Nicholson and Mike Forman; you can expect a consistently exciting and important selection of work in every issue.

Address: 17 Priory Gardens, London, N6 5QY
Mag Frequency: Quarterly
Subscription: UK £22 (institution £33)
Single Issue: £6 (institution £9)
Overseas £8/$16 (institution £11/$22)
Back Issue: £10 (institution £12)
Overseas £12/$24 (institution £14/$28)
Overseas: £24/$48 (institutuion £35/$70)
Payment in: Cheque/PO/Visa/Mastercard/American Express
Payable to: Ambit
Inserts accepted: Yes
Terms: £170 per 1000
Circulation approx: 3,000
Payment terms to contributors: £5.00 per printed page
Accept/rejection approx times: 3 - 4 months

AMERICAN MARKETS NEWSLETTER

Highlights American and international markets accepting articles and stories from writers. Gives press tips, book reviews, writers' tips, guidelines of the month, and readers' letters. Free syndication of articles is offered to all subscribers.

Editor Name(s): Sheila O'Connor
Address: 175 Westland Drive, Glasgow, Scotland G14 9JQ
Telephone: 415 753 6057 (USA)
Fax: 415 753 6057 (USA)
Email: sheila.oconnor@juno.com
Mag Frequency: 10/year
Subscription: £29
Single Issue: £2.95
Overseas: £37
Payment in: £ sterling
Payable to: S O'Connor
Inserts accepted: Yes
Terms: £25 per issue
Advertising Rates: 25p per word
Payment terms to contributors: 3 months sub extension
Accept/rejection approx times: 2 months

AMMONITE

Ammonite has become known for publishing the unexpected, the surprising, the unusual. Contributors stretch their imaginative boundaries when writing for Ammonite. A wealth of new writing imagination beyond the straight rules of the speculative genre. Ammonite brings new dimensions to the thinking of all those who seek the challenge of ideas and images that stir the human mind and spirit to part the veil of mundane, accepted views of reality. Ammonite is presented in A5 format with 36 pages of poetry, fiction and ideas within a decorative art card cover.

Address: Ammonite Publications, 12 Priory Mead, Bruton, Somerset, BA10 0DZ
Mag Frequency: Occasional
Subscription: £5
Single Issue: £3
Back Issue: £2.50
Overseas: £8
Payment in: Cheque/IMO/PO/ Discount of 20% of total order value if 5 or more copies ordered
Payable to: Ammonite Publications
Inserts accepted: No
Circulation approx: 200
Payment terms to contributors: 1 free copy
Accept/rejection approx times: 8 weeks

ANARCHIST ANGEL

Anarchist Angel aims to promote the voice of young poetry. In so doing we encourage young poets (under 25 yrs) to read comtemporary poetry of different styles and influences. Our magazine also includes information on poetry competitions, poetry readings, general news and information of interest to young writers. We have interviewed established and experienced poets (eg Mathew Sweeney & Gerda Mayer) who have given valuable advice to our readers. The magazine also reviews new books and other publications that are of interest to young writers. Our readership includes the UK, Europe and the USA. We welcome contributors and subscriptions from all young poets and, in many cases, offer advice and information.

Address: Ms E Berry, 5 Aylesford Close, Sedgley, West Midlands DY3 3QB
Mag Frequency: Quarterly
Subscription: £6
Single Issue: £1.50
Back Issue: £1.50/£1
Overseas: £10
Payment in: IMO or sterling only
Payable to: Angel Press
Inserts accepted: Yes
Circulation approx: 300
Payment terms to contributors: No payment to contributors
Accept/rejection approx times: 2-6 weeks

ANCHORS AWEIGH

Anchors Aweigh is an informative chatty and friendly newsletter aimed at poets who enjoy simple accessible poetry. Packed with news and views on the poetry world, Anchors Aweigh offers poets the chance to communicate with each other. Sections include: * Worm's Eye View * Readers' News & Reviews * Mini workshop * Rebecca Reports * Booklet Reviews * Competition News * Articles * Poets' Contact Section.

Editor Name(s): Heather Killingray
Address: 1-2 Wainman Road, Woodston, Peterborough, Cambs, PE2 7BU
Telephone: 01733 230746
Fax: 01733 230751
Email: pete@forwardpress.co.uk
Website: www.forwardpress.co.uk
Mag Frequency: Quarterly
Subscription: £6
Single Issue: £1.75
Overseas: £6
Payment in: Visa/Cheque/PO
Payable to: Forward Press
Inserts accepted: Yes
Terms: Free
Circulation approx: 1800
Payment terms to contributors: Letters £2, Compass Points £5, Articles £10, Worms Eye View £5, Book Reviews £5
Accept/rejection approx times: 6-8 weeks

ANGEL EXHAUST

The space, normally 128 pages, is divided equally between poetry and documentation on poetry. We are interested in the realm where formally innovative work overlaps with socially radical ideas, also in Gothic and New Age poetry. We do not publish work comfily snuggled inside the behavioural rules established before 1970. Ideal poets for this magazine would be Allen Fisher, Denise Riley, Maggie O'Sullivan, and JH Prynne. The prose arm aims at making visible the achievements of the British Poetry Revival as the history of the present, via interviews, survey articles, and in-depth reviews of new books. Special issues have been on the schools of Cambridge poetry, and London; an anthology of new poets; art and politics; the history of Cambridge poetry; and Socialist, Northern poetry. Special interests include Scottish informationism, socialist poets of South Wales, Gothic poetry of the Seventies, the Left, the critique of subjectivity, navigating in new information landscapes, the milieu of the text and peripheral or minority traditions, neoprimitivism, sociobiology, the periodization of the past 30 years of style history, and the nincompoop school of poetry. An elite team of reviewers is dedicated to the unswathing of brilliance, the massacre of the insignificant, and the incomprehension of the incomprehensible.

Editor Name(s):
Address: 27 Sturton Street, Cambridge, CB1 2 QG, Cambs
Mag Frequency: Twice yearly
Subscription: £7
Single Issue: £4
Back Issue: Two for £7, one for £4
Overseas: £9 for a year
Payable to: Angel Exhaust
Inserts accepted: Yes
Circulation approx: 300
Payment terms to contributors: In offprints
Accept/rejection approx times: 1 week

ANSIBLE

Informal newsletter edited by David Langford, covering doings in the science fiction community, primarily in Britain. The first series ran from 1979 to 1987; the current incarnation (2pp A4 each issue) has appeared since 1991. Ansible received Hugo awards - the international SF 'Oscars' - in 1987, 1995 and 1996. Coverage includes events, meetings, gossip, award results, authors' and publishers' misbehaviour, humourous items of related interest (e.g. examples of grotesquely bad writing from current SF/fantasy), and whatever else suits the editor's whim. Many noted SF authors have contributed. Ansible may be examined on the web at http://www.dcs.gla.ac.uk/SF-Archives/Ansible (there is no charge).

Address: 94 London Road, Reading, Berks RGI 5AU.
Subs to: SAEs to above address
Fax: 0118 966 9914
Email: ansible@cix.co.uk
Website: http://www.dcs.gla.ac.uk/SF-Archives/Ansible
Mag Frequency: Monthly
Subscription: Free
Single Issue: Send SAE
Back Issue: N/A (available on World Wide Web)
Overseas: US & Australian details on request
Inserts accepted: Flyers for non-commercial, non-profit SF events etc only - by arrangement
Circulation approx: 2100 + unknown on web
Payment terms to contributors: Free copies and drinks only
Accept/rejection approx times: 1 month

ANTHEM

All poetry is considered on its own merits although a general theme of individuality and searching for one's inner flame runs through most issues. However, so long as our editors and issue/submitting readers consider a poem has integrity - even on religious themes - poems are accepted.

Address: 36 Cyril Avenue, Bobbers Mill, Nottingham NG8 5BA
Mag Frequency: 2 a year
Subscription: £2 per year
Single Issue: £1.25
Back Issue: Not available
Overseas: £1.60 per issue £3 per annum
Payment in: Cheque/PO
Payable to: C Hufton
Inserts accepted: No
Circulation approx: 500-600
Payment terms to contributors: No payment is made except on issues featuring one poet
Accept/rejection approx times: 4-6 weeks

APOSTROPHE

Apostrophe is a bi-annual publication of poetry, both modern and in translation. The editorial policy is to encompass the whole spectrum of human emotions and aspirations, not forgetting the importance of wit and humour. New poets are encouraged and there is always a balance between unknown and experienced contributors. There is an international readership. The editor welcomes well-crafted poetry on any topic and in any style. Shorter, rather than longer, poems are preferred, as the editor feels that the A5 format and number of pages (32-36) do not lend themselves to lengthy poems. In each issue a small number of poems are illustrated by Apostrophe's resident artist, John West. Apostrophe has a dearth of subscribers but a wealth of would-be contributors, many of whom can be found in the Poetry Library of the South Bank Centre, London, preferring to read, rather than buy Apostrophe. There are also occasional reviews of poetry collections and anthologies.

Editor Name(s):
Address: The Editor, Mr Pillows Press, 41 Canute Road, Faversham, Kent ME13 8SH
Mag Frequency: Twice yearly, March/September
Subscription: £5.50
Single Issue: £2.50 + 25p postage
Back Issue: £1.50 inc postage
Overseas: IRCs x14 or £6.50
Payment in: Overseas IMO/IRC
Payable to: Mr Pillows Press
Inserts accepted: Yes
Terms: £5 per 100
Circulation approx: 100 and rising
Payment terms to contributors: Complimentary copy
Accept/rejection approx times: 4-6 weeks Editor's office closed for submissions during August and 14th December - 1st January

A

AQUARIUS

A serious poetry magazine bought by individuals and institutions world wide. Has featured work from George Barker to Fay Weldon. This magazine is one of the essential outlets for poetry. The editor likes writers who have bought and studied the style and form of the work published in the magazine.

Address: Aquarius, Flat 10, Room A, 116 Sutherland Avenue, Maida Vale, London W9
Mag Frequency: Yearly
Single Issue: £5 plus post 70p
Overseas: $17
Payable to: Aquarius
Inserts accepted: Yes
Terms: £50
Circulation approx: 2,000
Payment terms to contributors: By agreement

THE ARCADIAN

The Arcadian was founded in 1991, and includes editorial, reviews, news, readers letters as well as poems and essays. A regular feature is a chronological history of the Poets Laureate, with a different incumbent highlighted in each issue. The editor has a blind spot concerning haiku, but otherwise all forms are considered. However most of the poems accepted tend to come out of a traditional/mainstream background. Poets published in previous issues include Sophie Hannah, William Oxley, Geoff Stevens and John Ward amongst many others, although submissions from new or unknown writers are particularly welcomed. No preference is given to subscribers, although it is strongly recommended that would-be contributors study the magazine before submission.

Editor Name(s): Mike Boland
Address: 11 Boxtree Lane, Harrow Weald, Middlesex HA3 6JU
Mag Frequency: Bi-annual
Subscription: £4 pa
Single Issue: £2
Overseas: £5 pa
Payment in: IMO/PO/Cheque in sterling
Payable to: Mike Boland
Inserts accepted: Yes
Terms: £2 per 100
Circulation approx: Growing
Payment terms to contributors: 2 copies of magazine
Accept/rejection approx times: Hopefully within 3 weeks

AREOPAGUS MAGAZINE

Areopagus is an A4-sized 32-page special interest magazine, aimed mainly at Christian writers. Established in 1990, it covers market news and writing events, and focuses on issues which will be of interest to writers of all backgrounds. Published material is sourced exclusively from subscribers, and there is also a subscribers-only competition in each issue, with a £10 prize. Areopagus also publish an annual Guide to (UK) Christian Organisations (price £3 from same address).

Editor Name(s): Julian Barriitt
Address: 101 Maytree Close, Budger Farm, Winchester, Hants SO22 4JF
Reviews to: 5 Foxglove Close, Dunkeswell, Honiton, Devon EX14 0QE
Email: jbarritt@hantslife.co.uk
Mag Frequency: Quarterly
Subscription: £10 (£8 unwaged)
Back Issue: £1
Overseas: £12.50 Europe/£15 RoW
Payment in: Cheque/PO - sterling
Payable to: Areopagus Publications
Inserts accepted: Rarely
Advertising Rates: 10p per word; £4 per ½ page A4
Circulation approx: 119
Payment terms to contributors: From £2 - £5 for items
Accept/rejection approx times: 2 weeks

THE ARGOTIST

. . . a deeply dilettante review. 'In the best tradition of the independent magazine' Michael Schmidt, Carcanet Press. 'Down to earth, sincere and in your face - I dig it' Benjamin Zephania. The Argotist provides a platform for interaction between popular and academic writing in the arts. Each issue is loosely focused on a particular theme (issue one: performance poetry/issue two: cartoons and cartoonists) and is supported by a guest-edited 'poetry portfolio'. The magazine has featured exclusive interviews with top artists (from Joseph Brodsky to John Cooper Clarke). Articles are normally commissioned, though examples from new writers are welcome.

Editor Name(s): Nick Watson
Address: The Argotist, PO Box 278, Liverpool Central, Liverpool L69 6DU
Email: radged@liv.ac.uk
Website: www.cyberramp.net/~mdbutler/argotist
Mag Frequency: Irregular - 1-2 issues a year
Subscription: £2 per issue
Single Issue: £2
Back Issue: £1.50 (issues 1&2)
Overseas: £3 per issue(Europe)/£4 per issue(ROW)
Payment in: UK drawn cheques
Payable to: The Argotist
Inserts accepted: Yes
Terms: £50 per 500
Advertising Rates: £120 full page
Circulation approx: 2000
Payment terms to contributors: Complimentary copies
Accept/rejection approx times: 2 months max

ASWELLAS

Aswellas, now in its sixth year, aims to give new writers (poetry and prose) a voice alongside the more well known - particularly writers who have an oblique and quirky view of life. From Issue Four we also feature drawings and B/W photographs.

Address: John Steer, 69 Orchard Croft, Harlow, Essex CM20 3BG
Mag Frequency: Yearly
Subscription: £3 per copy
Single Issue: Same
Back Issue: £1.50
Overseas: £4 - £2 Back Issue
Payment in: Sterling cheque
Payable to: West Essex Literary Society
Inserts accepted: No
Circulation approx: Growing all the time
Payment terms to contributors: Free copy of magazine
Accept/rejection approx times: Approx 3 - 4 weeks. Greater favour shown to those who subscribe

AUALLAUNIUS

The journal is that of the society which offers the life and writing of Arthur Machen, the 1890s (mystery and imagination genre). Our president: Barry Humphries; Patron: Julian Lloyd Webber

Address: Rita Tait, 19 Cross Street, Caerlean, Gwent NP6 1AF
Mag Frequency: 2 a year
Subscription: £15
Single Issue: £3.50
Back Issue: £4
Overseas: £18
Payable to: The Arthur Machen Society
Inserts accepted: No
Circulation approx: 300
Payment terms to contributors: None
Accept/rejection approx times: N/A

AUTO QUEUE

It is proposed to initiate a magazine of biography and poetry, with biographical details of establishment poets (past & present) and small press poets, along with poems by the small press poets featured, and poems about poets. The name may be changed from that listed above. Write with SAE for details. First issue scheduled for 1999.

Editor Name(s): Geoff Stevens
Address: 25 Griffiths Road, West Bromwich B71 2EH
Mag Frequency: Not decided
Subscription: Not decided

AVON LITERARY INTELLIGENCER

Poetry, fiction, criticism, news. ALI is a sweet smelling yellow-eyed alley cat quarterly literary jumped up newsletter. There is a sample on the Web: www2.bath.ac.uk/~masdr/ali.html

Address: 20 Byron Place, Clifton, Bristol BS8 1JT
Email: dsr@maths.bath.ac.uk
Website: www2.bath.ac.uk/~masdr/ali.html
Mag Frequency: Quarterly
Subscription: £4 yearly
Single Issue: £1
Back Issue: £2
Overseas: $10 bills/one year
Payable to: Avon Literary Intelligencer
Inserts accepted: Yes
Terms: £10
Circulation approx: 200
Payment terms to contributors: 1 copy
Accept/rejection approx times: 6 weeks

AXIOM

Axiom requires quality material on fiction, sci-fi, fantasy, horror, poetry, thoughts - nothing too sentimental. Contributors must enclose an SAE and a covering letter with work.

Address: Michelle Oliver, 60 Greenfarm Road, Ely, Cardiff, CF5 4RH
Subs to: TBA
Subscription: TBA
Single Issue: £1.25
Payment terms to contributors: £10 prize for best published work

BACK BRAIN RECLUSE (BBR)

BBR publishes some of the most startling and daring SF currently being written, and has developed a cult following around the world through a policy of emphasising the experimental and uncommercial end of the form. Recent contributors have included Richard Kadrey, Paul Di Filippo, Michael Moorcock, Misha, Don Webb and Mark Rich, as well as many exciting new names making their first professional appearance. 'If you think you know what science fiction looks like, think again' - Covert Culture Sourcebook.

Address: BBR, PO Box 625, Sheffield S1 3GY
Email: bbr@bbr-online.com
Website: www.bbr-online.com
Mag Frequency: Annual
Single Issue: UK £4
Payment in: Ireland/USA/Australia enquire with SAE for local agents
Payable to: Chris Reed
Inserts accepted: No
Circulation approx: 3000
Payment terms to contributors: £10 ($15) per 1000 words, on publication
Accept/rejection approx times: 1 month

B
BAD POETRY QUARTERLY

Bad Poetry Quarterly is a weekly poetry magazine with an open door publishing policy. Submissions are invited from anywhere in the known universe and beyond provided suitable means of replying are supplied (eg SAE, IRCs). Payment to contributors is one complimentary copy. Subscriptions are even more welcome provided payment is made in sterling, cheque or PO. Poems can be in any language as long as it is English. We look forward to hearing from everyone. Earthlings are especially welcome as they are currently under-represented among our subscribers/contributors.

Editor Name(s): Gordon Smith
Address: Bad Poetry Quarterly, PO Box 639, London E11 2EP
Mag Frequency: Weekly
Subscription: 99p + 1st class stamp
Single Issue: 99p + 1st class stamp
Overseas: 99p + 50p p&p (sterling only)
Payment in: Sterling - Cheque/PO
Payable to: G Smith
Inserts accepted: Yes
Terms: Swap
Advertising Rates: Full page £80 and pro rata
Circulation approx: 500
Payment terms to contributors: Complimentary copy
Accept/rejection approx times: 4 weeks

BALDIE

Baldie is a zine that covers all/any styles of music with a strong bias towards underground/independent releases. We also like to include short pieces of fiction, especially sci-fi orientated, cyberpunk or anything of a weird and bizarre nature. Length between 500 - 2,000 words.

Address: 605 Portswood Road, Portswood, Southampton SO17 3SL
Mag Frequency: Every 2 months
Subscription: Free with SAEs
Single Issue: Free with SAE
Back Issue: None available
Overseas: Free for cost of postage
Payment in: N/A
Inserts accepted: No
Circulation approx: 300-500
Payment terms to contributors: None - copy of relevant zine
Accept/rejection approx times: 2 months or less

B

BEAT SCENE

Beat Scene is a magazine about America's Beat Generation. We include news, features, interviews, profiles by and about such writers as Jack Kerouac, William Burroughs, Charles Bukowski, Allen Ginsberg, Gary Snyder, Lawrence Ferlinghetti, Hunter S Thompson and many others. We publish in a standard A4 format in a three colour photo glossy cover. We consider it a news magazine. Our latest issue has 68 pages. We are now up to issue no 32.

Address: Kevin Ring, 27 Court Leet, Binley Woods, Nr Coventry CV3 2JQ
Subs to: £16 for 5 issues
Mag Frequency: Quarterly
Subscription: £16 for 5 issues
Single Issue: £3.85
Overseas: $35 payable to Mr D Hsu, PO Box 105, Cabin John, Maryland 20818, USA
Payable to: M Ring
Inserts accepted: No
Payment terms to contributors: Negotiable/to 'You must be joking'
Accept/rejection approx times: 1 Week

BEDSPRINGS UNITE

One of the few fanzines to have lasted longer than the music papers' identity crises, Bedsprings still manages to talk about spanking while deliciously challenging all traditional conventions of music press. This includes interviewing diverse, groovy bands like Lambchop, Date of Birth, Frente and Ben Folds Five while reviewing records by the gullet-load, and representing underground music via the soon-to-be-set-up record label Play Muzak and signing star band George. Revolution is the name of the game with Bedsprings Top 50 Wankers cards free with every issue, and culture ALWAYS gets a look in with poetry, film, book and gig reviews . . . 50 pages of wit, wisdom, sarcasm and ventage of spleen plus a therapeutic 2-colour card cover . . . Ooh Monsieur.

Address: c/o Sara Wingate-Gray, Norfolk Terrace, University of East Anglia, Norwich NR4 7TJ (term time) otherwise
1 Southside, Shadforth, Durham DH6 1LL
Email: s.wingate-gray@vea.ac.uk or sara@shindig.demon.co.uk
Mag Frequency: Quarterly (when not absconding to Hong Kong for 6 months)
Subscription: £8.50 inc p&p for a year's supply
Single Issue: £1.50
Back Issue: Limited available
Overseas: Circa £10 dep on postage price. $accepted
Payment in: Cash OK if well-hidden/ Cheque/PO better.
Payable to: S W Gray
Inserts accepted: Yes
Circulation approx: 200
Payment terms to contributors: Free copy of relevant issue (generally)
Accept/rejection approx times: Oct/Feb/May/August

B
BLACK CAT BOOKS

Black Cat Books publishes magazines and anthologies of tales of the unexpected/ mystery/horror/crime. We need authors of short tales of up to 4000 words, any type of tales accepted - send £5.75 for our authors' package, with this you receive a free copy of one of our books plus information on being published with us. We started in 1995 and have published 78 authors so far. Our latest anthology is the 9th edition! Upcoming title Hands of Fear needs more tales. You must send SAE with all correspondence for a reply. We will help all authors who help us by buying a book! As Vincent Price said 'I need my pound of flesh!'

Editor Name(s): Neil Miller
Address: Mount Cottage, Grange Road, St. Michaels, Tenterden, Kent TN30 6EE
Mag Frequency: 2 a year
Single Issue: £3 25
Overseas: $6
Payment in: UK Cheque/Cash
Payable to: Millers Publications
Inserts accepted: No
Circulation approx: 3000+
Payment terms to contributors: Free copy + £50-£20 for our novel
Accept/rejection approx times: 6 weeks

BLACK ZINE

This irregular origami publication is truly interactive. Its 'create to destroy to create' ethos makes it one of the most ingenious and unusual poetry zines currently on offer. Formed into a varity of weird and wonderful creations, the Black Zine has to be seen to be believed. The individual style and design of the zine reflects the distictive poetry contained within. All submissions are considered although, obviously, the shorter the better. Contributors should write with a covering letter and an sae.

Address: Denude Studio (Black Zine), PO Box 72, Manchester, M14 5SD.
Mag Frequency: Irregular
Subscription: N/A
Single Issue: £1 + sae (A5)
Back Issue: £1 + sae (A5)
Payment in: Secured sterling/cheque/PO
Payable to: M. McNamara
Inserts accepted: Yes
Terms: Free
Circulation approx: Not known
Payment terms to contributors: 1 issue
Accept/rejection approx times: Immediate response with sae

BLADE

Poetry and reviews of clarity and incisive nature. Occasional free supplement with news and extra reviews. Editorial-based, each issue attacks and explores different facets of the UK poetry scene. 56 average pages. New and well-known names. No-one sensitive to strong criticism should submit work. A 'boring' stamp policy is in operation. 'One of Britain's gutsiest poetry magazines' - Neil Astley. 'I both admire and am provoked by its ebullience' - G Allnutt, Poetry Review.

Address: 'Maynrys', Glen Chass, Port St Mary, Isle of Man IM9 5PN
Mag Frequency: Twice yearly
Subscription: £10 annual
Single Issue: £5
Back Issue: £3
Overseas: £15 Sterling
Payment in: Cash or IMO to Blade Press
Payable to: Blade Press
Inserts accepted: Yes
Terms: Swop
Circulation approx: 170-200
Payment terms to contributors: 1 x copy
Accept/rejection approx times: 6 - 8 weeks

BLITHE SPIRIT - Journal of the British Haiku Society

Journal containing original haiku, senryn, tanka, renga in English, with learned articles in this field. Published by The British Haiku Society, it accepts only haiku and haiku-related material from members of the society. We welcome diverse statements about the writing and appreciation of haiku as well as poetry, on the understanding that none of the work submitted is under consideration elsewhere. Please provide publication details of any item submitted which has already appeared in print.

Editor Name(s): Caroline Gourlay
Address: Caroline Gourlay, Hill House Farm, Knighton, Powys LK7 1NA
Subs to: Colin Blundell, Longholm, East Bank, Wingland, Nr Sutton Bridge, Lincs PE12 9YS
Telephone: 01547 528 542
Mag Frequency: Quarterly
Subscription: £15 pa Society membership/£12 magazine only
Single Issue: £3
Back Issue: Some years £2.50
Overseas: £20 (US$32) Society membership/£16(US425) magazine only
Payment in: Sterling/US bills
Payable to: The British Haiku Society
Inserts accepted: No
Advertising Rates: No ads
Circulation approx: 400
Payment terms to contributors: None
Accept/rejection approx times: 1 month

B

THE BLOODY QUILL

The Bloody Quill is a bi-annual magazine of international vampire and gothic horror, publishing exciting new work by writers from Britain, North America and Australia. TBQ regularly receives excellent reviews and they are getting better with each issue. As well, we offer one of the best subscription rates around. TBQ is looking for poetry and fiction that takes the vampire genre into new territory; offers fresh ideas on an old theme. SF work is of special interest. Each issue contains reviews of current Horror/SF publications and editors/writers are urged to send in their magazines and chapbooks. Contributors are asked to view a copy of The Bloody Quill before submitting their work. SAE/IRCs are mandatory.

Editor Name(s): J & E L Rogerson
Address: The Bloody Quill, Silver Gull Publishing, West Lodge, Higher Lane, Liverpool L9 7AB
Mag Frequency: Twice yearly
Subscription: £2 for two
Single Issue: £1
Overseas: 3 IRCs or 6IRCs for two
Payment in: Cheque/PO/IMO/IRC
Payable to: J Rogerson
Inserts accepted: Yes
Terms: By trade
Circulation approx: 50 - 100
Payment terms to contributors: Copy
Accept/rejection approx times: Up to 2 months

BOGG

Uses contemporary poetry, short prose, articles, reviews, letters, graphics. It is actually an American publication. George Cairncross is purely the British editor.

Address: John Elsberg, 422 N Cleveland Street, Arlington VA 22201 USA/George Cairncross 31 Belle Vue Street, Filey, N Yorks YO14 9HU
Mag Frequency: Irregular
Subscription: £6
Single Issue: £2.50
Overseas: £8
Payment in: Cheque or Postal Order
Payable to: George Cairncross
Inserts accepted: No
Circulation approx: 700
Payment terms to contributors: Two free copies of mag
Accept/rejection approx times: As soon as possible

BORDERLINES

Magazine published by Anglo-Welsh Poetry Society, a group founded to promote poetry in the Marches / Welsh border area. Open to contributions from anyone. No axe to grind. The editors say 'We try not to have preconceived ideas about what poetry should be and try to be catholic in our choice of material - more instinctive than analytical. We are aware of needing to maintain a reasonable standard while providing encouragement where possible. We always seem to end up with a magazine with plenty of variety, a generally high standard and some first class material.' Orbis said, 'This excellent magazine lives up to everything the editors say about it.' Peter Finch says, 'Well worth the £1.50 asked for it.'

Editor Name(s): Dave Bingham/Kevin Bamford
Address: Nant y Brithyll, Llangynyw, Welshpool, Powys SY21 OJS
Telephone: 01938 810263
Mag Frequency: Twice yearly
Subscription: £3
Single Issue: £1.50
Overseas: £5
Payment in: Sterling IMO
Payable to: Anglo-Welsh Poetry Society
Inserts accepted: Yes
Terms: Negotiable
Circulation approx: Print run 200
Payment terms to contributors: Complimentary copy of magazine

BOX OF DRAGONS

Published by Hot Sticks. Looking for exciting, original, short fiction, 2000 words maximum, that pushes the envelope and bursts from the page. We're looking for drama, fire and passion - and a good story! No science fiction, no horror, no poetry. Competitions run three times a year - details on application.

Editor Name(s): Meredith Knight
Address: Whitesmiths, Smelt Road, Coedpoeth, Wrecsam LL11 3SH
Telephone: 01978 757167
Mag Frequency: 3 times per year
Subscription: £9 pa
Single Issue: £3.25
Overseas: £12 pa
Payment in: Sterling cheques drawn on UK bank
Payable to: M Knight
Inserts accepted: Yes
Terms: On application
Advertising Rates: On application
Circulation approx: 120
Payment terms to contributors: Voucher copies only at present. Hope to offer payment by autumn '99
Accept/rejection approx times: 2 months

B
BRAQUEMARD

Like all magazines, Braquemard has its own distinctive flavour, and it is obviously best to see a copy before submitting. As a rough guideline, we tend to bad taste, black humour and the sick side of human nature. We avoid explicit religion, politics, ecology and PC attitudes. No style limitations - we have used sonnets, villanelles, haiku etc as well as free verse. Short story writers should note that we use only micro-fictions, 1000 words or less, and at most two per issue; we have had to return many excellent stories that were simply too long. Original black-and-white artwork is welcomed, but suitable work may be kept on file indefinitely, so please send only photocopies. Braquemard's past contributors have included Fiona Pitt-Kethley, Sean O'Brian, Benjamin Zephaniah, Geoff Hattersley, Douglas Houston, Brian Patten, Joolz, Michael Daugherty, Ian MacMillan, Alison Chisholm, Margot K Juby and TF Griffin as well as many lesser-known quality writers.

Address: David Allenby, 20 Terry Street, Hull HU3 1UD
Mag Frequency: Twice yearly
Subscription: £5 per 2 issues
Single Issue: £2.90
Back Issue: £1.50
Overseas: £4 per issue, £7 for two
Payment in: Sterling cheques payable as above
Payable to: David Allenby
Inserts accepted: Yes
Terms: Terms on application
Payment terms to contributors: Copy of the magazine
Accept/rejection approx times: Variable, up to 2 months

BRASS BUTTERFLY

Brass Butterfly seeks only to publish good poetry. It has no biases other than those the editor was born with. In its thirty or so A4 comb-bound pages you may find haiku and dialogue poems, political satire, high theology, poems about works of art, sex, death, the condition of the oppressed classes, by-passes, and cats. 'If it's good it will get in' is our motto. Brass Butterfly was launched in 1998 with considerable success, and in its first two issues has featured work by David Scott, Sam Smith, Geoff Stevens, Keith Bennett and Anna Monroe to name a few of its authors. It has received critical acclaim and has received several submissions from overseas. We try our best to make constructive comments on work submitted to us. SAE essential.

Address: 17a Edward Road, Dorchester, Dorset DT1 2HL
Mag Frequency: Twice yearly
Subscription: £5 pa
Single Issue: £3
Overseas: Same
Payment in: By cheque to editorial address
Payable to: A Hawthorn
Inserts accepted: Yes
Terms: On application
Circulation approx: 100
Payment terms to contributors: Copy of issue
Accept/rejection approx times: 1 month

B

BREAKFAST ALL DAY

Breakfast All Day, aka BAD, is a quarterly magazine of fiction, poetry, humour, comment, cartoons and graphics, drawing contributions from Britain, mainland Europe and North America. A4, 40pp, b&w, coloured cover. We publish short fiction (up to 4000 words), poetry (maximum 50 lines), articles (up to 1500 words, any subject matter, but preferably with an original viewpoint, or humorous slant), cartoons, comic strips. Line illustrations and b&w photographs very welcome. Written contributions should be in clear black typescript on white paper, or saved as an ASC11 file on a 3.5" disk, and accompanied by a hard copy. Line art and cartoons should be sent as good quality photocopies. Contributions should be accompanied by one or more IRCs. We do not usually return manuscripts unless particularly requested, in which case sufficient return postage must be sent. Send 4 IRCs and an A4 envelope for a sample issue.

Editor Name(s): Philip Boxall
Address: 43 Kingsdown House, Amhurst Road, London E8 2AS/or/4 rue Bonne Nouvelle, 76200, Dieppe, France
Fax: 033 (0)2 35 40 33 26
Email: boxall@badpress.com
Mag Frequency: Quarterly
Subscription: £6.50
Single Issue: £1.80
Overseas: US $24/Europe £9
Payment in: Sterling/US dollar cheques or cash
Payable to: B A D Press
Inserts accepted: Selectively
Terms: By arrangement
Circulation approx: 300
Payment terms to contributors: 1 free copy of magazine
Accept/rejection approx times: 2-3 months

THE BRITISH FANTASY SOCIETY NEWSLETTER

There is a group of people who know all the latest publishing news and gossip. They enjoy the very best in fiction from some of the hottest new talents around. They can read articles by and about their favourite British Fantasy Society. Foremost amongst the BFS's publications is the acclaimed Newsletter. Published on a bi-monthly schedule, it contains genre news, exclusives, publication information, interviews, features and other items of interest to members. The Newsletter also contains informed book reviews, and reviews of all other genre-related material including films, magazines, fanzines, small press magazines, television and radio productions, video and much more. There are regular celebrity columns, members' letters, artwork and lots more besides. Members also receive magazines of fiction and comment as well as occasional 'specials.' These have included free BFS-published/funded paperback books. Members also receive discounted attendance to the BFS' FantasyCon event. The BFS is dedicated to genre works of all ages, so expect material on authors old and new, classic and forgotten, popular and unknown.The BFS has enjoyed the patronage of many established authors, artists and journalists. The BFS' own publications are regularly looked to by editors when selecting material for numerous 'Best Of' anthologies and numerous members have gone on to become published authors in their own right.FantasyCon is the convention organised by the BFS. Guests and attendees travel from around the world to take part, meet old friends and make new ones. Recent Guests of Honour have included Brian Lumley, Stephen Laws, Dan Simmons, Katherine Kurtz, Tom Holt, Christopher Fowler and Graham Joyce.

Address: 46 Oxford Road, Birmingham B27 6DT
Subs to: 2 Harwood Street, Stockport SK4 1JJ
Mag Frequency: Bi-monthly
Subscription: £20 UK - £25 Europe - £40 rest of world
Single Issue: N/A
Back Issue: Write for details
Payable to: The BFS C/O 2 Harwood Street, Stockport SK4 1JJ
Inserts accepted: Yes
Terms: £50 per mailing (plus pro rata postage if insert pushes rate up)
Circulation approx: 500 and rising steadily
Payment terms to contributors: Complimentary copy of work
Accept/rejection approx times: 1 month from receipt

B

THE BROOM CUPBOARD

A quarterly newsletter aimed at writers, illustrators, publishers and performance artists in the pagan community. The aim is to improve the multi-media aspects of esoteric writing/art. Opportunities for short articles, stories, poetry etc. Send two first class stamps for a free back issue.

Address: BCM Writer, 27 Old Gloucester Street, London WC1N 3XX
Mag Frequency: Quarterly
Subscription: £6
Single Issue: £1.50
Back Issue: Free
Payment in: Cheques/PO
Payable to: Flying Witch Publications
Inserts accepted: Yes
Circulation approx: 300
Payment terms to contributors: Complimentary copy
Accept/rejection approx times: 1 month max

BYPASS

Bypass is a review magazine covering all forms of small press publishing with over 400 reviews in every issue alongside a few related articles and lots of contact addresses for useful resources. All lines received are reviewed by a varied panel of readers. A resource for publishers and goldmine for readers. Reviewers are needed, especially bilingual ones.

Address: P.O. Box 148, Hove BN3 3DQ
Mag Frequency: Twice yearly
Subscription: £5 for 3
Single Issue: £2.20 inc. p & p
Back Issue: £1.50 inc. p & p
Overseas: $10
Payment in: Cash
Payable to: Bypass
Inserts accepted: No
Circulation approx: 2000
Payment terms to contributors: Free copy of magazine
Accept/rejection approx times: N/A

C

THE CADMIUM BLUE LITERARY JOURNAL

The journal of the Cadmium Blue Communion of romantic poets. Spearhead of the romantic renaissance movement. Poetry and articles aligned to the romantic school of poetry and to contemporary spiritual romanticism. Traditional rhyme and rhythm favoured, and elegance and beauty of expression. Poems of reflection, heart and soul. Articles about the great romantics, spiritual philosophy, new age concerns. Elevated and inspirational poetry.

Address: Peter Geoffrey/Paul Thompson, 71 Harrow Crescent, Romford, Essex, RM3 7BJ
Mag Frequency: Bi-annual
Subscription: £10
Single Issue: £5
Back Issue: £5
Overseas: £15
Payment in: British or foreign currency
Payable to: Precious Pearl Publications
Inserts accepted: No
Circulation approx: 500
Payment terms to contributors: 1 complimentary copy
Accept/rejection approx times: Usually within 1 month

C

CAMBRENSIS

A quarterly magazine, founded 1988, devoted solely to short stories by writers born or resident in Wales; no payment offered other than writers' copies; short stories under 2500 words; only other material used - book reviews and features of Anglo-Welsh literary interest; art-work, mainly cartoon and line-drawings by Welsh artists; sae with submissions or IRC with overseas inquiries; not more than one manuscript at one time; the magazine is supported by The Arts Council of Wales.

Address: 41 Heol Fach, Cornelly, Bridgend, CF33 4LN
Telephone: 01656 741 994
Mag Frequency: Quarterly: Spring/Summer/Autumn/Winter
Subscription: £6 for year's 4 issues, post paid
Single Issue: £1.50 post paid
Back Issue: £1.50 (some available)
Overseas: Via Blackwell's Periodicals, Oxford or Swets & Zeitlinger BV, PO Box 800, 2160 Lisse, Holland
Payment in: Overseas: sterling via these two companies
Payable to: Cambrensis Magazine
Inserts accepted: Yes
Terms: Negotiable
Circulation approx: Print run 350-400
Payment terms to contributors: Copies to writers
Accept/rejection approx times: By return of post mainly

C

CANDELABRUM POETRY MAGAZINE

A5 saddle-stitched 40pp; established 1970. Preference for metrical and rhymed poetry, but free verse not excluded. English 5/7/5 haiku accepted. Any subject but NB no racialist or sexist matter SAE essential. Overseas poets IRC and self addressed envelope. NB IRC must be stamped on the left side by the issuing post office. 'A magazine of well-crafted poetry, and not one a dud' New Hope International. 'Well crafted writing' Tenth Muse.

Editor Name(s): Michael Leonard McCarthy
Address: 1 Keyham Court, Star Mews, Peterborough PE1 5NH
Mag Frequency: Twice yearly (April & October)
Subscription: £11.50 volume 9 (1997/99)
Single Issue: £2
Overseas: US $22 the volume - single copy US $4
Payment in: British: cheque/PO; USA & Canada: US$ bills only - no cheques
Payable to: The Red Candle Press
Inserts accepted: No
Circulation approx: 900
Payment terms to contributors: Complimentary copy
Accept/rejection approx times: 8 Weeks

C

CARTILAGE

He (the previous resident)
Was an extraordinarily tall man, perhaps a giant, and conscious of his peculiar height.
This is why he wasn't put in the basement.
There wasn't room.

Living here must have made him feel yet taller.
Which in turn must be why he put his mattress on the floor:
To get as low to the ground as possible.
Below the window
So no passing plane or pigeon
Could peer in and be privy

To his private peculiarity,
His abominable tallness
Two stories above the rooms of the living.

It's getting dark now, I've had to switch the lamp on.
Soon, should the clouds clear,
I will be able to stare out the stars.

I would not have been able to do that before
And here is the irony:
That for the last year,
He (the previous resident)
Has had access to the night sky,
While I have not.

Yet he is the one
Who has stuck plastic stars
To the ceiling.

Editor Name(s): Wes White
Address: Wes White, 37 Caledonian Road, Chichester, West Sussex PO19 2LJ
Telephone: 01243 539831
Email: postslave@postmaster.co.uk
Mag Frequency: Irregular
Subscription: £5 for 4
Single Issue: £1.50
Payment in: Preferably cheques made out to Wes White
Payable to: Wes White
Inserts accepted: No
Circulation approx: 100, signed & numbered
Payment terms to contributors: No longer accepts unsolicited contributions
Accept/rejection approx times: Instant

C

CASABLANCA

This magazine of politics, satire and the arts has been variously described as devastating (Private Eye), peppery (The Guardian), spirited (Sunday Telegraph), clean, true and fearless (The Face), a literary hand grenade (New Statesman & Society), and unlimited cultural subversion (The Sunday Times). The select subscription list includes film stars, MPs, novelists and a raft of investigative journalists who use Casablanca to find out where their next story is coming from.

Address: 31 Clerkenwell Close, London EC1R 0AT
Telephone: 0171 608 3784
Fax: 0170 608 3865
Subscription: £12/Students £7/Institutions £20
Single Issue: £2.20
Back Issue: £1.50
Overseas: £16 (Europe airmail); £19.50 (RoW)
Payment in: Cheque/credit card - credit card phoneline 0171 608 3784 FREE extra issue if so
Payable to: Casablanca
Inserts accepted: Yes
Terms: £60
Payment terms to contributors: Most contributions are voluntary
Accept/rejection approx times: 1 month

C

CASCANDO

Cascando (founded 1991) features poems, stories, reviews, translations, drama, literary articles and interviews . . . all by students in Britain and around the world. Tomorrow's great writers are discovered and published here in their own forum, which is shaped by their particular concerns. Interviews with writers of all persuasions have been included, Tom Paulin, Eleain Ni Chuilleanain, Colm Toibin, Dermot Bolger, Tom Morrison, Tony Harrison, Benjamin Zephaniah, Ranjit Bolt, John Hegley and Jung Chang. Young student writers we published include Sinéad Morrissey (youngest ever winner of the Patrick Kavanagh Poetry Award), David Wheatley and Tobias Hill. Cascando includes magazine listings and a literary diary.

Address: Cascando Press Ltd, PO Box 1499, London SW10 9TZ
Mag Frequency: Irregular - at least annually
Subscription: £13.50
Single Issue: £4.50
Back Issue: £3
Overseas: $30 US/£15.50 Europe
Payment in: Sterling/Cheque/PO/Bankers Draft/Foreign Currency (must allow for exchange comm)
Payable to: Cascando Press Ltd
Inserts accepted: Yes
Terms: £65
Circulation approx: 3000
Payment terms to contributors: Free copies of relevant magazine
Accept/rejection approx times: 4 months

CELTIC HISTORY REVIEW

Celtic History Review aims to explore the histories of the six Celtic nations, Ireland, Scotland, Isle of Man, Wales, Brittany and Cornwall, from their own perspectives plus inter Celtic, and not as peripheral areas to British and French history.

Address: Micheal O Siochrie Rye Bothar, Na Eaglaise, Mulloch Ide, Co Athachatt, Eire
Mag Frequency: Quarterly
Subscription: £7
Single Issue: £1.50
Overseas: $US 15 / FF 70
Payment in: Cheque/cash/PO
Payable to: An Clochan
Inserts accepted: Yes
Terms: £40
Circulation approx: 400
Accept/rejection approx times: 2 weeks

THE CELTIC PEN

The Celtic Pen, started in 1993, is primarily in English but deals with literature written in the six Celtic languages (Lush, Scots, Gaelic, Manx, Welsh, Breton and Cornish) - for example, features on writers or genres. It also carries inter-Celtic and English-Celtic translations of poetry etc, and a book review section. All periods of literature are covered.

Address: 36 Fruithill Park, Belfast BT11 8GE
Mag Frequency: Quarterly
Subscription: £5
Single Issue: £1(plus 25p p & p)
Overseas: US $15 / FF 40
Payment in: Cheque/cash/PO
Payable to: The Celtic Pen
Inserts accepted: Yes
Terms: £55
Circulation approx: 800
Accept/rejection approx times: Two weeks

C

CENCRASTUS

Cencrastus covers Scottish and international literature,arts and affairs. Submission of articles, short stories, poetry and reviews welcomed speculatively, payment by negotiation. Editor: Raymond Ross; Managing Editor: Richard Moore . The magazine was first published in 1979 by students and staff at Edinburgh University and takes its name from Curly Snake, the Celtic serpent of wisdom, the symbol of energy and infinity as embraced by Hugh MacDiarmid in his poem 'To Cicumjack Cencrastus'. The magazine also took its international motto - 'If there is ocht in Scotland that's worth ha'en/There is nae distance to which it's unattached' - from the same poem. Cencrastus is at the cutting edge of literary, artistic and political affairs. The magazine has lately interviewed Iain Banks and Alisdair Gray and constantly publishes unseen material from established writers.

Editor Name(s): Raymond Ross, Editor/reviews & subs to Richard Moore, Managing Editor
Address: Cencrastus, Unit 1 Abbeymount Techbase, 2 Easter Road, Edinburgh EH8 8EJ
Fax: 0131 661 5687
Mag Frequency: Four times a year
Subscription: £12 (4 issues) £15 (institutions)
Single Issue: £2.95
Overseas: £15 (4 issues) £17 (institutions)
Payment in: In advance
Payable to: Cencrastus
Inserts accepted: Yes
Terms: N/A
Circulation approx: 2,000
Payment terms to contributors: Negotiable
Accept/rejection approx times: Approx 6-8 Weeks

A CHANGE OF ZINERY

Peterborough Science Fiction Club's website at www.btinternet.com/~c.ayres/ psf.htm and part of this is the online fanzine A Change of Zinery. We post SF, fantasy and horror short stories and poetry. We have also started a gothic-dedicated site, Nightmare Alley. We tend to use work from the Peterborough area (north Cambridgeshire, east Northamptonshire, Rutland, South Lincolnshire and west Norfolk), though this has flexible boundaries. Check out the site first and ask the Site Manager (Chris Ayres) about submitting on either disk, down the wire or in hardcopy. We are especially interested in using pieces that have previously been printed elsewhere due to the very nature of the internet.

Address: 58 Pennington, Orton Goldhay, Peterborough PE2 5RB
Website: www.btinternet.com/~c.ayres/psf.htm
Mag Frequency: Constantly updated
Payment terms to contributors: No

C

CHAPMAN

Chapman is Scotland's leading literary magazine, controversial, influential, outspoken and intelligent. Founded in 1970, it has become a dynamic force in Scottish culture, covering theatre, politics, language, and the arts. Our highly-respected forum for poetry, fiction, criticism, review and debate is essential reading for anyone interested in contemporary Scotland. Chapman publishes the best in Scottish writing - new work by well-known Scottish writers in the context of lucid critical discussion. With our strong commitment to the future, we energetically promote new writers, new ideas and approaches. Several issues have been landmarks in their field, in Scots language, women's writing, cultural politics in Scotland, and we have published extensive features on important writers: Hugh MacDiarmid, Tom Scott, Iain Crichton Smith, Ian Hamilton Finley, Alasdair Gray, Naomi Mitchison, Hamish Henderson, Jessie Kesson, to name but a few. We also publish poetry and short fiction by up-and-coming writers, as well as critical articles, book reviews and items of general cultural interest. Our coverage includes theatre, music, visual arts, language, and other matters from time to time. Each issue includes Scots and Gaelic, as well as English although most of the work is in English. Although the focus is on Scotland, Chapman has a long history of publishing international literature, both in English by non-Scots and in translation from other languages.Chapman will interest anyone researching British and Scottish literature. It has a natural outlet in universities and institutions of secondary education. With its emphasis on new creative writing, it is of interest to anyone with a love of literature.We also publish poetry collections and plays under the heading of Chapman Publishing. Our New Writing Series is dedicated to giving first publications to promising young writers. The Theatre Series brings the best of Scottish theatre before a wider audience.

Address: 4 Broughton Place, Edinburgh EH1 3RX
Mag Frequency: Quarterly
Subscription: £15
Single Issue: £3.80 inc p&p
Back Issue: £3 (inc p&p)
Overseas: £20
Payment in: Cheque/PO/IMO
Payable to: Chapman
Inserts accepted: Yes
Terms: £50 per 1000
Circulation approx: 2000
Payment terms to contributors: Copies
Accept/rejection approx times: 1-3 months

CHEAP DATE

C

28 page A4 magazine about 2nd hand stuff, especially clothes. Explores a glamorous lifestyle of being imaginative about what you wear/listen to/read/drive etc. The extensions of which become wider: ideas of individuality, identity and avoidance of consumer culture. Meanwhile it's got guides to good charity shops, psychological analysis on the nature of collecting/wearing something someone could have died in . . . sexy centre spreads (so far starring Sophie Dahl and Rachel Weisz). My guy-style photo-story starring Iris Palmer and all sorts of stupid stuff.

Editor Name(s): Kira Jolliffe
Address: PO Box 16778, London EC1M 5SH
Telephone: 0966 498 078
Fax: 0171 689 6887
Email: cc.magazines@dial.pipex.com
Mag Frequency: Quarterly
Subscription: £7
Single Issue: £1.50
Back Issue: £2.10
Overseas: £10 Europe/£12 USA
Payment in: Cheque/cash/PO
Payable to: Cheap Date
Inserts accepted: Yes
Advertising Rates: 1pg £400; 1 year's classified box £15
Circulation approx: 4000
Payment terms to contributors: No pay I'm afraid. Small expenses covered
Accept/rejection approx times: 2 weeks

CITY WRITINGS MAGAZINE

City Writings Magazine, whose production team is currently led by editor Megan Miranda, is the magazine of City Writers, the Southampton-based literary organisation. City Writers brings poets and novelists of national acclaim to our readings at the Gantry Arts Centre. City Writings Magazine supports these activities by publishing a wide range of poetry, short prose writers, events, publications. We encourage submission from all corners of Britain and beyond. We regularly recieve submissions from Ireland, Spain, Italy, America, etc. We publish well-known poets' work next to 'up and coming' writers. We tend to centre issues around themes, so it may be helpful to check the 'Call for Submissions' in a recent issue. Our editorial tastes are eclectic in style and content, but we particularly favour writing that engages with the larger community and current debates in contemporary writing. We are pleased to receive experimental submissions on controversial topics. Located in Southampton, we also strive to link the realms of the University with that of the southern writing community as a whole, and we are constantly broadening our interests as we expand our readership and submission pool. We are a non-profit, community-based group and thus try to keep the price of the magazine one of the lowest around to maximise its accessibility. Submissions should come from writers willing to view their own work critically in the context of contemporary prose and poetry. Reading City Writings first is helpful but not compulsory. Submissions should be addressed to the Editor; we will consider up to six poems and/or 2,500 words of prose at a time, preferably typed. All submissions should be accompanied by sufficient return postage, and obviously we accept no responsibility for work lost in the post so please do not send originals. All submissions eventually receive a personal reply from the editor, so please be patient. We look forward to hearing from you and reading your work.

Editor Name(s): Megan Miranda
Address: Editor, City Writings Magazine, c/o The Gantry Arts Centre, Off Blechynden Terrace, Southampton SO15 16W
Mag Frequency: 2 per year
Subscription: £3 inc postage
Single Issue: £1.50 inc postage
Overseas: Write for details
Payment in: Cheque/PO - no cash
Payable to: City Writings
Inserts accepted: Yes
Terms: Consult editor
Circulation approx: 300
Payment terms to contributors: No payment - we are a non-profit community magazine
Accept/rejection approx times: Up to 6 months depending on when submitted

COMMUNITY OF POETS

Community of Poets Press is an independent poetry publishing organisation based at Hatfield Cottage, Chilham, Caterbury, England. The Press, run by Philip and Susan Bennetta, produces and publishes special poetry publications, including an international magazine, handmade poetry collections; and it sells secondhand poetry books by post. The international quarterly magazine Community of Poets focuses on community and organisational life and learning. The magazine, like all our publications, is in A5 format and produced to a high standard. One of our imprints, launched in 1997, is Pamphlet Poets. This series showcases the work of contemporary poets in an individual collection. The pamphlets are hand sewn, in the traditional style of the 20s and 30s; some of the collections are illustrated. We also produce Poems by Post. These slim pamphlets contain one poem and are hand sewn with a woodcut print. They are complete with a matching handmade envelope, ready to post.

Editor Name(s): Philip Bennetta
Address: Hatfield Cottage, Chilham, Kent CT4 8DP
Telephone: 01227 730787
Fax: 01227 732134
Email: cpoets@globalnet.co.uk
Mag Frequency: Quarterly
Subscription: UK £8 pa. (incl p & p)
Single Issue: £2 + 30p postage
Overseas: £12 pa (incl p & p)
Payment in: Cheque preferred
Payable to: Community of Poets Press
Inserts accepted: No
Circulation approx: Increasing
Payment terms to contributors: Free copy of magazine to non-subscribers
Accept/rejection approx times: 1 month

C

CONNECTIONS

Connections publishes new work - articles, short stories (up to 2500 words), poetry - anything to do with writing matters including reviews, letters, information on events and competitions. There are also articles from professional writers, and we hold our own annual mini-saga competition which runs from January to end of May each year. This year we are to publish the best fifty in booklet form, plus the four winners. We welcome submissions from the UK and abroad but we do advise those wanting to send work to us to see a copy of the magazine first.

Editor Name(s): Narissa Knights
Address: 13 Wave Crest, Whitstable, Kent CT5 1EH
Mag Frequency: 4 a year
Subscription: £9
Single Issue: £2.50
Back Issue: £2
Overseas: £12
Payment in: Overseas - IRCs
Payable to: Connections
Inserts accepted: Yes
Advertising Rates: £50 back cover/£25 half/£20 qtr inside pgs
Circulation approx: 300
Payment terms to contributors: Over 1000 words £10/under £5
Accept/rejection approx times: 6 weeks

CORPSES AND CLARINETS

Corpses And Clarinets began as a forum for Brighton Writers, but in its second issue expanded into perfect-bound and Europe-bound horizons. Initally a periodical for poetry and fiction, we welcome other modes such as articles, but are holding back on this till the third issue; the same applies to reviews and other prose. The second issue concentrates on the new Bavarian poetry. Our taste is as catholic as the title suggests, the editors themselves both tend to the innovative that doesn't marginalise itself in ritual gardisms. Originality that can burn one's fingers is more fun, and needs less surgery. The poetry of one editor, Simon Jennor, is accused of density by lovers of the accessible, and accessible by some modernists as a term of abuse. He has two volumes out in Germany, and reckons he must have got the balance about right. David Kendall, the other editor, is a short-story writer and novelist who lectures on the gothic and cultural studies.

Editor Name(s): Simon Jennor/David Kendall
Address: 51 Waterloo Street, Hove, Sussex BN3 1AH
Telephone: 01273 202867
Mag Frequency: Biannual
Subscription: £8
Single Issue: £4 (perfect-bound)
Back Issue: Sold out
Overseas: £10
Payment in: IRC overseas
Payable to: Corpses and Clarinets
Inserts accepted: Yes
Circulation approx: 400
Payment terms to contributors: None
Accept/rejection approx times: We try by return of post

C

THE COTTAGE GUIDE TO WRITERS' POSTAL WORKSHOPS

The Guide is a pocket-sized directory of postal workshops / foliod giving 16 names and addresses of 16 editors and a brief description of 16 types of workshop, viz miscellaneous, poetry, short stories etc. The directory is desktop published so that it can be upgraded as soon as new information is received.

Address: Croftspun Publications, Drakemyre Croft, Cairnorrie, Methlick, Ellon, Aberdeenshire AB41 7JN
Mag Frequency: On request
Subscription: N/A
Single Issue: £2 post free
Payable to: Catherine Gill
Inserts accepted: No
Payment terms to contributors: None
Accept/rejection approx times: N/A

CRIMEWAVE

Modern crime fiction gives writers the freedom to discuss ideas, to create characters and explore locations, and above all to investigate human psychology and society. The genre is broader in scope than others - humour, horror, satire, escapism and political analysis are all encompassed in crime fiction - and Crimewave aims to cover the entire territory, from the misnamed 'cosy' to the deceptively subtle 'hardboiled'. Every issue contains stories by authors who are household names in the crime fiction world (Ian Rankin, Julian Rathbone, Maureen O'Brien, Michael Z Lewin, etc), but we also constantly find room for lesser-known or even unknown writers. The magazine is beautifully designed in a unique and colourful B5 format, with at least 60 pages per issue.

Editor Name(s): Mat Coward
Address: TTA Press, 5 Martins Lane, Witcham, Ely, Cambs CB6 2LB
Telephone: 01353 777931
Email: ttapress@aol.com
Website: http://purl.oclc.org/net/ttaonline/
Mag Frequency: Quarterly
Subscription: £11 (4 issues)
Single Issue: £3
Overseas: Europe £3.50/£13; USA $6/$22; RoW£4/£15
Payment in: Cheque/PO/Eurocheque, etc
Payable to: TTA Press
Inserts accepted: Yes
Terms: Negotiable
Advertising Rates: Query
Circulation approx: 20,000
Payment terms to contributors: Contract on acceptance, payment on publication
Accept/rejection approx times: 1 month

CRIMSON

Crimson, the world's leading vampire magazine is published four times a year by The Vampire Guild. It regularly features articles, stories and poetry by both established and up-and-coming writers. Articles cover factual cases, supposition, reviews (music, cinema, theatre, and literature), celebrity interviews, plus art and cartoons. It also covers all the top vampiric events and meetings giving the most comprehensive guide to vampire fandom anywhere. Get infected!

Address: TVG 82 Ripcroft, Portland, Dorset DT5 2EE
Email: vampire.guild@zetnet.co.uk
Mag Frequency: Quarterly
Subscription: £12
Single Issue: £3.25
Back Issue: £2.75
Overseas: £16
Payment in: IMO/Cash
Payable to: Thee Vampire Guild
Inserts accepted: Yes
Terms: £12
Circulation approx: 1000 copies (18 countries)
Payment terms to contributors: N/A
Accept/rejection approx times: 2 months

C

CRITICAL WAVE

Founded in 1987, now established as the leading independent European journal of science fiction, fantasy and horror news/criticism. Contributors have included Michael Moorcock (who called it the 'most consistently interesting and intelligent' magazine of its kind), Clive Barker, Andrew Darlington, Terry Pratchett, Steve Sneyd, Graham Joyce, Storm Constantine and Joel Lane. Also features regular art portfolios (those featured include Jim Porter, Dave Carson, Jim Pitts, Harry Turner and Alan Hunter) and the most extensive conventions listing available in print. Placed in the SFX 'Top Ten' Readers' Poll 1996. Does not carry poetry, but reviews genre poetry collections and carries historical analysis of the field (including Sneyd's landmark essays on SF poetry).

Address: Steve Green, 33 Scott Road, Olton, Solihull B92 7LQ
Subs to: Martin Tudor, 24 Ravensbourne Grove, Off Clarkes Lane, Willenhall WV13 1HX
Mag Frequency: 5 a year
Subscription: £11.50
Single Issue: £2.45
Overseas: Send reply-paid envelope for rates
Payable to: Critical Wave Publications
Inserts accepted: No
Terms: By negotiation
Circulation approx: 800-1000
Payment terms to contributors: Complimentary copy of issue
Accept/rejection approx times: Six weeks (enclose SAE)

C

CULT FICTION

Cult Fiction, as the name suggests, is a fiction based A5 magazine publishing short stores unrestricted by length, poetry unrestricted by style and writer reviews unrestricted by bad taste in writer choice. We are particularly interested in work that challenges thoughts and perceptions about the world around us, not the usual 'fluffy bunny' stories of love and sunshine. We also accept A5-size artwork, plays, monologues, and song lyrics. But not sheet music!

Address: Canada, Poppy Publishing, PO Box 144, Preston Central, Preston PR1 3GH
Mag Frequency: Irregular
Single Issue: £2
Back Issue: £1
Payment in: Cheque/PO
Payable to: Poppy Publishing
Inserts accepted: Yes
Terms: Negotiable
Circulation approx: 400
Payment terms to contributors: A copy of the issue
Accept/rejection approx times: 1 month

CURRENT ACCOUNTS

Mainly features poetry and prose by members of Bank Street writers, but high-quality submissions from non-members are welcome. No restriction on subject matter apart from usual considerations of taste and decency. Previous contributors include M R Peacocke, Pat Winslow & Gerald England.

Address: 16-18 Mill Lane, Horwich, Bolton BL6 6AT
Email: 100417.3722@compuserve.com
Mag Frequency: 2 per year
Subscription: £3
Single Issue: £1.50
Overseas: £5
Payment in: Sterling cheque/PO/cash
Payable to: Bank Street Writers
Inserts accepted: Yes
Terms: Free
Circulation approx: Increasing
Payment terms to contributors: Free copy of magazine
Accept/rejection approx times: 1 month

CUSTARD PIE - The Magazine of Funny Stuff

Fresh, light, genuinely funny and flavour-filled magazine. Contains the very best cartoons, poems, short stories and oddments. Some of the humour is dark, some is risqué. Comments: 'Had me in hysterics' . . . 'Excellent magazine' . . .. 'Try this one for size' . . . 'It did tickle the old funny bone.'

Editor Name(s): Jason Ingham
Address: 76c Granville Road, Finchley, London N12 0HT
Mag Frequency: Annual
Subscription: £4 for 2 issues
Single Issue: £2.20
Overseas: + IRC if outside EU
Payment in: Cheque/PO
Payable to: Custard Pie
Inserts accepted: Yes
Terms: Negotiable
Advertising Rates: Negotiable
Circulation approx: 500
Payment terms to contributors: Copy of mag
Accept/rejection approx times: 3 months

CYPHERS

Poetry, prose, criticism, translations.

Editor Name(s): Leland Bardwell/Pearse Hutchinson/Eiléan Ní Chuilleanáin/
Macdara Woods
Address: 3 Selskar Terrace, Dublin 6
Mag Frequency: 2-3 yearly
Subscription: £6
Single Issue: £2
Back Issue: £1.50
Overseas: $20
Payment in: Cheque
Payable to: Cyphers
Inserts accepted: No
Circulation approx: 350
Payment terms to contributors: £10 a page
Accept/rejection approx times: 3 - 6 months

D

DADAMAG

The more Dadamag refuses to exist, the mightier it becomes . . . active cooperation is encouraged, passive enjoyment is not. Dadamag teeshirts soon to be made. £100 & £2 postage. Very ordinary quality . . . only buy if you have money to waste. Size XL only.

Address: PO Box 472 Norwich NR3 3TS
Mag Frequency: Sometimes, perhaps
Subscription: N/A will vary
Single Issue: N/A
Payment in: ££'s/cheques/PO only
Payable to: W L Walker
Accept/rejection approx times: Don't send unsolicited work. Enquiries only for now with sae

DAM (Disability Arts Magazine)

DAM is a quarterly magazine which promotes the arts activities of disabled people and promotes access to the arts for disabled people. The magazine is run, staffed and controlled entirely by disabled people, through DAM Publishing Ltd, a registered charity. All art forms are regularly featured and reviewed: visual arts: paintings and sculpture; creative writing: fiction and poetry; performance arts: theatre, cinema and television etc. Venues visited by reviewers are assessed for accessibility for other disabled people. As the original full name Disability Arts Magazine suggests DAM focuses on Disability Arts, where the subject matter of a piece of artwork draws on the experience of the disabled artist as disabled people.This magazine should be of interest to anyone who has an interest in art: the art disabled people produce and access issues disabled people have.

Address: DAM, 11A Cleveland Avenue, Lupset Park, Wakefield, WF2 8LE
Mag Frequency: Quarterly (March, June, September, December)
Subscription: £12 (four issues)/£6 concession unwaged
Single Issue: £2
Overseas: £20 (outside EU)
Payment in: Cheques in pounds sterling through UK bank
Payable to: DAM
Circulation approx: 1500+ copies printed
Accept/rejection approx times: Variable

DANDELION ARTS MAGAZINE

Dandelion Arts Magazine is an international non-profitmaking publication created and founded in 1978 in London by Jacqueline Gonzalez-Marina who has been the publisher ever since. Its aims have always been to provide an outlet for poets, journalists and illustrators world-wide. Contributions are welcome but subscription is a must if seeking publication. All submissions should be accompanied by a SAE. Personal advice will be gladly given on an individual basis.

Address: Fern Publications - Casa Alba, 24 Frosty Hollow, East Hunsbury, Northants NN4 0SY
Mag Frequency: Bi-annual
Subscription: £8 UK
Single Issue: Half subscription cost
Back Issue: Subscription cost
Overseas: £18 Europe/£18 USA/£20 Australia & NZ
Payment in: In sterling by cheque, bankers draft or postal order
Payable to: J Gonzalez-Marina
Inserts accepted: Yes
Terms: £8 per 100/£80 per 1000
Circulation approx: Up to 1000
Payment terms to contributors: No payment given, just the publicity and advice
Accept/rejection approx times: 2 weeks

THE DARK FANTASY NEWSLETTER

The newsletter is a forum for dark fantasy/horror writers, featuring guidelines, news, markets, websites, reviews, fiction, poetry and prose. Previously unpublished writers are welcome! There is no word count for fiction/prose; poetry must be under 40 lines. Articles and features are welcome on all aspects of the dark world. With submissions, send a 50-word (approx) biography. Fantasy fiction/prose also considered, and artwork.

Editor Name(s): Sian Ross
Address: Springbeach Press, 11 Vernon Close, Eastbourne, East Sussex BN23 6AN
Mag Frequency: Quarterly
Subscription: £4.50 for 4
Single Issue: £.25
Overseas: SAE/IRC for details
Payment in: Cheque/PO/IMO (sterling)
Payable to: S Ross
Inserts accepted: Yes
Terms: Exchange only - by arrangement
Advertising Rates: A5 page - £5/smaller - exchange basis
Circulation approx: Over 150 - evergrowing
Payment terms to contributors: Complimentary copy
Accept/rejection approx times: A few days!

D

DARK HORIZONS

Dark Horizons is the journal of the British Fantasy Society. It publishes a mix of fiction (stories and poetry) and non-fiction, covering all aspects of fantasy, horror and SF. The definitions of these three words are as wide as the authors' imaginations - although we tend not to publish gratuitous matter for its own sake. A story can be of any style, but ultimately it must entertain. In the past, Dark Horizons has published material by professionals (such as Ramsey Campbell, Thomas Ligotti and Storm Constatine) and non-professionals. Although we do publish poetry, only a few poems are included each issue. We encourage new writers. Dark Horizons also publishes artwork, ranging from that produced to illustrate specific stories and articles, to 'spot' pieces.

Address: Peter Coleborn, 46 Oxford Road, Acocks Green, Birmingham B27 6DT
Subs to: 2 Harwood Street, Stockport, Cheshire SK4 1JJ
Email: peter@alchemypress.demon.co.uk
Mag Frequency: 1-2 times a year
Subscription: £17 UK BFS Membership
Single Issue: £3-£4 depending on issue
Overseas: £20 Europe/$35 USA
Payable to: The British Fantasy Society
Inserts accepted: Yes
Terms: £20 for complete mailing
Circulation approx: 500-600
Payment terms to contributors: Contributor copies
Accept/rejection approx times: Varies

DATA DUMP

This publication gathers and disseminates information on genre poetry - science fiction poetry as a priority, but also fantasy and horror. Topics covered include new collections/anthologies, articles on the field, early work, novels incorporating poetry, poetry in fantasies, humorous SF poetry, SF poetry on the net, picturesque/human-data, SF poetry in unusual settings (media, film, opera, radio). Aim is an ongoing update on the field, plus a backfill of its past, with a preponderance of attention to the UK but some coverage of USA, Australia, Europe etc. Information on any of these topics welcomed/credited. Otherwise no unsolicited MSS. Original poetry is not sought.

Editor Name(s): S Sneyd
Address: 4 Nowell Place, Almondbury, Huddersfield, West Yorks HD5 8PB
Mag Frequency: 6 Monthly (approx)
Subscription: See payment details
Single Issue: 70p inc. post
Back Issue: Ordinary issues - photostat reprints only. Special double issues, send SAE for details
Overseas: Indiv. copies US$2 cash or small denomination (50¢ or less) US stamps to that amount. For Special Issue prices enquire w/ SAE/IRC. Dist. in USA by NSFA.
Payment in: No advance subscriptions as price/format may vary, but those wanting each copy as produced can place a 'till cancelled' order and pay for each issue when received.
Payable to: S Sneyd
Inserts accepted: Yes
Terms: Exchange basis by prior arrangement
Circulation approx: 100
Payment terms to contributors: None
Accept/rejection approx times: No MSS accepted as such. Information of relevance welcomed, and as and when included, source acknowledged.

D

DAY BY DAY

Founded 1963, Day By Day is a news commentary, digest of national and international affairs and review of the arts, independent of all major political parties, with an emphasis on non-violence and social justice. Anti-war and anti-racialist, it is concerned about conservation, pollution, cruelty to animals, arms trade, poverty, unemployment, homelessness and moral and civilised values. It publishes short poems, reports cricket, reviews exhibitions, films, plays, opera and musicals. It very rarely publishes short stories. No illustrations.Reviews books on art, cricket and other sport, current affairs, economics, education, films, conservation, music, history, politics, religion, peace, non-violence, literature, war etc. Unsolicited manuscripts must be accompanied by a sae. It is worth studying an issue or two first, since we like outside contributions to harmonise with the spirit of our editorials.

Address: Woolacombe House, 141 Woolacombe Road, Blackheath, London SE3 8QP
Mag Frequency: Monthly
Subscription: £10.45 UK
Single Issue: 85p
Overseas: Europe £14/RoW$26
Payment in: UK cheque/PO/Euro cheque/sterling cheque/IMO
Payable to: Day By Day
Inserts accepted: No. But will accept exchange of advertisement
Circulation approx: 24,000
Payment terms to contributors: By arrangement
Accept/rejection approx times: 14 days provided accompanied by SAE

DAYDREAMS, NIGHTMARES AND . . .

Centralised around art, music and fiction. Content: art, articles on bands and labels, contact list, reviews. Any black & white artwork welcome. No larger than A4 but magazine is A5. Anything factual is wanted as well as science fiction and horror but no poetry, work no longer than 2 A4 pages. Please enclose SAE for return of unused work.

Address: Tony, PO Box 471, Peckham, London, SE15 2JX
Mag Frequency: Biannual
Subscription: £1.50 two copies
Single Issue: £1 Europe/£1.50 Row
Back Issue: Negotiable
Overseas: £2
Payable to: Tony Eaton
Inserts accepted: No
Circulation approx: 750
Payment terms to contributors: Complimentary copy
Accept/rejection approx times: As soon as decided

D

THE DEVIL

We commission the best in new writing and accept some unsolicited material, but only if it suits our profile. We publish interviews, essays, polemic, short fiction and poetry. We are particularly interested in the interface between culture and politics. We have included interviews with Jeffrey Archer/Helena Kennedy/Christopher Hampton/Julie Birchill and articles by Richard Gott/Marina Warner/Ronan Bennett.

Address: 247 Gray's Inn Road, London WC1X 8JR
Email: thedevil@play-333.demon.uk
Mag Frequency: Twice a year
Subscription: £15 for 3 issues
Single Issue: £5.99
Back Issue: £4.99 / £5.99 from issue 9
Overseas: £25 for three issues
Payment in: Mail order from 247 Gray's Inn Road, London WC1X 8JR
Payable to: The Printer's Devil
Inserts accepted: No
Circulation approx: 1500
Payment terms to contributors: £50 fiction/£25 poems
Accept/rejection approx times: 3 months

DIAL 174

An A5-size magazine of 60+ pages with A4-sized large print version available. Wide variety: poetry, short fiction, articles, travelogues, book reviews, news. Artwork accepted, printed in colour, specially when accompanying and enhancing submissions. Resident artists illustrate suitable submissions for featuring on the cover or as centre pages spread. The editor's policy: to help and encourage those deriving pleasure from writing and reading the writing of others. Debate on the art of writing and social issues derives from the content of submissions, articles and readers' letters. Dial involves itself with charity work, including: discretionary free subscription or reduced rates to those not so 'financially fortunate', so mention your circumstances if you wish to be considered and would like to belong to this 'literary family'. The magazine reaches a wider audience than mere subscription, being on permanent display at the Internet, South Bank Centre Poetry Library, universities in the USA - and it is free to establishments such as schools and prison education departments. It also produces anthologies and books featuring selected subscribers.

Editor Name(s): Joseph Hemmings
Address: 21 Mill Road, Watlington, King's Lynn, Norfolk PE33 0HH
Telephone: 01533 811949
Email: apoet@globalnet.co.uk
Mag Frequency: Quarterly
Subscription: $12 (£16 A4 format)
Single Issue: £3 (£4 A4 format)
Overseas: £16 or $30
Payment in: PO/Cheque/IMO/sterling, dollar, DM notes
Payable to: Dial 174
Inserts accepted: Yes
Terms: Exchange basis
Advertising Rates: Exchange basis
Circulation approx: 400
Payment terms to contributors: None (non-funded/non-profit)
Accept/rejection approx times: See 'publishing policy' sent with info pack

THE DRAGON CHRONICLE

The Dragon Chronicle (Founded 1993). Editor Ade Dimmick. Published by Dragon's Head Press. Special interest journal dedicated entirely to dragons in all their forms and aspects. Features dragon-related and dragon-inspired myth, magic, paganism, astrology, folklore, fantasy, spirituality and tradition. Plus artwork and poetry. A dracophile's delight! Dragon's Head Press is an independent small press publishing project specialising in dragon-interest. Publishes The Dragon Chronicle as well as publishing and distributing books about dragons. Mail order book service.

Editor Name(s): Ade Dimmick
Address: PO Box 3369, London SW6 6JN
Email: dragonet@vtx.ch
Website: http://freespace.virgin.net/huw.rees/dc/
Mag Frequency: 3 times a year
Subscription: £7 per 4 issues
Single Issue: £2
Back Issue: £1.50 pre-1998
Overseas: $15/$5 Single Issue
Payment in: UK: cheques to Dragon's Head Press/Overseas: cash only - dollars or sterling
Payable to: Dragon's Head Press
Inserts accepted: Yes
Terms: Free to dragon-orientated flyers from subscribers/supporters
Circulation approx: 1000
Payment terms to contributors: Articles/features/poems/illustrations - free copy
Accept/rejection approx times: Generally acknowledged by return

DRAGON WYND: A Collection Of Dragon Stories

Little sister of The Dragon Chronicle. Specializes in draconic and serpentine works of fiction writing and poetry. Published by Dragon's Head Press: the independent small press publishing project. (Founded 1993.)

Editor Name(s): Ade Dimmick/Alastair Mcbeath
Address: Dragon's Head Press, PO Box 3369, London SW6 6JN
Email: dragonet@vtx.ch
Website: http://freespace.virgin.net/huw.rees/dc/
Mag Frequency: 2 per year
Subscription: £5 / 4 issues
Single Issue: £1.50
Overseas: $12 (4 issues)/$4 (single)
Payment in: Cash only US$ or sterling
Payable to: Dragon's Head Press
Inserts accepted: No
Advertising Rates: Negotiable
Circulation approx: 500
Payment terms to contributors: Free copy
Accept/rejection approx times: Generally acknowledged by return

D

DRAGON'S BREATH

The international small press review and independent monthly newsletter. Here's why you should subscribe . . . 'Comments definitely not sycophantic' - Dreamberry Wine / 'Well worth checking out' - ByPass / 'Handy and useful for budding writers and the like' - Monas Hieroglyphica / 'Micro reviews . . . wide net' - Fans Across the World / 'Genuine enthusiasm for the subject' - A Riot of Emotions / 'Stuffed with close-typed punchy reviews' - The Wizard's Knob / 'Reviews of the latest issues of most popular zines' - Sierra Heaven / 'Can be quite scathing . . . but useful and informative' - NHI Review / 'Densely packed with a swift content overview and Zine Kat's wry observations' - The BBR Directory / 'Information-dense, essential, and free' - Matrix / 'Does sterling service to the genre' - BFS Newsletter / 'Brings you sharp reviews of (the) Small Press' - Zine Zone / 'Comment on lots of magazines, excellent taster' - Iota / 'Pulls no punches so you can tell which is overpriced junk and which is good value . . . Try one - it's compellingly intriguing' - Krax.

Address: Zine Kat, c/o Pigasus Press, 13 Hazely Combe, Arreton, Isle Of Wight PO30 3AJ
Subs to: To Tony Lee at Pigasus Press
Mag Frequency: Monthly
Subscription: £2.50
Single Issue: Sample free for SAE
Overseas: 1 IRC per issue
Payment in: Cheque/PO
Payable to: Tony Lee
Inserts accepted: Yes
Terms: See **Advertising Rates:**
Advertising Rates: Available on request - send SAE/IRC
Circulation approx: Unknown
Payment terms to contributors: N/A
Accept/rejection approx times: N/A

DRAGONSPHERE

The Scrying Glass of Esoteric and Strange Publishing. A 'Magic Press' review and listings bulletin. Published by Dragon's Head Press: the independent small press publishing project.

Editor Name(s): Ade Dimmick
Address: Dragon's Head Press, P O Box 3369, London SW6 6JN
Email: dragonet@vtx.ch
Website: http://freespace.virgin.net/huw.rees/dc/
Mag Frequency: 3-4 times pa
Subscription: 4 x 2nd class stamp/IRC or donation
Single Issue: SAE/IRC or donation
Overseas: IRC or cash donation in US$ bills
Payable to: Dragon's Head Press
Inserts accepted: No
Circulation approx: 1000
Payment terms to contributors: N/A
Accept/rejection approx times: N/A

D

DREAMBERRY WINE

Dreamberry Wine is primarily a mail order catalogue, specialising in science-fiction, fantasy and related areas of books and magazines. However, DW also carries an average of 2-3 pages of book reviews, occasional author interviews, news from the SF field; even, rarely, short fiction - very short fiction.

Address: 233 Maine Road, Manchester M14 7WG
Email: mike.don@btinternet.com
Mag Frequency: Bimonthly (approx)
Subscription: £6
Single Issue: £1
Overseas: £10
Payment in: IMO/Sterling cheque/UK postal order
Payable to: Dreamberry Wine or Mike Don
Inserts accepted: No
Circulation approx: 400
Payment terms to contributors: None
Accept/rejection approx times: Variable

DREAMS FROM THE STRANGERS' CAFE

Beautifully set, printed and designed, Dreams From The Strangers' Cafe emanates genuine strangeness through its fiction, poetry and art. Stories between 2,000 - 10,000 words; poetry: 40 lines; and art is commissioned, although artists are welcome to send examples of work. We recommend seeing a recent issue before submitting.

Address: 15 Clifton Grove, Clifton, Rotherham, South Yorkshire S65 2AZ
Reviews to: Allen Ashley, 74 Hewison Street, Bow, London E3 2HY
Mag Frequency: Irregular - usually 2 per year
Subscription: 4 issues - £9
Single Issue: £2.50
Back Issue: £1.50
Overseas: US $25/RoW £18
Payment in: Dollars cash/sterling
Payable to: John Gaunt
Inserts accepted: No
Circulation approx: 500+
Payment terms to contributors: Contractual basis dependent on profit of each issue
Accept/rejection approx times: 2 months

E

EASTERN RAINBOW

Eastern Rainbow is a magazine which focuses on 20th century culture via poetry, prose & art. Will appeal to a wide range. Has featured Elvis Presley, Marilyn Monroe, George Best, Martin Luther King, George Orwell, Star Trek, Dr Who, The Prisoner, etc, in the past. Looking for enthusiastic work, but not hero-worshipping, deification of celebrities/TV programmes/films, etc. We also run poetry competitions and forms are available for an SAE/IRC. Full guidelines for contributions are available for an SAE/IRC.

Address: 17 Farrow Road, Whaplode Drove, Spalding, Lincs PE12 OTS
Mag Frequency: Once yearly
Subscription: £7.50 for 4 issues
Single Issue: £1.75
Back Issue: £1
Overseas: $16
Payment in: UK cheque/PO; Overseas IMO/banknotes
Payable to: Peace & Freedom
Inserts accepted: Yes
Terms: £20/$50 per 1000. Free to magazines who are willing to exchange circs
Circulation approx: 300
Payment terms to contributors: Free issue of magazine when work is published
Accept/rejection approx times: Less than 3 months

ECLIPSE POETRY MAGAZINE

Non-genre poetry magazine aimed at bringing new and untried poets into print. All forms of poetry accepted on any subject (subject to the law and the rules of decency).

Editor Name(s): Elizabeth Boyd
Address: Everyman Press, 53 West Vale, Neston, South Wirral L64 9SE
Mag Frequency: Bi-monthly
Subscription: £18 for 6 issues
Single Issue: N/A
Overseas: £20 EU/£24 RoW
Payment in: £ sterling
Payable to: Everyman Press
Inserts accepted: Yes
Terms: By arrangement
Advertising Rates: By arrangement
Payment terms to contributors: None - £25 per issue for readers' choice 'Poem of the Month'
Accept/rejection approx times: 2-3 weeks

E
ECTO 1

Ecto 1 is an exciting and eccentric and eclectic mix of poetry, pics, news clippings, bits, pieces and 'Biology for Life'-derived illus. Focus is on 'smart and experimental', and influences include pop culture, Futurism, the paranormal, sci-fi and cartoons. Issue One features work by, amongst others, Chris Bell, Andrew Darlington, T Kretz, Brendan McMahon, Paul Pinn, J Rogerson and Geoff Stevens and comes complete with Tango-orange front cover and ace 'Teenage Mutant Ninja Turtles' dot-to-dot on the back cover. Issue Two will include work by Jon Aylett, DF Lewis, Steve Harris, Robert Hrdina, Steve Sneyd, Peter Tennant, Johan de Wit, plus many, many more. Issue Three could feature you. Poetry with a (post-) modern edge preferred, but anything considered, and multiple submissions more than welcome. Ideas for future covers also required (photcopies only). Always enclose an SAE and hope to hear from you soon.

Editor Name(s): Mao
Address: 4 Pen-y-Cwm, Pentyrch, Cardiff CF4 8PS
Mag Frequency: Quarterly
Subscription: £6.25 for 4
Single Issue: £1.75
Back Issue: £1.50
Overseas: £2.25/£8 for 4
Payable to: M Oliver
Inserts accepted: Yes
Terms: Ad swap only
Advertising Rates: Ad swap only
Circulation approx: 125
Payment terms to contributors: Complimentary copy
Accept/rejection approx times: 1-2 months

THE EDGE

52-page A4 glossy, full-colour covered semi-pro publishing fiction, interviews, book, film, video, TV, graphic novel reviews. Published Michael Moorcock, Graham Joyce, Iain Sinclair, Christopher Petit, Peter Whitehead, John Shirley and many others alongside complete newcomers. 'Unusual', 'uncommercial' work published; 'modern' & 'postmodern' and 'borderline' 'horror', 'SF', sequels to work published elsewhere. No poetry. Nothing accepted if first submitted on disk or by email. No genre-clichés. Originality will be rewarded. No reprints. Much (about 30%) of our fiction has been republished in book form; The Edge is read by many professional writers and editors (by which we don't mean one or two 'Year's Best Fantasy' etc editors). Articles are 1000-16000 words so far. Cartoons & strips considered. Send disposable photocopies. We've never published an unsolicited review - send us a sample, whether previously published or not. Most of what we're sent is wildly unsuitable. Read the magazine first. Always send return postage. UK: SAE; Europe: 1 IRC; USA/RoW: 2 IRCs or 2 US dollars.

Editor Name(s): Graham Evans/Gerald Houghton
Address: 111 Guinness Buildings, Fulham Palace Road, London W6 8BD
Telephone: 0181 741 7757
Email: Yes - address in magazine
Website: www.users.globalnet.co.uk/~houghtong/edge/htm
Mag Frequency: 5 times a year
Subscription: £9.50 (4 issues)
Single Issue: £2.75 post free
Overseas: $20 US (4 issues) $6 US single copy
Payment in: Overseas - US cash/US cheques
Payable to: The Edge
Inserts accepted: Yes
Terms: Phone to discuss
Advertising Rates: Negotiable
Payment terms to contributors: Negotiable (£15-400)
Accept/rejection approx times: Anything from 1 week to 6 months

E

EDIBLE SOCIETY

Edible Society is a web-based magazine featuring short stories, featured poetry and a fine art gallery. It is part of Black Cat Communications' *words-music-vision* multi-art website, which is growing all the time. EdSoc features a creative use of words, visual art and sound - and is idealistic, visionary and disturbing in orientation, in varying proportions. Contributors are recommended to have a look before submitting anything. Contributors keep their own copyright.

Address: Black Cat Communications, PO Box 2864, Brighton, East Sussex BN1 4TH
Email: edsoc@mistral.co.uk
Website: http:www3.mistral.co.uk/blackcat
Mag Frequency: Monthly (approx)
Subscription: Local phone calls
Single Issue: Local phone calls
Back Issue: £2.50 inc p&p
Overseas: As UK
Payable to: Black Cat Communications
Inserts accepted: No
Circulation approx: Unlimited - growing number of visitors
Payment terms to contributors: Publication in a good website
Accept/rejection approx times: Up to 2 months

EDINBURGH REVIEW

This acclaimed literary and cultural review publishes a wide range of original and topical material with a new emphasis on the literary by both new and established writers. Lively, controversial and eclectic, Edinburgh Review is the only forum which positively asserts the rich diversity of Scottish arts and culture while attending to international literary and cultural events.

Address: Edinburgh University Press, 22 George Square, Edinburgh EH8 9LF
Mag Frequency: Twice a year
Subscription: Individual £15/Institution £30
Single Issue: £7.95
Overseas: Individual £16.95/Institution £33
Payable to: Edinburgh University Press
Inserts accepted: Yes
Terms: £135
Circulation approx: 800
Payment terms to contributors: By negotiation
Accept/rejection approx times: 2 months

E

END OF MILLENNIUM

Quarterly journal (Spring, Summer, Autumn & Winter issues) primarily for new writers and eclectic readers, aiming to celebrate this historic time in history through literature (hence the title). 92 A5 pages each issue with a well-balanced and wide mixture of poetry and prose from a plethora of brand new and contemporary writers. Radically different themes, forms, and styles have been explored in work hitherto published - more traditional poetry hangs out with modern forms, and short stories have come from genres as diverse as romance, sci-fi, historical, and contemporary and metaphysical themes. Articles also published, especially essays on literary or philosophical themes. No reviews published, but news of relevance to readers and writers may be mentioned in editorials. Concerning lengths: short stories can be anything from a few hundred up to 8,000 words. Our longest poem so far was 190 lines and we could comfortably consider longer pieces. Non-fiction should be between 500-3,000 words. All submissions are gratefully received and carefully considered.

Editor Name(s): G A Coyle
Address: End of Millennium, Porcine Publications, PO Box 7367, Kilmarnock, Ayrshire KA3 1RA
Mag Frequency: Quarterly
Subscription: £14 for 4 issues (inc p&p)
Single Issue: £4 each (inc p&p)
Back Issue: Back issue cost £3.50 (inc p&p)
Overseas: + £2 for non-EU Europe & RoW
Payment in: Sterling cheque/money order
Payable to: Porcine Publications
Inserts accepted: No
Circulation approx: 350
Payment terms to contributors: 2 free copies of journal & free entry into magazine prize prose and poetry competitions
Accept/rejection approx times: Generally 6-8 at weeks for decisions. Please send SAE for acknowledgement

ENIGMATIC TALES

Enigmatic Tales publishes supernatural ghost and horror stories with the emphasis on a beginning, middle and end. We prefer believable characters, realistic dialogue, and a strong storyline. We are unlikely to publish anything with strong swearing or explicit sex in it, we prefer to keep that to our private lives. We publish new stories as well as reprints, from new writers and more established ones. We also publish rare stories from the past. Any length will be considered, as we also run an occasional series, Enigmatic Novellas. Traditional supernatural ghost stories are our favourites, but we enjoy the whole range of the supernatural tale. The overriding factor is the quality of the story. We also publish artwork.

Address: 1 Gibbs Field, Bishops Stortford, Herts CM23 4EY
Website: www.magician.force9.co.uk
Mag Frequency: Quarterly
Subscription: £10
Single Issue: £3
Overseas: US$20 ($6 single)/Europe £12 (£4 single)
Payment in: Cheque/PO/IMO
Payable to: M Sims
Inserts accepted: Yes
Terms: Reciprocal
Circulation approx: 200 for 1st issue - just launched
Payment terms to contributors: 1 issue of magazine
Accept/rejection approx times: 1-3 weeks

ℰ
ENVOI

Current editor Roger Elkin. Subscription brings you * 176 pages each issue* Groups of poems (up to 8) by any one writer* Long(er) poems, over 40 lines of most magazine* Sequences, or extracts from longer sequences* Poems in collaboration* Poems in translation* First Publication feature for new writers* Articles on poetry, creativity and style* Competition and Adjudicator's Report each issue* Comparative reviews of current poetry publications* Letters and Comment* Free critical comment (3 poems per year) on request* And oodles of poems.

Editor Name(s): Roger Elkin
Address: 44 Rudyard Road, Biddulph Moor, Stoke-on Trent, ST8 7JN
Mag Frequency: 3 issues per annum (Feb; June; Oct)
Subscription: £12 per annum
Single Issue: £4
Back Issue: Sample £3
Overseas: £15 or $30 pa/current copy £4 or $8
Payment in: Preferably in US dollar bills if sterling not available
Payable to: Envoi
Inserts accepted: Yes
Terms: £50 per 1000
Circulation approx: 800-1000
Payment terms to contributors: 2 complimentary copies
Accept/rejection approx times: 6-8 weeks

E

EPIPHYTES

The journal of the Epiphytic Plant Study Group: covers all aspects of the cultivation of epiphytic plants. Line drawings and colour photographs to illustrate articles. A must for all interested in epiphytic plants.

Editor Name(s): John F Horobin
Address: 1 Belvidere Park, Great Crosby, Lancs L23 0SP
Telephone: 01509 413541
Email: csd@mcmail.com
Mag Frequency: Quarterly (Feb/May/Aug/Nov)
Subscription: £7.50
Overseas: £8.75 surface mail
Payment in: Sterling only
Payable to: EPSG
Inserts accepted: No
Circulation approx: 200

E
EPOCH

Epoch (founded 1991) features Scottish material in the context of European and world literature & art. Epoch is open to politics, philosophy, poetry. Leading article is usually on a major figure in Scottish literature (eg RB Cunninghame Grahame) plus articles on European artists (eg Goya) and writers (eg Victor Serge). Liberal/socialist ethos but not dogmatic - have carried articles on Nietszche in the past!

Address: 57 Murray Street, Montrose, Angus, Scotland, DD10 8JZ
Mag Frequency: Depending on funds
Subscription: £7 for 5 issues
Single Issue: £1.50
Overseas: £15 Europe/America
Payment in: IMO/Sterling cheque/PO; foreign currencies must allow for exchange charge
Payable to: The Corbie Press
Inserts accepted: Yes
Terms: Free if reciprocated
Circulation approx: 300 (increasing)
Payment terms to contributors: 1 copy
Accept/rejection approx times: About one in ten acceptances, usually over-subscribed with poetry! Decision time about 6-10 weeks

EQUINOX

E

Equinox - a 32pg b/w anthology title - featuring top writers and artists on comic strips. Sci-fi, superheroes and adventure are its staple diet. A collection of fast-paced action-packed strips, inspired by Hollywood blockbusters! New contributors very welcome - please send copies of samples to the editors, Lee Davis or Julie Henderson at the featured address. Equinox is attempting to increase its frequency and format . . . we're entering exciting times!

Editor Name(s): Lee Davis/Julie Henderson
Address: North London Comics, 140 Amersham Ave, Edmonton, London, N18 1DY
Subs to: Mark for 'subscriptions'
Mag Frequency: Quarterly
Subscription: £7
Single Issue: £1.75
Back Issue: £1.50
Overseas: Please write for details
Payable to: Lee Davis/Julie Henderson
Circulation approx: 100-150

E

ESCAPED

Escaped is the regular magazine for members and supporters of Escape. Escape is a cutting edge campaign group which works for the freedom of animals, humans and the earth. Escape operates peaceful and legal public education campaigns, aimed at exposing and fighting against animal abuse, erosion of civil liberties, medical fraud and dangerous foods. Each issue of Escaped complements the Escape campaign work with in-depth articles about Escape's work, alternative health, animal liberation and other issues. Escaped is the magazine for the informed intelligent campaigner with the latest news, views, contacts and light-hearted features. Escaped - until all are free.

Address: Escaped Magazine, @ Escape, PO Box 2801 Brighton BN1 3NH
Mag Frequency: Quarterly
Subscription: £5 as membership of Escape campaign group
Single Issue: £1.50
Overseas: Overseas members £8 subs
Payment in: Cheque/PO/Cash at own risk
Payable to: Escape
Inserts accepted: Yes subject to approval
Terms: Donation to Escape
Circulation approx: 260 copies currently increasing
Payment terms to contributors: No payment
Accept/rejection approx times: Replies within 1 month

ESPYLACOPA (ESP)

A fast-growing publication, Espylacopa is an irreverent sideways look at the world as we know it. Including interviews with the likes of Paul Grist as well as short fiction ranging from science fiction to satire.

Address: 5 Bove Town, Glastonbury, Somerset BA6 8LE
Mag Frequency: Quarterly
Subscription: £5 for 4 issues
Single Issue: £1.50
Payment in: Cheque/PO
Payable to: Ben Graham
Inserts accepted: Yes
Terms: Reciprocal - contact editor
Circulation approx: 100
Payment terms to contributors: Free issue
Accept/rejection approx times: Within 1 month

E
ESSENCE OF BEING

This is a collection of thoughts by Andoon Hinley Dink and Faene Nuff; other people's work may be included.

Address: Andoon & Steph, c/o 13 Spencer Drive, Sutton Height Telford, Shropshire, TF7 4JY
Mag Frequency: Irregular
Single Issue: 50p each plus SAE

EXILE

E

Poetry magazine for new writers, contributions accepted from round the world. No short stories or poems longer than 40 lines. Poetry not returned but copyright remains with author. Exile has been established for ten years and is used by various universities throughout America, Canada, Israel as a study aid to students of contemporary poetry.

Editor Name(s): Ann Elliott / John Marr
Address: Four Winds, Guston Road, East Langdon, Kent CT15 5JE
Telephone: 01304 852986
Mag Frequency: Quarterly
Subscription: £8
Single Issue: £2.50
Overseas: £8 for 4 issues
Payable to: Exile
Inserts accepted: No
Circulation approx: 500
Payment terms to contributors: None
Accept/rejection approx times: 6 months

F
FACTS & FICTION

Facts And Fiction celebrates the world of oral storytelling. Each edition includes information of what is going on - plus news from around England (and overseas) - interviews with storytellers - 'how to' type articles - reviews of relevant books and tapes - and stories to share. It has been published since Autumn 1991 and is done very much on a non-profit basis with no payments being made to contributors etc. We all do it for the love of the art form. For the last three years it has received a fairly small funding from West Midlands Arts. As the editor and a working story-teller, my aim is to produce a magazine I'd want to buy and enjoy myself - a fanzine of storytelling.

Address: 16 Severn Way, Cressage, Shropshire SY5 6DS
Mag Frequency: Quarterly - October, January, April, July
Subscription: £9
Single Issue: £1.80 (plus 50p post + package)
Back Issue: £ (incl post + package)
Overseas: £10 (EU)/£12 RoW
Payable to: Facts and Fiction
Inserts accepted: Yes - only if they relate to storytelling events
Terms: Price per 100 - £10
Circulation approx: 200
Payment terms to contributors: None
Accept/rejection approx times: With SAE - 1 month

THE FAIRACRES CHRONICLE

The journal of the Anglican contemplative religious community, The Sisters of the Love of God. A mix of community news and articles on prayer and spirituality with a bias towards contemplative prayer. Current books on Christian spirituality/prayer are reviewed. Poetry not accepted for publication.

Address: The Sister in Charge, S.L.G. Press, Convent of the Incarnation, Fairacres, Oxford OX4 1TB
Mag Frequency: 3 issues per year
Subscription: £4.50 (p&p incl)
Single Issue: £1
Back Issue: As priced on cover
Overseas: Europe (air) £5 / **Overseas:** surface £5 (US$ 9); airmail £6.50 (US$ 21)
Payment in: Cheque or cash only (not credit card)
Inserts accepted: No
Circulation approx: 1200
Payment terms to contributors: A proportion of print run, no royalties
Accept/rejection approx times: At earliest opportunity, by return

F
FELINE FABLES

Feline Fables is an anthropomorphic fiction magazine. Any type of animal story or poem is considered for publication. Cat stories are most highly featured, most humorous and mostly told from the animal's point of view. Feature - reader's photo featured on cover back and front (feline reader). The magazine is generously laid out with larger than average print size for easy reading. Stories of all types from both new and established authors are featured. Unsolicited material welcomed and always replied to providing an sae is enclosed. Note, standard rejections never given.

Editor Name(s): Amanda Gillies
Address: Suite 2, 39 Heathhill Industrial Estate, Dawley, Shropshire TF4 2RH
Telephone: 01952 275290
Email: Feline.Fables@writers.brew.clara. net
Website: http://www.writers.brew.clara.net/ff/
Mag Frequency: Quarterly
Subscription: £30 - but request info on current special offer. Special rate for OAPs £22 UK.
Single Issue: £7.50
Overseas: $66 sub/£20 single copy
Advertising Rates: Full pg £15/half £12/quarter £5
Payment terms to contributors: Free copy or sub extension

F

FIRE

Fire is a magazine for new and experimental writing - mainly poetry but also some prose; it does not align itself with any particular group or style but will publish a broad range of work from anywhere in the UK or the world. It is particularly interested in work which might not easily be accepted elsewhere - longer poems, sprawling works of the heart or soul, work that is experimental or 'alternative' or just simply unfashionable. It is also concerned to promote young, new or little-known writers.

Editor Name(s): Jeremy Hilton
Address: Field Cottage, Old White Hill, Tackley, Kidlington, Oxfordshire OX5 3AB
Mag Frequency: 2 times a year
Subscription: £7 (3 issues)
Single Issue: £4
Back Issue: £3
Overseas: Add postage to UK sub
Payable to: Fire
Inserts accepted: No
Circulation approx: 150 expanding steadily
Payment terms to contributors: 2 copies
Accept/rejection approx times: 5-8 weeks

F

THE FIRING SQUAD

Poetry of complaint or protest. Requires volunteers to copy a dozen copies or more each and distribute. This is not just a poetry sheet but a vehicle for protest by people desperate to say something.

Address: 8 Beaconview House, Charlemont Farm, West Bromwich B71 3PL
Mag Frequency: Occasional
Subscription: £1
Single Issue: N/A
Back Issue: 50p
Overseas: N/A
Payment in: Cash or cheque
Payable to: Purple Patch
Inserts accepted: Yes
Terms: Make a donation
Circulation approx: 100
Payment terms to contributors: None
Accept/rejection approx times: Two weeks

F

FIRST IMPRESSION

First Impression is a unique combination of poetry competition and self-publication. First poem can be entered free of charge. Subsequent poems are entered for £7.50. All poems are published and all participating poets vote for monthly winning poem and runner up. Prize money £20 + £10. Please send sae for details. Poems to be no longer than 40 lines (approx) and not to contain unsuitable language.

Address: PO Box 11, Mablethorpe, Lincs LN12 2GA
Fax: 01507 443909
Email: frstimpoem@aol.com
Mag Frequency: Monthly
Subscription: £18 for 6 issues
Single Issue: £3
Overseas: N/A
Payable to: First Impression
Inserts accepted: No
Circulation approx: Increasing
Payment terms to contributors: Copy of magazine plus chance of winning competition
Accept/rejection approx times: All poems conforming to Editor's rules (see above) are published

ℱ

FIRST OFFENSE

The magazine is for contemporary poetry and is not traditional, but is received by most ground-breaking poets.

Editor Name(s): Tim Fletcher
Address: Syringh, Stodmarsh, Canterbury, Kent CT3 4BA
Mag Frequency: 1 or 2 yearly
Subscription: £2.75
Single Issue: £2.75
Back Issue: £2.50
Overseas: £2.75
Payment in: Cheque
Payable to: Tim Fletcher
Inserts accepted: No
Circulation approx: 300
Payment terms to contributors: N/A
Accept/rejection approx times: N/A

F

FIRST TIME

A well established magazine / too large to be called little. I publish work of all kinds and welcome work from disabled people who are in institutions. A bi-annual magazine designed to encourage first time poets. Note: 1. Poems submitted must not exceed 30 lines / 2. Poems must not have been published elsewhere and must be author's original work / 3. Name and address must be printed on each sheet / 4. Manuscripts cannot be returned unless sae envelope enclosed / 5. The editor's decision is final. No correspondence can be entered into regarding choice for publication.

Address: Burdett Cottage, 4 Burdett Place, George Street, Hastings, E. Sussex TN34 3ED
Mag Frequency: Bi-Annual
Subscription: £6 per annum plus £1 postage
Single Issue: £3 plus p&p
Back Issue: £1.25 plus p&p
Overseas: US $13
Inserts accepted: Yes
Terms: £20 per 1000
Circulation approx: 1000
Payment terms to contributors: No
Accept/rejection approx times: 2 months

F

FLAIR FOR WORDS

Flair For Words was established in 1988. Cass and Janie Jackson are professional writers/lecturers/critics who offer a wide range of services to beginning or experienced writers. Flair Comments is the assessment, editiing and advisory service. We also publish handbooks, Yellow Pages and audio tapes on all aspects of writing. Our positive thought newsletter, Flair For Living, is published on alternate months and has now been running for two years. Further details on request.

Editor Name(s): Cass Jackson/Janie Jackson
Address: 57 Hillside Road, Whyteleafe, Surrey CR3 0BR
Telephone: 01883 626540
Email: caja@compuserve.com
Mag Frequency: Alternate months
Subscription: £6 pa
Single Issue: £1
Overseas: £6 + postage
Payment in: Cheque/PO. Overseas payment in £ sterling or drawn on UK bank.
Payable to: Cass & Janie Jackson
Inserts accepted: Yes
Terms: Reciprocal

FLAMING ARROWS

Literary journal, contemporary styles of fiction and poetry. New writers sought with distinctive style; polished prose, coherent, lucid, direct and strong poetry. Contemplative metaphysical, mystical, spiritual themes are sought which are grounded in physical senses. Also interested in Earth/Gaia sensibility, sensitivity to sacred space in landscape. Where is the sacred in contemporary life, how is it identified and sustained? Flaming Arrows receives financial assistance from The Arts Council of Ireland.

Address: Leo Regan, VEC, Riverside, Sligo, Ireland.
Fax: +353 71 43093
Email: leoregan@tinet.ie
Mag Frequency: Annual
Subscription: £2.65
Single Issue: £2.65
Back Issue: Issues 1, 2, 3 - £5.00. Issues 4, 5, 6 - £2.65
Payment in: Cheque or PO
Payable to: Flaming Arrows
Inserts accepted: No
Circulation approx: 500
Payment terms to contributors: One comp copy, copies at cost on request.
Accept/rejection approx times: 3 months - final selection, October

F
FOCUS

Focus is the writers' magazine of the British Science Fiction Association. It specialises in articles on the creative processes of SF from the original spark of ideas to
publication, and publishes material by both aspiring and published writers. We feature a forum where a particular issue is discussed by several writers. Focus also
publishes fiction, poetry and artwork - also 'drabbles' (stories of exactly 100 words).
Contributors have included John Brunner, Gwyneth Jones, Diana Wynne Jones,
Dave Langford, Steve Sneyd and Sue Thomas, also a regular column by author and
critic Colin Greenland. Submissions should be up to 5000 words for fiction and
articles, a maximum of 50 lines for poetry; forum pieces should be of 600-800
words (contact the editors for details of the current forum. Previous subjects have
included Characters, Worldbuilding, Aliens and Other Animals and Writers' Workshops). Artists should ideally send photocopied examples/submissions in the first
instance (sorry, no colour). We are open to submissions from members and non-
members.

Address: Julia Venner, 42 Walgrave Street, Newland Avenue, Hull HU5 2LT Carol
Ann Green, Flat 3, 141 Princes Avenue, Hull HU5 3EL
Subs to: Membership secretary: Paul Billinger, 82 Kelvin Road, New Cubbington,
Leamington Spa, Warwickshire CV32 7TA
Mag Frequency: Bi-annual
Subscription: Included in BSFA Membership £18 UK
Single Issue: £1 + p & p
Back Issue: Some back issues available at 50p + p & p
Overseas: Contact Membership secretary for details
Payment in: UK Sterling cheque/British PO/IMO
Payable to: In UK BSFA Ltd/In US Cy Chauvin (BSFA)
Inserts accepted: By negotiation with the BSFA
Circulation approx: 900* The BSFA is the British Science Fiction Association.
Members receive Vector (the critical journal); Matrix (the news magazine) and Fo-
cus (the writers' magazine).
Payment terms to contributors: Contributor's copy
Accept/rejection approx times: 8-12 weeks. Receipt is acknowledged

FOOTSTEPS

Footsteps is devoted to tales of quiet horror, tales that give the reader a shiver or a shudder at their conclusion. It also includes poetry and illustrations.

Address: Huntiegouke Press, 32 Caneluk Avenue, Carluke, Scotland ML8 4LZ
Mag Frequency: Quarterly
Subscription: £9
Single Issue: £2.50
Overseas: £20
Payment in: Cheque/PO
Payable to: Ian Hunter
Inserts accepted: Yes
Circulation approx: 100
Payment terms to contributors: £3 per 1000 words, £3 per poem, £5 per illustration
Accept/rejection approx times: 12-14 weeks

F
FORTNIGHT

Independent review of politics and the arts.

Address: 7 Lower Crescent, Belfast BT7 1NR
Reviews to: John O'Farrell/Martin Crawford
Subs to: John O'Farrell
Fax: 01232 232650
Email: mairtin@fortnite.dnet.co.uk
Mag Frequency: Monthly (11 issues per year - combined Jul/Aug)
Subscription: £28
Single Issue: £2.20/Ir £2.30
Back Issue: £2.10
Overseas: Rep of Ireland Ir£33/Europe £33/RoW£47; Institutions add £10
Payment in: Cheque/PO/IMO
Payable to: Fortnight
Inserts accepted: Yes
Terms: £45
Circulation approx: 4500
Payment terms to contributors: Arranged individually

FORUM

Forum (Founded 1967) is the international journal of human relationships, dealing with all aspects of sex and sexuality. It features serious medical and relationship-based articles, interviews, erotic fiction by leading names in the genre and newcomers. Expert advice to readers' problems and a world-famous letters page. A regular feature offers budding poets the chance to see their work in print.

Address: Northern & Shell Tower, PO Box 381, City Harbour, London E14 9GL
Subs to: 43 Mill Harbour, London E14 9TR
Fax: 0171 308 5075
Email: forum@norshell.co.uk
Mag Frequency: 13 annually
Subscription: £32 (13 issues)/£17 (6 issues)
Single Issue: £3.50
Back Issue: £3.50 + £1 p & p
Payable to: Northern & Shell
Inserts accepted: Yes
Terms: £15
Advertising Rates:
Circulation approx: 35000
Payment terms to contributors: £10 per poem/£125 per short story
Accept/rejection approx times: 2-3 months

$\mathcal{F}$
FreeHand

FreeHand has traditionally been a magazine for writers who want to share their work with like-minded people. Under new editorship since October 1998, FreeHand maintains its A4 format and easygong style. Each issue contains a seasonal section, a pause for thought section of memories and reminiscence, and a feature on one of the subscribers as well as the usual mix of stories and poems. It is hoped that one page will in future develop as a young subscribers' page to encourage promising youngsters to make contributions and submissions. Submissions are invited in poetry, prose, article or short story form . . . up to 2000 words. Puzzles and word-searches are also invited. Illustrators capable of producing good quality black & white line art are actively sought. Rather than becoming a competitive publication, FreeHand aims to remain a platform for mainstream writing and artwork and a vehicle for the promotion of those poets/writers who have acheived publication in a small way either through self-publishing or acceptance of short-run publications. If you write, FreeHand wants to read it! Submissions from subscribers only. Annual competition will be launched in 1999. Monthly award of $5 for most promising/appealing submission in any form.

Editor Name(s): Jo Wood
Address: 5 Island Court, Riversdale Road, West Kirby, Wirral L48 4EZ
Telephone: 0151 625 0969 or 0777 590 3462
Fax: 0151 625 0969
Email: josephinewood@compuserve.com
Mag Frequency: Bi-monthly
Subscription: £12 pa
Single Issue: £2
Overseas: £18 pa/£2.50 single
Payment in: Cheque
Payable to: Footprints
Inserts accepted: Yes
Terms: On application or reciprocal
Advertising Rates: On request
Circulation approx: 250
Payment terms to contributors: £5 award each month
Accept/rejection approx times: ASAP

FREELANCE MARKET NEWS

Established in 1968, Freelance Market News is a monthly newsletter giving news, views and advice about new publications - plus the trends and developments in established markets, at home and abroad. With feature articles, author profiles, book reviews, news of competitions, festivals and residential courses, professional advice and problem solving - writers can be sure they are kept up to date with what is happening on the writing scene.

Address: Sevendale House, 7 Dale Street, Manchester M1 1JB
Fax: 0161 228 3533
Mag Frequency: Monthly (not published in July)
Subscription: £29 per year (11 issues) £17 (6 issues)
Back Issue: £2.50
Overseas: As UK
Payable to: Freelance Market News
Inserts accepted: Yes
Terms: £50 perr 1000
Circulation approx: 4000+ subscribers
Payment terms to contributors: £35 per 1000 words, guidelines available for SAE
Accept/rejection approx times: 2 weeks

$\mathcal{F}$

THE FROGMORE PAPERS

The Frogmore Papers publish poetry and prose by new and established writers. Founded in 1983, the magazine has featured work by a wide variety of poets from Linda France, John Mole and Sophie Hannah to Elizabeth Garrett, Pauline Stainer and Katherine Pierpoint. The annual Frogmore Poetry Prize, founded in 1987, was won by Russ Cogan in 1998; previous winners include John Latham, Tobias Hill and Mario Petrucci.

Address: 18 Nevill Road, Lewes, East Sussex BN7 1PF
Subs to: The Frogmore Press, 42 Morehall Avenue, Folkestone, Kent, CT19 4EF
Mag Frequency: Bi-annual (March/September)
Subscription: £7
Single Issue: £3.80 (inc p&p)
Back Issue: £2
Overseas: US $20, Europe £10
Payment in: US subs in bills only no US cheques
Payable to: The Frogmore Press
Inserts accepted: No
Circulation approx: 500
Payment terms to contributors: Complimentary copy
Accept/rejection approx times: 1-3 months

F

FRONT & CENTRE

Front & Centre Magazine is a biannual fiction magazine published jointly in Great Britain and Canada. Submissions of new fiction between 50-4000 words are welcome. We are interested in fiction set in a realistic tone, concerning the obsessions of contemporary life. We want fiction that moves swiftly. That roars in the ear of complacency. That is not cloaked with stylized diversions and distractions but has instead clarity, conflict and characterization at its core. Above all, make it meaningful. Each issue contains new fiction from approximately a dozen writers from both sides of the Atlantic, plus book reviews, features and commentary. Please include a SASE with alll submissions. No electronic submissions, queries only.

Editor Name(s): Matthew Firth
Address: 4-C Alexandra Place, St Andrews, Fife KY16 9DX
Telephone: 01334 470250
Email: af11@st-andrews.ac.uk
Mag Frequency: Biannual
Subscription: £4 two issues
Single Issue: £2
Payment in: Sterling
Payable to: M Firth
Inserts accepted: No
Circulation approx: 300
Payment terms to contributors: 2 copies
Accept/rejection approx times: 1-3 months

F

FRONTAL LOBE

Prose, poetry, articles, music, cartoons, artwork, short stories - max 4000 words; poems, articles - 1000 words: all must be typed. Please enclose SAE for return of work. Also a short review.

Address: 18 Stile Common, Primrose Hill, Newsome, Huddersfield, W. Yorks HD4 GDY
Mag Frequency: Quarterly
Subscription: £5 for 4 issues
Single Issue: £1.25 inc p&p
Payment terms to contributors: Free copy of the magazine

FUTURION

Futurion: Neo-sci-fi fanzine features the short stories, poetry, artwork and collages of Leigh Smith. After years of pumping out free artwork, collages, poetry and short stories Leigh Smith decided to create his own fanzine. Two and a half issues exist so far, may mutate into a one-page A4 newsletter or explode and go weekly knocking 2000 AD off the shelves. Futurion has come to save sci fi ! Come to meet the dark inhabitants of Unicorn Park! No X piles or Star Tat fans need write. Futurion is best described as a mix of The Ghosts of Motley Hall/ Bladerunner/ Dune/ Spawn and Louise Clifford. They offer us no future thus we must create our own! Also home of geek star puppet video!

Address: 16 Bridge Street, South Quay, Maryport, Cumbria CA15 8AE.
Mag Frequency: Every couple of months
Subscription: £5
Single Issue: £1
Overseas: Beware U-Boats
Payment in: Make it cash and fast
Payable to: Mr L J Smith
Inserts accepted: Yes
Terms: Free
Circulation approx: 100
Payment terms to contributors: Copy of fanzine
Accept/rejection approx times: 1-2 weeks

G
GAIRM

A quarterly publication, in Scottish Gaelic, encompassing fiction, poetry, current affairs, articles on technical topics, folklore, song, reviews with some pictorial features. The periodical was founded in 1951-52. Gairm Publications also publish a wide range of books: dictionaries, grammars, novels, short stories, poetry, children's books, Gaelic music books etc. Only Scottish Gaelic contributions accepted.

Address: 29 Waterloo Street, Glasgow G2 6BZ
Mag Frequency: Quarterly
Subscription: £8 UK
Single Issue: £1.60
Back Issue: Variable; pack of 50 back issues £28 (£40 overseas)
Overseas: £10
Payable to: Gairm Publications
Inserts accepted: Yes
Terms: £30 per 1000
Circulation approx: 2000
Payment terms to contributors: Approx £10 per page
Accept/rejection approx times: 2-3 weeks

GEEK LOVE

G

Founded in 1995, Geek Love is innovative in style and layout. Dedicated to further-ing writers at all levels it features some of the best writing from around the world. Enhancing poetry with graphic design, Geek Love is one of the most original poetry publications available. All submissions will be used at some point whether they are good, bad or ugly. Although due to the format and demand of space, shorter contri-butions will be looked upon favourably, Geek Love doesn't believe in any form of censorship and abhores the elitist attitude of some poetry publications. Often let-ters and other correspondence are incorporated into the layouts. This booklet, infa-mous as it is unique, will interpret your work like no other. Due to its phenomenal success in the first year publication has been reduced to just two issues per year, (June and December). Buy one.

Address: Denude Studio (Geek Love), PO Box 72, Manchester M14 5SD
Mag Frequency: Twice yearly (June/December)
Subscription: N/A
Single Issue: £1 plus postage
Payment in: Secured sterling/cheque/PO
Payable to: M McNamara
Inserts accepted: Yes
Terms: Free
Circulation approx: 400
Payment terms to contributors: 1 issue/kudos
Accept/rejection approx times: Immediate response with SAE

G
GHOSTS & SCHOLARS

Ghosts & Scholars publishes new ghost stories in the M R James tradition (no other kind of ghost story will be considered). The M R James tradition is not the same as traditional. Prospective contributions should be familiar with M R James' work. Research on aspects of MRJ's stories especially encouraged. Mss up to 8000 words. Non-fiction on MRJ and other writers in the James tradition also welcome (up to 8000 words).

Address: Rosemary Pardoe, Flat One, 36 Hamilton Street, Hoole, Chester CH2 3JQ
Fax: 01244 313685
Email: pardos@globalnet.co.uk
Mag Frequency: Twice a year
Subscription: £14
Single Issue: £4
Overseas: £15
Payment in: No foreign cheques
Payable to: Rosemary Pardoe
Inserts accepted: No
Circulation approx: 450
Payment terms to contributors: Contributor copies only (3)
Accept/rejection approx times: Two weeks maximum

GIBBERING MADNESS

Horror/art/punk zine with short stories, interviews, articles, reviews and artwork. No poetry! Contributors wanted of any of the above . . . especially stories (max length about 4 pages long). I run this zine on a non-profit basis - that is why it is cheap . . . but because of that I can't afford to pay any contributors (sorry!) The last issue (#5) has stories by Tim Drage and Leigh Smith, articles about censorship, Aleister Crowley, Sea Heads, & Mail Art, interviews with Paul Petard (Anarchist Cartoonist) & David Dellafiora (Mail Artist) plus loads of artwork and masses of reviews.

Address: Gibbering Madness, PO Box 298, Sheffield, S10 5XT
Mag Frequency: About once a year (but sometimes twice!)
Single Issue: 50p (+sae)
Back Issue: #4 - 50p/#3 - 20p
Overseas: $2 per issue - including postage
Payment in: £sterling or US$ only please
Payable to: E Griffiths (UK only)
Circulation approx: 400 copies printed
Payment terms to contributors: Copy of issue work appears in
Accept/rejection approx times: I hardly get much sent . . . so I haven't had the luxury of being too picky!

$\mathcal{G}$
GLASSHOUSE ELECTRIC

Glasshouse Electric is a randomly published double-sided A4 sheet of experimental poetry, word art, phonetic graphics, etc. Editorial selection is looser than with other Silver Gull publications due to the nature of Glasshouse Electric. Each issue will be sent to a large number of magazines for review as well as libraries, colleges and universities around the country. Please send submissions 'camera ready'.

Editor Name(s): J Rogerson
Address: Silver Gull Publishing, West Lodge, Higher Lane, Liverpool L9 7AB
Mag Frequency: Random
Subscription: N/A
Single Issue: Free for SAE/IRC
Inserts accepted: By trade
Circulation approx: 50-100
Payment terms to contributors: Complimentary copy
Accept/rejection approx times: 2-6 weeks

GLOBAL TAPESTRY JOURNAL

A manifestation of exciting creativity. Innovative prose writing and novel extracts. Contains 'PM Newsletter' - reviewing small alternative networks and large publishing house releases. Bohemian, post-Beat and counter-culture orientation.

Address: Spring Bank, Longsight Road, Copster Green, Blackburn, Lancs BB1 9EU
Mag Frequency: Irregular
Subscription: £8 - 4 postal issues
Single Issue: £2.20 single postal copy
Back Issue: Usually out of print
Overseas: £10 sterling
Payment in: Sterling cheques/USA currency
Payable to: BB Books
Inserts accepted: Yes
Terms: £10 per 1000
Circulation approx: 1050 to 1500
Payment terms to contributors: Issue of magazine
Accept/rejection approx times: 2 - 6 weeks

G
GOOD STORIES

Quarterly magazine of original short stories of all kinds.

Editor Name(s): A Royle
Address: Oakwood Publications, 23 Mill Crescent, Kingsbury, Warwickshire B78 2LX
Telephone: 01827 873435
Mag Frequency: Quarterly
Subscription: £10 pa (4 issues)
Single Issue: £2.95
Back Issue: £2
Overseas: £17.50
Payment in: Sterling only
Payable to: Oakwood Publications
Inserts accepted: Yes
Terms: By negotiation
Advertising Rates: Media pack on request
Circulation approx: 3000
Payment terms to contributors: On publication
Accept/rejection approx times: 6 weeks

GUTTER GIRL

Gutter Girl is Lancaster's answer to Vogue, Cosmo, Women's Own (without the recipes, glamour and knitting patterns!). Original concept was to create a magazine for women to air their views, promote women's issues and challenge the mainstream 'glossies'. Packed full of articles, poems, reviews, cartoons (there's even a rant corner to get it off your chest too!). Gutter Girl is reasonably priced feminism for all women. And every woman is a potential Gutter Girl.

Address: Gutter Girl c/o Single Step, 78A Penny Street, Lancaster LA1 1XN
Mag Frequency: Quarterly (sometimes 6 a year)
Subscription: £5 yearly
Single Issue: 50p
Overseas: Negotiable
Payment in: Cheque/PO
Payable to: Gutter Girl
Inserts accepted: Yes
Circulation approx: 500-800
Payment terms to contributors: Unpaid contributions only
Accept/rejection approx times: As long as it's sound, we won't reject anything

𝓗
HA!

Ha! has turned electronic and is now available on the Internet via: www.humour.co.uk. Dedicated to writing of a humorous, satirical and whimsical nature, the magazine also contains cartoons and caricatures. Articles are sometimes related to topical events, but we do not constrain ourselves to trying desperately to reflect the times. Basically, we like being *silly* and hope it amuses the occasional reader/viewer.

Address: 5 Longholm Way, Barnet, Herts EN5 2SP
Fax: 0181 449 1368
Email: simon@gcsl.co.uk
Website: www.humour.co.uk
Mag Frequency: Bi-monthly/Quarterly
Terms: Advertising space on the website is available
Circulation approx: Internet
Payment terms to contributors: (Non-profit, at present!)

HALLOW-ZENE

An exploration of halloween & connected 'things' in poetry, prose, fact, fiction & art - though not as serious as that sounds . . . Celtic/Pagan/Horror/Magick/Forteana. We're interested in far more things than we believe . . .

Address: Neil Rhind, Birchview, Longmorn, Elgin, Moray, Scotland IV30 3SL
Reviews to: Music reviews - Alan Ferguson, 2 Birnie Crescent, Elgin, Moray, Scotland
Mag Frequency: Annually
Back Issue: Trade/£350
Payable to: Neil Rhind
Circulation approx: 200-250 limited edition covers - 300 'normal'
Payment terms to contributors: You'll be lucky
Accept/rejection approx times: 1 acceptance per 5 rejections

$\mathcal{H}$

HANDSHAKE

Handshake is a very specialised magazine, consisting of a single sheet of A4 devoted entirely to SF poetry. One side of the magazine consists of news and information about genre poetry - information submitted should be typed, single-spaced, ready for photocopying. Adverts are OK if small. Side two has now evolved into a 'poetry magazine' - but being only one side of a single sheet means I can take no epics! Short poems preferred, and as I always have more poems than information I prefer the latter. You are advised to see a copy before submitting. All rights revert to author on publication. All submissions must be accompanied by an sae, and have not been published elsewhere.

Address: J.F. Haines, 5 Cross Farm, Station Road, Padgate, Warrington WA2 OQG
Mag Frequency: Irregular
Subscription: SAE/IRC/Stamps/Trade
Single Issue: Same
Back Issue: Same - very few ever available
Overseas: SAE/IRC/Stamps/Trade
Inserts accepted: Yes - genre poetry related only
Circulation approx: 60+
Payment terms to contributors: Copy of newsletter
Accept/rejection approx times: Soon as I can and within a month if possible, though if you're close to an issue being printed it could be longer

HARD COPY

A personal website full of stuff I like - mostly artwork and short prose pieces about comic strips, TV, movies, media, northern soul - but nothing too serious, important or worthy. I'm looking for artwork that spoofs news, people and media of the moment; witty writing and criticism of same; and even both together - no poetry unless it's very funny.

Editor Name(s): Michael Perridge
Address: http:// website.lineone.net/~m.perridge/index.html
Email: m.perridge@lineone.net
Mag Frequency: Site updated every month
Subscription: Free
Single Issue: Free
Back Issue: Free
Overseas: It's free
Payment in: No really - it's free
Payable to: No - it's free
Advertising Rates: No advertising
Payment terms to contributors: None
Accept/rejection approx times: 1 week via email

ℋ
HAWKEYE

Hawkeye is a Hawkwind and related publication, looking at recent events/news and CD, LP and video releases. Each issue has lengthy articles on Hawkwind to date and past, using artwork and adverts throughout. There's also a list of useful contact addresses for other publications and mail order companies that are connected with Hawkwind or the many spin-offs, solo and related bands. In addition to Hawkeye there are other, more in-depth reference publications related to Hawkwind, that may be of interest. Send SAE for further information to Adrian Parr at mag address.

Address: 6 Conifers Close, Teddington, Middlesex TW11 9JG
Mag Frequency: Twice yearly
Single Issue: £2.50 incl p&p
Overseas: £3 Europe - £3.50 elsewhere
Payment in: Cheques/Postal Orders/IMOs
Payable to: Mr A Parr
Inserts accepted: Yes if related to Hawkwind
Circulation approx: 250

HEADLOCK

Wall-to-wall poetry, occasional prose essay on the state of poetry. Famous biographies. Some illustration (B/W only). No reviews. Submissions always welcome, must be accompanied by sae. Overseas submitters, send disposable copies and IRC. Editor's tastes are eclectic - experimental/provocative work elbows with good traditional writing. South-West contributors encouraged, but not given special preference.

Address: Tony Charles, Old Zion Chapel, The Triangle, Somerton, Somerset TA11 6QP
Mag Frequency: Twice yearly
Subscription: £6.50
Single Issue: £3.50 UK only
Back Issue: £2.50
Overseas: £7.50 EC/£8.50 worldwide
Payment in: All payments in sterling
Payable to: Headlock Press
Inserts accepted: Yes
Terms: £10
Advertising Rates:
Circulation approx: 150
Payment terms to contributors: Free copy
Accept/rejection approx times: Usually 1 month

ℋ
HEADPRESS

Headpress is the journal of sex religion death. For several years it has enjoyed considerable cult status at the forefront of 'transgressive' writing. Incisive and cutting-edge essays on films and filmmakers, religious manias, fanaticism, weird crime cases, sex queens, curious music, art, pornography, trash and sleaze. Headpress does not publish poetry, prose or non-fiction. As of no 18 (published early 1999) Headpress has increased its page count to 144pp. Critical Vision is a book publishing imprint of Headpress, always on the lookout for fresh, interesting, esoteric manuscripts of a non-fiction nature. Write to Headpress for further information.

Address: 40 Rossall Avenue, Radcliffe, Manchester M26 1JD
Fax: 0161 796 1935
Email: david.headpress@zen.co.uk
Mag Frequency: Three times a year
Subscription: £16 for two editions
Single Issue: £8.50 (as of issue 18)
Back Issue: £4.95
Overseas: £18 Europe, £20 USA & RoW (two edtions)
Payment in: UK bankable cheque/Post Giro
Payable to: Headpress
Inserts accepted: No
Circulation approx: 2,500
Payment terms to contributors: Complimentary copy
Accept/rejection approx times: 3 to 4 weeks

HELICON POETRY MAGAZINE

A5 format, card cover, 44 pages. Non-genre poetry of very high standard. We reject a lot of work so it is essential to study at least a back issue before submitting. An increasingly popular magazine with a lively letters page and regular competitions. Competitions are open to non-subscribers, entry fee a few postage stamps. Send SAE for details.

Address: Linden Cottage, 45 Burton Road, Little Neston, South Wirral L64 4AE
Fax: 015 353 0967
Email: helicon@globalnet.co.uk
Mag Frequency: Quarterly
Subscription: £9 for 4 issues
Single Issue: £2.50
Back Issue: £2
Overseas: Send IRC for price list
Payment in: Sterling/IRCs
Payable to: Cherrybite Publications
Inserts accepted: Yes
Terms: Reciprocal
Circulation approx: 300
Payment terms to contributors: £2 per poem & free copy or credit note
Accept/rejection approx times: 2 weeks

ℋ
HJOKFINNIES SANGLINES

Poetry should play for high stakes and the internet is a good forum. A place for visionary verse is on the screen. Technology is the soul of printing - as the daily newspaper and the glossy magazine become anachronisms, the silicon chip makes possible a revival of artisanal publishing and polemical pamphleteering.

Where Finnie's At *(editor's poem 1998)*
I need poetry with the wherewithal to charter a schooner
that hazards Shelley's balls with Auchie seamanship
that can work her crew of warrior picts and actresses
through an equinoxal Pentland Firth unfazed as a scarfie.

There are those who write poems, create inspirational artworks and there are various arts funding rackets. Maybe on occasion compatible. HFJS attempts to continue on an honest commerical basis. An e-zine can take some advertising without it overwhelming the enterprise as often happens with a print magazine. For the price of a local newspaper ad go global with Hjokfinnies Sanglines.

Editor Name(s): Jim Inglis
Address: Electronic only till further notice
Email: seamus@yfinnie.demon.co.uk
Website: http://www.yfinnie.demon.co.uk
Mag Frequency: Convinces by its presence
Subscription: Free
Single Issue: Paper copy £3 (includes p&p)
Overseas: No
Payable to: Jim Inglis
Inserts accepted: Yes
Advertising Rates: Please ask
Circulation approx: The thistle also rises
Accept/rejection approx times: Varies

H

HOLLYWOOD MUSICALS SOCIETY

Founded in 1989 featuring articles, photos and drawings of stars, directors, etc, of Hollywood musicals and related genres. Members in every continent. Free small ads to subscribers. Free service to find photos, videos etc, autographed photos received from stars eg Doris Day, Jane Powell, Deborah Kerr, Deanna Durbin, Debbie Reynolds, Howard Keel, Ricardo Montalban etc. Sister magazine: Deneuve Centre dedicated to Catherine Deneuve.

Address: 1 Pond Meadow, Milford Haven, Pembs, Wales, UK
Mag Frequency: 3 / Year (4 / Year 1989 - 1994)
Subscription: £5
Single Issue: £2
Overseas: $20 cash only or £15
Payment in: UK cheques/US $ bills
Payable to: P Gent
Inserts accepted: Yes
Terms: Free
Circulation approx: 300
Payment terms to contributors: Free copy
Accept/rejection approx times: Few rejections

ℋ
HOLOGRAM TALES

Hologram Tales is the leading on-line science fiction & fantasy magazine, found on the internet of http://www.sf-fantasy.com. It is available to access free of charge and acts as a platform for new writers and authors, publishing fiction, book and film reviews, author interviews, articles and debate. It has become one of the most popular magazines on the worldwide web. Hologram Tale's house style is light-hearted and accessible.

Address: 12 Shannon Court, 1 Tavistock Croydon, Surrey CRO 2AL
Website: http://www.sf-fantasy.com
Mag Frequency: Monthly
Subscription: Free
Single Issue: Free
Inserts accepted: No
Circulation approx: 668,000 people a month visit the site
Payment terms to contributors: No payment
Accept/rejection approx times: 1 month

HQ POETRY MAGAZINE (The Haiku Quarterly)

HQ (founded in 1990) is an international poetry magazine that publishes a broad range of work - from the highly experimental to the very traditional. The emphasis is on quality and originality. About one third of the magazine's space is given over to haiku and haikuesque poetry; the rest to mainstream poetry and reviews/articles. HQ encourages the publication of new work by established writers (Kirkup, Redgrove, Brownjohn, Middleton, Clemo, Gross, Stryk, Lydiard etc in previous issues) and developmental/experimental work by new poets (Hogan, Rollinson, Savage, Marks, McMahon, etc). It should be noted that Howard Sargeant and Roland John at Out-posts and Mike Shields at Orbis have been a strong influence on HQ's editor, and this is reflected in the magazine's style.

Address: 39 Exmouth Street, Swindon, Wiltshire SN1 3PU
Mag Frequency: Quarterly
Subscription: £9 UK/£12 Non-UK
Single Issue: £2.60
Overseas: £12
Payment in: Cheque, PO UK/Cash, sterling cheques non-UK
Payable to: The Haiku Quarterly
Inserts accepted: Yes
Terms: By arrangement
Circulation approx: 500 (readership via libraries etc, 1000+)
Payment terms to contributors: Free copies of magazine - some financial assistance to contributors in need
Accept/rejection approx times: Up to 6 months depending upon workload

ℋ

HU

The North of Ireland's premier literary magazine, celebrating 30 years of publishing the best poems, stories, interviews, articles and book reviews. Past contributors include Seamus Heaney, Paul Muldoon, Tony Harrison, Carol Rumens and many more. Get a back issue and see for yourself.

Editor Name(s): Tom Clyde
Address: 49 Main Street, Greyabbey, County Down BT22 2NF
Mag Frequency: 3 a year
Subscription: £12 UK&Ireland
Single Issue: £3
Back Issue: Varies
Overseas: £17
Payment in: Sterling
Payable to: HU Publications
Inserts accepted: Yes
Terms: On application
Circulation approx: 1000
Payment terms to contributors: Token & 2 copies
Accept/rejection approx times: 3 months

HYBRID

Hybrid (founded in 1990) is probably the most accessible magazine in the world. New writers are found alongside established writers and those established writers have included Lawrence Ferlinghetti, Linda France, Barry Graham plus a host of writers from all over the planet. Occasional reviews are accepted but the magazine is devoted to poetry, poetry of all kinds. The editor has an open mind and likes to read good poetry of whatever ilk.

Address: 42 Christchurch Place, Peterlee, Co. Durham SR8 2NR
Mag Frequency: Twice yearly (from 1997)
Subscription: £4 annually
Single Issue: £2
Overseas: $8US/£6 Europe
Payment in: IMO/Cheque in sterling/PO. Foreign currencies must allow for exchange
Payable to: Kevin Cadwallender
Inserts accepted: Yes
Circulation approx: Increasing
Payment terms to contributors: Free copy of magazine
Accept/rejection approx times: N/A

I

IMPACTE MACABRE

Thoughtful thought provoking fiction in SF/horror/fantasy genre. Whimsical, metaphysical and profound with simple and surreal illustrations. Simple presentation.

Address: 8 Chamberlain Street, Crawcrook, Tyne & Wear NE40 4TZ
Mag Frequency: Irregular
Subscription: N/A
Single Issue: £2.50
Overseas: N/A
Payment in: Cheques/POs
Payable to: T Gay
Inserts accepted: Yes - generally by exchange
Advertising Rates: Free by exchange
Circulation approx: Small but national
Payment terms to contributors: Free copy of magazine
Accept/rejection approx times: Unpredictable

THE INTERPRETER'S HOUSE

We started as a Bedfordshire magazine, and our title comes from Pilgrim's Progress ' . . . the house of the Interpreter, at whose door he should knock, and he will show him excellent things.' We now get submissions from all over the world, and I am looking for excellent poems and short stories (up to 2000 words), so please don't send me your second-best work. We welcome new and established writers, normally publish only one piece per person, and don't do reviews. We are associated with the Bedford Open Poetry Competition, and the winners are published in October each year.

Editor Name(s): Merry Williams
Address: 10 Farrell Road, Wootton, Bedfordshire MK43 9DU
Subs to: Anne Chisholm, 38 Verne Drive, Ampthill, Beds MK45 2PS
Mag Frequency: Feb, June & Oct each year
Subscription: £8.50
Single Issue: £2.50 + 38p postage
Overseas: At present the same
Payable to: The Interpreter's House
Inserts accepted: Yes
Circulation approx: 300
Payment terms to contributors: No
Accept/rejection approx times: Fast

I

INTERZONE

Interzone publishes science-fiction and fantasy short stories, plus reviews, interviews, etc. It does not publish verse, and therefore is not a 'poetry-related' magazine.

Address: 217 Preston Drove, Brighton BN1 6FL
Mag Frequency: Monthly
Subscription: £32
Single Issue: £3
Overseas: £38
Payment in: Overseas: IMO/Eurocheque/credit card
Payable to: Interzone
Inserts accepted: No
Circulation approx: 8000
Payment terms to contributors: £30 per 1000 words
Accept/rejection approx times: 2 months

I

INTIMACY

Intimacy is an irregularly-produced journal seeking to gather together differing response to a common theme, or themes; collating diverse topologies, dialogue, contradiction, openings, closures, etc, and the play of text/images which exist both in their own right, and as sites that feed off, and into, each other. The journal devotes itself to innovative writers and artists, and has developed a tendency to couple archival material (Artaud, Bataille, Bellmer, Krafft-Ebing, etc) with a contemporary arena. Influences are multiple, although, if a magazine has to be cited as a reference point, Paul Buck's seminal Curtains must rank as an indication of editorial policy. Subjects of interest: Art, Writing, Literature (particularly French), Philosophy, Psychology, Crime and Criminology, Sexuality, Poetry, Music, Film. A specialism would be in the area of how a writer constitutes his, or her, identity in the act of writing (from an earlier editorial statement). The journal does not operate as a catch-all forum for writers and compulsive submitters, and thus, some knowledge of the journal's concerns is recommended prior to sending material. All feedback is very welcome.

Address: Apt C, Ramney House, 1 Charles Street, Maidstone, Kent ME16 8EU
Mag Frequency: Irregular
Subscription: Varying dependent on issue size
Single Issue: Varying
Back Issue: Issues 1 - 4 £15 inc
Payment in: In sterling only
Payable to: Adam Mckeown
Inserts accepted: Yes but only for journals of interest
Circulation approx: 200
Payment terms to contributors: What planet are you on

I

IOTA

Looking for well-crafted poetry with something to say and the ability to say it with economy and force. The longer the poem, the harder it is to fit it in, so shorter pieces have the edge and epics are definitely out. There is no limitation on style or subject; the magazine aims to include the complete range of poetry, so light verse, as well as more serious poetry, is always welcome. However, the editor claims no expertise (or facilities) for concrete poetry - apart from that, anything goes. The magazine also carries book reviews and a round-up of interesting magazines received.

Editor Name(s): David Holliday
Address: 67 Hady Crescent, Chesterfield, Derbyshire S41 0EB
Telephone: 01246 276532
Mag Frequency: Quarterly
Subscription: £8
Single Issue: £2
Back Issue: £1
Overseas: As above, or US$4 per issue/$15 per year (plus $10 if by cheque). Or equivalent in other currencies.
Payment in: Anything negotiable
Payable to: Iota or David Holliday
Inserts accepted: Yes
Terms: Free assuming space
Advertising Rates: No adverts - no space
Circulation approx: 400
Payment terms to contributors: 2 complimentary copies
Accept/rejection approx times: 2 weeks for first reaction (unless prep of next issue takes precedence); final decision may take up to a year.

JOURNAL OF CONTEMPORARY ANGLO-SCANDINAVIAN POETRY

The original aim was for the magazine to be a showcase for Scandinavian poetry in translation alongside contemporary poetry written in English. Scandinavian contributions, however, continue to arrive in fits and starts; so, issue by issue, I have been casting my net Europe-wide for other-language contemporary poetry translated into English.

Editor Name(s): Sam Smith
Address: 11 Heatherton Park, Bradford on Tone, Taunton, Somerset TA4 1EU
Mag Frequency: Biannual
Subscription: £7
Single Issue: £4
Back Issue: £2
Overseas: £9 (USA £11)
Payment in: Cheque/IRCs/cash. No barter.
Payable to: Sam Smith
Inserts accepted: No
Circulation approx: 150
Payment terms to contributors: 1 complimentary copy
Accept/rejection approx times: Within 4 weeks

J
THE JOURNAL OF SILLY

The best in single panel cartooning, by the world's top professional cartoonists. See the gags even before they appear in the likes of Private Eye, The Times, The Observer, The Express, The Telegraph, Independent, Punch and the rest + exclusives to JOS.

Address: Flat 12, Cholmeley Lodge, Cholmeley Park, London N6 5EN
Fax: 0181 883 5250
Email: HAM@DIRCON.CO.UK
Website: www.ham.dircon.co.uk
Mag Frequency: Quarterly
Subscription: £6 one year/£12 three years
Single Issue: £1.50
Back Issue: £5
Overseas: £10 EU/£24 RoW for one year
Payable to: The Journal Of Silly
Inserts accepted: Yes
Terms: £40 per 1000
Circulation approx: 1000
Payment terms to contributors: N/A
Accept/rejection approx times: 1/10

K

KICKIN' & SCREAMIN'

Kickin' & Screamin' want poetry that shouts emotion and leaves the reader gasping. Poems that liberate the spirit and help us find our place in space. Social and political comment that uplifts and inspires - no deep, bleak, dark despair. Poems that rise to the challenge, deal with the difficult and offer a creative alternative. Poetry in any style - rhymed, unryhmed, not too long - enclose sae for return. See the world anew, strange and wonderful.

Address: 5 Canberra Close, Greenmeadow, Cwmbran, Gwent, S. Wales NP44 3ET.
Mag Frequency: Monthly
Subscription: N/A
Single Issue: Free (send SAE)
Overseas: Free (with appropriate SAE)
Inserts accepted: No
Circulation approx: Increasing
Payment terms to contributors: Free copy
Accept/rejection approx times: 1-3 months, work returned only with SAE.

K
KIMOTA

Illustrated small press magazine concentrating on SF fantasy and horror as well as genre reviews and articles. The emphasis is on good readable stories and stylish production values. New fiction by established writers rubs shoulders with up-and-coming talent. Potential contributions should see a copy before sending manuscripts in.

Address: 52 Cadley Causeway, Fulwood, Preston, Lancs, PR2 3RX
Email: g.hurry@virgin.net
Mag Frequency: Twice yearly
Subscription: £9 for 4 (free p&p in UK)
Single Issue: £2.50
Overseas: International money order - UK prices plus postage
Payment in: Cheque or postal order
Payable to: G Hurry
Inserts accepted: No
Circulation approx: Increasing
Payment terms to contributors: £2 per 1000 words & copy
Accept/rejection approx times: 6 weeks

K
KINO THERAPY

A 32-page A5 zine about film, film-making, cinema, etc. Includes illustrations, essays, rants, poems, creative writing. Contributors include Dr Steg, Steve Sneyd, Myk T, Geiger Counter & Exploding Cinema ex-scribers. Subject matter includes critiques of Stalker, Naked, Star Wars, Con Air, Coen bros. And a guide on how to be a commercial film student!

Editor Name(s): Roy
Address: C/O 43 Ewart Street, Brighton BN2 2UP
Mag Frequency: Once only (sequels if it's popular!)
Subscription: Send SAE for details
Single Issue: £1.50
Overseas: £2 Europe/£3 RoW
Payment in: Sterling - cash/cheque/PO/UK stamps
Payable to: V I Pollard
Inserts accepted: No
Payment terms to contributors: Free copy of the issue your work in
Accept/rejection approx times: 1 week (send SAE)

𝒦
KONFLUENCE

Konfluence is a new magazine with a West Country slant. Based in the Five Valleys converging on Stroud, Glos, the magazine aims to provide a platform for local voices to be heard. It also aims to showcase the work of talented minor poets who haven't won that competition/caught a commercial publisher's eye . . . but could with luck and in time. The Editor is also interested in poetry written by people whose main creative medium lies in related fields: musicians, sculptors, visual/conceptual and performance artists etc. No genre of peotic style is preferred but the poems must broach that intangible marrige of form and content that makes them 'zing'. Any length of poem, though ideal length is approx 40-50 lines.

Address: Bath House, Bath Road, Nailsworth, Glos GL6 0JB
Mag Frequency: 1 per year
Single Issue: £3
Payment in: Cash or cheque
Payable to: Mark Floyer
Inserts accepted: No
Circulation approx: Not known yet
Payment terms to contributors: Free copy of magazine
Accept/rejection approx times: Within a fortnight

KRAX

A light-hearted poetry magazine - witty, amusing and whimsical, interspersed with descriptive narrative. Usually contains some short fiction, an interview with a writer of interest and lots of illustration. There's a chunky review section of books and magazines for added variety, too. Quite a large proportion of American contributors. Some of the content is unsuitable for children although we don't actively seek risqué material.

Editor Name(s): Andy Robson
Address: C/O 63 Dixon Lane, Leeds LS12 4RR Yorkshire UK
Mag Frequency: Nine monthly approx
Subscription: £9 for 3 subsequent issues
Single Issue: £2.50
Back Issue: On request
Overseas: $18 for 3 issues
Payment in: Overseas - currency notes only
Payable to: A Robson
Inserts accepted: No
Circulation approx: 60% UK, 40% USA
Payment terms to contributors: Single copy of magazine (cover art payment on publication)
Accept/rejection approx times: Up to ten weeks overseas

L

THE LANCASTRIAN

Stories, poems, accounts & news all with a Lancashire flavour and portraying the true indentity of the real, historic and geographical county of Lancashire.

Address: 1 Belvidere Park, Great Crosby, Lancashire L23 0SP
Subs to: Mrs J Brooks, Oaklea Cottage, Meathop, Grange-Over-Sands LA11 6RB
Email: csd@memail.com
Mag Frequency: Annual
Subscription: £4 per annum
Single Issue: £1.31 inc postage
Back Issue: £1.31 incl postage
Overseas: £6
Payable to: Forl
Inserts accepted: No
Circulation approx: Members of Friend of Real Lancashire

LANGUAGE ALIVE

Writing for live action; developed through live action; directly related to live action. Poetics-related texts. No unsolicited poetry please.

Editor Name(s): Chris Cheek
Address: Sound And Language 85 London Road, South Lowestoft, Suffolk NR33 0AS
Email: cris@slang.demon.co.uk
Mag Frequency: Occasional
Single Issue: £4.50
Payable to: Sound And Language
Inserts accepted: No
Circulation approx: 400 copies

L

LATERAL MOVES

Lateral Moves (founded 1994) is the arts/literary magazine with extra tusk. Honest and forthright, the magazine features poetry, stories and miniatures (of around 250 words), articles on writing, philosophy, psychology, etc; an open letters page, a watchdog column, a futurism and computing section, reviews, news and regular humour columns. The small press world is examined with wit and a gruff (Northern?) sense of mischief. Described by Geoff Lowe as 'A really great little mag, packed with smart stuff and little quirky surprises in odd corners. The only magazine I know that, even without contributors' material, would still be worth reading and enjoying.' Lateral Moves is a magazine which subscribers and contributors can help to direct and certainly enrich. We welcome contributions of all kinds to the magazine, especially on disk in plain text format - however, potential contributors may like to view a copy first, as much of the accepted work is quite individual in nature. Lateral Moves eats curries! Come on, brighten our sad lives . . .

Address: Alan White & Nick Britton, 5 Hamilton Street, Astley Bridge, Bolton BL1 6RJ
Telephone: 01204 596369 (Answerphone)
Mag Frequency: 6 pa/bi-monthly
Subscription: £12 includes free p & p
Single Issue: £2.50 + 35p p & p
Back Issue: £1.50 + 35p/ £2.50 + 35p depending on issue
Overseas: £15 Europe £18 RoW
Payment in: Sterling cheques and postal orders only, please
Payable to: Aural Images
Inserts accepted: Free to partners/subscribers/exchange publicity
Circulation approx: 250
Payment terms to contributors: Free copy of magazine
Accept/rejection approx times: 3 months - may vary depending upon type of material

LEXIKON

Lexikon accepts poetry, short stories, articles, reviews; submissions can be printed, on disk or in braille. It is an A4 magazine which is also available on disk or audio tape for blind and print impaired people only. The magazine will appeal to all writers as it has information sections for writers detailing events and competitions. Runs regular competitions with cash prizes.

Editor Name(s): (Ed)Francis Anderson/(Fic Ed)Roger Bradley
Address: P O Box 754, Stoke-on-Trent ST1 4BU
Fax: 01782 285331
Mag Frequency: 4 issues a year
Subscription: £8
Single Issue: £2.25
Back Issue: Complimentary
Overseas: Depends on country
Payment in: Cheque/PO
Payable to: Lexikon
Inserts accepted: Yes
Terms: £80
Circulation approx: 200-300
Payment terms to contributors: Free copy
Accept/rejection approx times: Acceptance 2 weeks/rejection max 8 weeks

L
LINKS

Publishes quality poetry (unpublished); reviews, accepts unsolicited reviews, poems up to 100 lines any subject and style; all submissions given same consideration.

Address: Bude Haven 18 Frankfield Rise, Tunbridge Wells TN2 5LF
Mag Frequency: Twice a year
Subscription: £4 per year
Single Issue: £2
Back Issue: £2.25
Overseas: Sterling only £5 per year
Payment in: Cheques
Payable to: Links
Inserts accepted: Yes
Circulation approx: Up to 200
Payment terms to contributors: Complimentary copy of magazine
Accept/rejection approx times: 2 weeks

LITERARY REVIEW

Founded 1979. Monthly. Publishes book reviews (commissioned), features and articles on literary subjects. Prospective contributors are best advised to contact the Editor in writing. Unsolicited manuscripts not welcome. Runs a monthly poetry competition, the Literary Review Grand Poetry Competition, on a given theme. Open to subscribers only. Articles published in the magazine.

Address: 44 Lexington Street, London W1R 3LF
Subs to: Literary Review Subscriptions, 45-46 Poland Street, London, W1E 5HU
Fax: 0171 734 1844
Email: litrev@dircon.co.uk
Mag Frequency: Monthly
Subscription: £26 UK
Single Issue: £2.40
Overseas: £32 Eur/£36 (US$60) US&Canada Airspeed/£50 (US$84)RoW airmail
Payment in: Cheque/Mastercard/Visa/Amex
Payable to: The Literary Review
Inserts accepted: Yes
Terms: £34 (under 10gr per 1000)
Circulation approx: 15,000
Payment terms to contributors: Varies
Accept/rejection approx times: No unsolicited manuscripts

$\mathcal{L}$
LIVING POETS

One of the premier UK poetry websites - Living Poets continues to publish power-ful new poetry and offer a showcase to those artists at the threshold of the imagina-tion. Submissions are always considered provided an SAE is enclosed. House style is akin to Hughes, Eliot, Plath, Blake and Heaney.

Address: Executive Editor, Dragon Heart Press, 11 Menin Road Allestree, Derby DE22 2NL
Website: http://dougal.derby.ac.uk/lpoets
Mag Frequency: Occasional
Back Issue: £5/$10
Payable to: S Woodward
Inserts accepted: No
Circulation approx: 20 million (www)
Payment terms to contributors: Complimentary copy
Accept/rejection approx times: 2 months

LOCHS MAGAZINE

Celebrating its second anniversary, Lochs is a fast-evolving comedy publication, publishing work by some of the finest comic writers around. All kinds of comedy are catered for: black humour, short stories, satirical poetry, spoof news items, parodies, fantasy comedy, columns . . . Lochs also issues lairdships: legal-usage Scottish titles which come with ownership of a plot of land in Scotland. It's all included in the subscription price. The land and title can be passed on from generation to generation, and you get to choose between Laird of Camster and Laird of John O' Groats. Lochs will be taking a break between December '98 and May '99, before returning with a new design and style.

Address: Lochs Magazine, Kimbo International, PO Box 12412, London SW18 5ZL
Mag Frequency: Quarterly
Subscription: £6.90 (5 issues) (£16.90 including Lairdship - see below)
Single Issue: £1.50
Back Issue: 90p
Overseas: £7.90/$13
Payment in: PO, Cheque
Payable to: Kimbo International
Inserts accepted: Yes
Circulation approx: 400
Payment terms to contributors: Usually about £20 per thousand words, usually on publication, and sample copy
Accept/rejection approx times: 4 weeks

L
LONDON MAGAZINE

Poems, fiction, criticism, architecture, cinema, stories, memoirs, art, photography, theatre, architecture plus 40 pages of reviews. 'A fantastic magazine whose place in the history of 20th century literary life grows ever more secure and ignificant' - William Boyd, Evening Standard. 'If London Magazine shuts down nothing else whatever of that sort will ever take its place' - Anthony Powell, Journals.

Address: 30 Thurloe Place, London SW7 2HQ
Mag Frequency: Bi-monthly
Subscription: £28-50
Single Issue: £5.99
Back Issue: £3.50
Overseas: £33.50/£45 (airmail)
Payment in: Sterling cheques preferably
Payable to: London Magazine
Inserts accepted: Yes
Terms: £70 per 1000
Circulation approx: 3500+
Payment terms to contributors: Variable:poems £20-£50/stories £20-£75/reviews £25-£50
Accept/rejection approx times: 1 week

LONDON REVIEW OF BOOKS

In-depth reviews of current books on politics, literature, history, the arts.

Address: 28 Little Russell Street, London WC1A 2HN
Fax: 0171 209 1151
Email: subs@lrb.co.uk
Mag Frequency: Fortnightly
Subscription: £59.95
Single Issue: £2.50
Back Issue: £3
Overseas: On application
Payment in: Sterling cheque/International Girobank/Mastercard/DinersClub/Visa
Payable to: LRB LTD
Inserts accepted: Yes
Terms: £80 per 1000
Circulation approx: 29,293 (ABC Jan-June 1998)
Payment terms to contributors: £100 per 1000 words/ £50 per poem

THE LONG POEM GROUP NEWSLETTER

A4pp well-printed newsletter devoted to debating the long poem in our time, and publishing: the transactions of the Long Poem Group; a checklist of long poems published in Britain in the last 30 years; and one or two reviews of newly-published long poems.

Editor Name(s): William Oxley & Sebastian Barker
Address: 6 The Mount, Furzeham, Brixham, S. Devon TQ5 8QY
Email: pwoxley@aol.com.uk
Website: http://www.bath.ac.uk/-exxdgdc
Mag Frequency: Occasional
Subscription: Free - for SAE of 26p, A5 or larger envelope
Single Issue: Free - for SAE of 26p, A5 or larger envelope
Overseas: N/A
Inserts accepted: No
Circulation approx: 350
Payment terms to contributors: None
Accept/rejection approx times: N/A

MAD CARROT DISEASE

M

A freesheet (A3) devoted to folk music & blues, distributed to folk clubs mostly in Scotland. Reviews of new releases, articles on leading folk & blues singers.

Editor Name(s): Neil Mathers
Address: c/o The Corbie Press, 57 Murray Street, Montrose, Angus, Scotland DD10 8JZ
Telephone: 01674 672625
Mag Frequency: Depending on funds
Single Issue: Free (send SAE)
Inserts accepted: No
Advertising Rates: Approx £10
Circulation approx: 300 distributed
Payment terms to contributors: Nil
Accept/rejection approx times: Immediate decision for good articles

M
MAD COW

100 pages of college cartridge and coloured sugar paper cut to A5, spiral bound with stiff board covers on which the title is letterpress-embossed and packaged in a slip-case. Previous contributors include Thomas A Clark, Simon Cutts, Stuart Mills, Harry Gilonis, Colin Sackett, Robert Lax, Jonathan Williams, Cid Corman, Iliassa Seguin, Dick Higgins, Brendan McMahon, Rob Mackenzie. 'Beautifully presented new work by great poets' - Marie Claire.

Address: Jon T Whittington, 33 Kingsley Place, Highgate, London N6 5EA
Mag Frequency: 1 per annum
Subscription: £7
Single Issue: £7
Back Issue: None left - signed copies £60
Overseas: £10
Payment in: Cheque (dollars or sterling)
Payable to: J Whittington
Circulation approx: 500
Payment terms to contributors: No
Accept/rejection approx times: One poet, Brendan McMahon, was accepted after sending in material

MADAM X

Magazine of new writing by new and established writers. Emphasis on short stories, but also poetry, interviews, criticism.

Address: 18A Prentis Road, London SW18 1QD
Mag Frequency: Twice yearly
Subscription: N/A
Single Issue: £5
Payment in: Cheque/cash/credit card
Payable to: Colophon Press
Inserts accepted: Yes
Terms: Please apply
Circulation approx: 1000
Payment terms to contributors: Free copies, otherwise please apply
Accept/rejection approx times: Reasonably fast, but variable

M
MAELSTROM

Maelstrom is a genre fiction magazine, publishing short stories up to 10,000 words in length. We publish mainly science fiction, fantasy, horror and mystery stories, plus a few poems of a similar nature. We also publish a few book reviews and letters, as well as artwork illustrating the stories.

Address: 24 Fowler Close, Southchurch, Southend on Sea, Essex SS1 2RD
Mag Frequency: Twice yearly
Subscription: 2/£3.50; 4/£6.50
Single Issue: £1.80
Back Issue: Nos 1-5 £1/Nos 6&7 £1.80
Overseas: US 2/$10, 4/$20
Payment in: Equivalent in cash - no foreign cheques
Payable to: Sol Publications
Inserts accepted: Yes
Terms: 35p per 100g
Circulation approx: 250
Payment terms to contributors: £4 per 1000 words/£5 per 1000 words if supplied on disc
Accept/rejection approx times: 3 months

M

THE MAGAZINE

A publication of the Creative Writing Programme of Open Studies, Warwick University. Publishes poems and short stories. Poets submit 2-4 poems, up to 40 lines. Stories up to 2000 words. Subjects eclectic, tasteful. Submissions must be accompanied by stamped, self-addressed envelope for return or acknowledgement. We do not review or otherwise publicise poetry or short story collections. The Magazine is available by mail order or in local (Warwick area) bookstores.

Address: Sally Russell, c/o Open Studies Dept. of Continuing Education, University of Warwick, Coventry CV4 7AL
Mag Frequency: Twice a year
Subscription: N/A
Single Issue: £3.50 mailed/£3 in local shops
Back Issue: £4
Overseas: £1 extra postage
Payment in: Sterling cheques
Payable to: Warwick University, Open Studies
Inserts accepted: No
Terms: Unknown
Circulation approx: 250
Payment terms to contributors: 1 free copy
Accept/rejection approx times: 2-3 months

M
MAGMA

Founded in 1994 and published by the Stukeley Press. Each issue is edited by a different member of the Press within a common editorial approach. Poems in the mainstream-modernist range. Increasing interest in experimental work. Recent interviews with Mark Doty, Kate Clanchy, Ruth Padel and Tracey Emin. Occasional reviews/articles. Images (B/W) also welcome, whether accompanying poems or free-standing.

Address: The City Lit, Stukeley Street, London WC2B 5LJ
Mag Frequency: 3 times yearly
Subscription: £8
Single Issue: £2.50
Back Issue: £2
Overseas: £11
Payment in: IMO/Sterling cheque
Payable to: Magma
Inserts accepted: Yes
Terms: £10
Circulation approx: 300
Payment terms to contributors: Free copy of magazine
Accept/rejection approx times: Usually within 2 months, except for work submitted in July/August when City Lit is closed.

M
MAGNOLIAWORLD FRIENDS GAZETTE

A friendly magazine for those wishing to correspond with penpals worldwide. Includes long list of names worldwide, short story, craft ideas, recipes and much more.

Editor Name(s): Mrs B Jones
Address: 69 Pinhoe Road, Exeter EX4 7HS
Telephone: 01392 252605
Mag Frequency: Every 4 months
Subscription: UK - 4 issues £3.75 includes post
Single Issue: £1 includes post
Overseas: USA, Canada, NZ, Aust $10 buys 3 issues/RoW 4 IRCs for 1 copy
Payment in: Overseas: $ & IRCs
Payable to: B Jones
Circulation approx: 100+
Payment terms to contributors: None. Penpal names listed free

M
THE MAGPIE'S NEST

Poems of no more than 40 lines on any subject. Dislike too much repetition of words or phrases and clichés. Short stories of 1,000 - 2,000 words on any subject, preferably short stories with a 'twist' in the ending. Reviews also welcomed. SAE essential. Subscriptions welcomed to continue the magazine's survival.

Editor Name(s): Bal Saini
Address: 176 Stoney Lane, Sparkhill, Birmingham B12 8AN
Mag Frequency: Quarterly
Subscription: £6 per annum
Single Issue: £1
Overseas: £2 per issue
Payment in: Cheque
Payable to: The Magpie's Nest
Inserts accepted: Yes
Terms: £30 per 1000
Circulation approx: 400
Payment terms to contributors: 1 copy of issue
Accept/rejection approx times: 6-8 weeks

M
MAIN STREET JOURNAL

A cutting-edge, totally contemporary, lightning-fast literary magazine, with the idea of narrative rather than reviews/interviews forming the editorial basis. Highly professional and serious outfit. We publish a vast range of material, looking to connect the disparate threads of pitch, not subject matter. General subject areas are fiction, music, performance/narrative-based poetry and general 'cultural' essays, but we're always up for suggestions, treatments, synopses, canvassing for other ideas. Distribution: WH Smith nationwide; Dillons/Waterstones in the South-East; independents (Compendium etc). Review coverage: all broadsheets, Time Out etc. Aim: to build a real live Granta alternative for a generation that doesn't like Granta (and who can blame them?).

Address: 29 Princes Road Ashford Middlesex TW15 2LT
Mag Frequency: Twice yearly
Subscription: £12.99 (4 issues)
Single Issue: £4
Overseas: £25 (4 issues)
Payment in: Cheque/PO/IMO
Payable to: The Main Objective Ltd.
Inserts accepted: Yes
Terms: £300
Circulation approx: 1500
Payment terms to contributors: Minimup £10
Accept/rejection approx times: 3 weeks

M
MALFUNCTION PRESS

Poetry must have a s-fiction or fantasy slant. Works with an Italian connection regarded with interest. Castle & fortification studies also considered for Postern Magazine.

Address: Malfunction Press (PE Presford) Rose Cottage 3 Tram Lane Buckley Flintshire Wales CH7 3JB
Subs to: Postern only £1.25 per issue
Mag Frequency: Not fixed
Subscription: 1st class SAE only
Single Issue: Same
Payable to: PE Presford
Inserts accepted: No
Circulation approx: To demand

M

MARKINGS

Now in its 4th year and established as one of Scotland's leading arts and literary mags that has integrated itself into its local community as well as reaching major cultural centres nationwide. Markings is not afraid of controversy, is committed to providing a platform for new talent, and is insistent on quality. It has an ingenious editorial policy of finding work and helping develop its writers through articles and extracts on or from writers who deserve encouragement but need greater exposure to criticism; it also publishes extensive, often serialised, critical articles. Line drawings are welcome and we are always on the lookout for good short stories!

Editor Name(s): John Hudson
Address: 77 High Street, Kirkcudbright, Dumfries & Galloway DG6 8JW Scotland
Telephone: 01557 331557
Fax: 01557 331557
Email: j.hudson@btinternet.com
Mag Frequency: 3 per year
Subscription: £5
Single Issue: £2
Overseas: Same
Payment in: Sterling
Payable to: Markings
Inserts accepted: Yes
Terms: Free to good causes (contact editor)
Advertising Rates: Full pg £70/half £45/qtr £25/Covers b/w£100, col £250
Circulation approx: 1000
Payment terms to contributors: Payment for commissioned articles
Accept/rejection approx times: 8 weeks max

M
MARQUIS

The fetish fantasy magazine. Stylish full colour magazine featuring the best fetishistic photographs, illustrations, stories and fetish scene news. Only fetish erotica stories published, which are illustrated by the publishers. Published in 3 language editions - English/German/French.

Editor Name(s): Peter W Czernich (Germany)/Neil Mather (UK)
Address: Marquis, PO Box 1426 Shepton Mallet Somerset BA4 6HH
Telephone: 01749 831 397
Fax: 01749 831380
Email: neal.v@ukonline.co.uk
Mag Frequency: Quarterly
Subscription: £55 (6 issues) £28 (3 issues)
Single Issue: £10
Overseas: USA $125 (6 issues)/$65 (3 issues)
Payment in: Cheque/credit card/PO/cash
Payable to: Marquis
Inserts accepted: No
Advertising Rates: Full pg £1000/smaller ad space available
Circulation approx: 50,000 (total 3 editions)
Payment terms to contributors: Upon publication, up to £50 per printed page (rates vary)
Accept/rejection approx times: 3 months

𝓜
MAYPOLE EDITIONS ANNUAL ANTHOLOGY

We publish plays and poetry in the main. Two to three titles a year. Titles: Snorting Mustard One; Snorting Mustard Two; Metallum Damnantorum; Love Sonnets; Chocolate Rose Memoriam. Neon Lily Tiger; A Crusty Tome. Next year's poetry collection - Black Ribbons. Unsolicited manuscripts welcome provided return postage included. Poetry always welcome for collected anthologies. Poetry should be approximately thirty lines long, broadly covering social concerns, ethnic minorities, feminist issues, romance, travel, lyric rhyming verse. No politics. The annual collected anthology is designed as a small press platform for first-time poets who might not otherwise get into print, and a permanent showcase for those already published who want to break into the mainstreaam. Catalogue £1, plus SAE. Please be patient when sending work because of the huge volume of submission. Exempt charity status.

Editor Name(s): Barry Taylor
Address: 22 Mayfair Avenue, Ilford, Essex IG1 3DL
Mag Frequency: 1 or 2 pa
Single Issue: £7.95
Overseas: £7.95 + p&p
Accept/rejection approx times: 2-3 years

M

MEMORY LANE

Memory Lane is a lively magazine covering popular music of the 1920s through to the 1950s. Our particular areas of interest are dance bands, vocalists, instrumentalists, big bands, jazz, personalities, music hall and variety. The accent is placed firmly on the British scene, although we do make the occasional excursions across the Atlantic. (We do not cover rock 'n' roll, pop music, classical music or opera.) Our readers come from all walks of life and span all age groups. In particular, Memory Lane has become a focal point for collectors of 'popular' 78 rpm records. Each quarterly issue contains articles and features by our team of top writers and journalists. We include biographical features, reviews of CD and cassette re-issues, book reviews, discographical information, obituaries and picture pages. We also have a very spirited readers' letters section and encourage well-researched articles from new writers. We also publish advertisements. It is all presented in a relaxed and informal style which makes Memory Lane both an informative and enjoyable read. Associated with Memory Lane is a cassette club through which registered subscribers are able to borrow especially made pre-recorded cassettes free of charge.

Editor Name(s): Ray Pallett
Address: P O Box 1939, Leigh-on-Sea, SS9 3UH
Email: raymemlane@aol.com
Mag Frequency: Quarterly (Feb, May, Aug, Nov)
Subscription: £10 (UK) £14 (Overseas surface mail)
Single Issue: £2.50 (UK) £3.50 (Overseas surface mail)
Payment in: UK: cheque, PO, cash/Overseas: draft in sterling drawn on bank in UK
Payable to: Memory Lane
Inserts accepted: Yes
Terms: £75 per 1000
Advertising Rates: From £5 (mini display) to £75 (full page display)
Circulation approx: 2000
Payment terms to contributors: Individually negotiated
Accept/rejection approx times: 3 weeks

MICROPRESS MIDLANDS POETRY

Small A5 magazine of poetry. Advice service and poem analysis available from UK's most published poet - details available of request. Dec'98/Jan'99 issue of Micropress Midlands Poetry will be the last one - to be replaced by new mag, provisionally titled Auto Queue (see that entry for further details).

Editor Name(s): Geoff Stevens
Address: 25 Gutter Road, West Bromwich B71 2EH
Mag Frequency: 3 per year
Subscription: £3
Single Issue: N/A
Back Issue: £1
Overseas: N/A
Payable to: Geoff Stevens
Inserts accepted: Yes
Terms: Negotiable
Circulation approx: Rising
Payment terms to contributors: No

M
MODERN DANCE

Music review magazine that reviews all types of music - mainly CDs (albums), occasional music-related videos and books. Pop, rock, jazz, classical, metal, blues and opera - indeed, everything!

Address: 12 Blakestones Road, Slaithwaite, Huddersfield HD7 5UQ
Fax: 01484 842324
Mag Frequency: 2-3-4 months
Subscription: Free with SAEs
Single Issue: Free with SAE
Back Issue: No back issues
Overseas: Not available
Payable to: N/A although donations welcome D Hughes
Inserts accepted: Yes
Terms: £10
Circulation approx: 4000
Payment terms to contributors: N/A
Accept/rejection approx times: N/A

M
MODERN POETRY IN TRANSLATION

MPT, an international journal founded by Daniel Weissbort and Ted Hughes in the 60s, has been relaunched by King's College London under Daniel Weissbort's editorship. Published twice a year, the journal is dedicated to new translations into English of poems from all over the world, with no restrictions on period and no ideological bias. MPT also publishes articles on translation (with the emphasis on practice rather than theory), reviews of new translations and occasional features on individual translators. There is generally a substantial 'themed' section: issues 1 to 13 have featured Yves Bonnefoy, Franz Baermann Steiner (a bi-lingual edition with previously unpublished poems and Michael Hamburger's translations), Anna Kamienska and other Polish and East European poets, the Jerusalem International Poetry Festival, Galician-Portuguese troubadours, Brazil, Wales, France, Filipino and Pacific Rim, Russian poetry, Peru, Dutch/Flemish poets and modern Greek poetry. Most issues of the New Series have run to over 248 pages; MPT is effectively a well-designed paperback book. Forthcoming issues will include Arabic and Hebrew poetry.

Address: Professor Norma Rinsler, MPT, School of Humanities, King's College London, Strand, London WC2R 2LS
Fax: 0171 873 2415
Website: www.kcl.ac.uk/mpt
Mag Frequency: Twice yearly
Subscription: £20 annually for individuals/£30 for institutions
Single Issue: £10
Back Issue: £7.50
Overseas: £24 or $36 (U.S. dollars) for individuals
Payment in: Sterling/IMO/AMEX money order
Payable to: King's College London
Inserts accepted: No
Advertising Rates: £90 full page/£45 half page
Circulation approx: 300+
Payment terms to contributors: £10 per poem or £12 per page as appropriate
Accept/rejection approx times: Usually 4-6 weeks

M
MONAS HIEROGLYPHICA

Monas Hieroglyphica provides an eclectic mix of magic, history and archaeology. The magazine is mainly also concerned with promoting the gothic music scene, and therefore includes interviews with gothic/darkwave bands, music reviews, gothic fiction and poetry. Artwork also features strongly in its pages, and is of a very high standard.

Address: 58 Seymour Road, Hadleigh, Benfleet, Essex SS7 2HL
Mag Frequency: 3 issues a year
Subscription: £4.50 for 3 issues
Single Issue: £1.50 + A5 40p SAE
Back Issue: By arrangement with the editor
Overseas: £7.50 for 3 issues
Payment in: Cheque/PO/cash/UK postage stamps/IRCs
Payable to: Jamie Spracklen
Inserts accepted: Yes
Terms: Free
Circulation approx: Growing with each issue
Payment terms to contributors: Copy of magazine
Accept/rejection approx times: 1 month

M

MOONSTONE

Moonstone was founded in 1979 'to keep the flag of pagan poetry flying in Abion.' The magazine features pagan poetry and short prose items of all descriptions. Regular contributors include Steve Sneyd, Patricia Prime and Kenneth C Steven. Notes on contributors, short reviews and exchange listings for other pagan magazines are included. Occasionally black & white artwork is accepted. Opinions given by contributors are not necessarily those of the Editors. Previously unpublished work, clearly typed with sae, should be sent to the address below.

Address: Talitha Clare, 'Moonstone' S O S, The Old Station Yard, Settle, N. Yorks BD24 9RP
Email: Increasing
Mag Frequency: Quarterly at the Festivals
Subscription: £6 pa
Single Issue: £1.60
Back Issue: £2
Overseas: $20 p.a. US/Canada/Australia/Europe
Payment in: Notes/bills only. No cheques except in sterling
Payable to: Talitha Clare
Inserts accepted: Yes
Terms: £1
Payment terms to contributors: Free copy of magazine - contributors retain their copyright, by request
Accept/rejection approx times: All contributions of a pagan nature considered within 6-8 weeks; sae essential, study of magazine advised

M
MOSTLY HARMLESS

Mostly Harmless is the magazine of ZZ9 Plural Z Alpha, the official appreciation society of Douglas Adams and the Hitch Hiker's Guide To The Galaxy. As well as news of forthcoming projects, exclusive merchandise and discounts, Mostly Harmless is a showcase for original writing that is either related to or in the style of Douglas Adams' works; a wide range of science fiction humour has been featured in the seventeen years since Mostly Harmless began. Honorary members and proven readers of Mostly Harmless include Douglas Adams, Neil Gaimen, Simon Jones, Mark Wing-Davey and John Lloyd. Douglas Adams' publishers and production company are in frequent contact.

Address: Stuart Bruce, 6 Sandown Road, Hazel Grove, Stockport, Cheshire SK7 4SH
Subs to: ZZ9 Plural Z Alpha, 37 Keens Road, Croydon, Surrey CR0 7AH
Email: stuart@atomizer.demon.co.uk
Mag Frequency: Quarterly
Subscription: £6 per year (UK)
Back Issue: £2
Overseas: £8 - £12
Payment in: Cheque (UK £/US $) or standing order
Payable to: ZZ9 Plural Z Alpha
Inserts accepted: Yes
Terms: £50 (negotiable)
Circulation approx: 1000
Payment terms to contributors: None
Accept/rejection approx times: 1 month (50/50)

MUTINY

Mutiny, n. open revolt against authority: Mutiny magazine. See that line of people against that brick wall? See that gun pointing at them? That's us taking aim at the literary establishment and having a pot-shot. We're here to confront, confuse and confound you, push you places you may not want to go. Each issue contains the best in underground/small press prose, poetry, drama, illustrations and reviews. Sick of all that cliched traditionalism? Then get Mutiny under your belt. #1 includes Jeff Noon's World of the Vurt, Exquisite Corpse poem and Poppy Z Brite's Exquisite Corpse novel. #2 has beautiful prose from Andrew McEwan, film reviews of Lost Highway and Irma Vep, a piece on French director Eric Rohmer, Steve Urwin on life's poisons and more outstanding poetry, prose and vitriolic column inches lacerating life . . . Mutiny is subversion, know your rights. Send an SAE for submission guidelines.

Address: Sara Wingate-Gray, Norfolk Terrace, University of East Anglia, Norwich NR4 7TJ (term time)
Otherwise ie holidays, 1 Southside, Shadforth, Durham DH6 1LL
Email: s.wingate-gray@uea.ac.uk or Sara@shindig.demon.co.uk
Mag Frequency: Quarterly
Subscription: £12 inc p&p and special Xmas gift
Single Issue: £2
Overseas: Equivalent in £ currency + extra £5 for postage
Payment in: Cash OK if well-hidden/Cheque/PO/IMO or $ for overseas good
Payable to: S W Gray
Inserts accepted: Yes
Advertising Rates: £50 per b&w page
Circulation approx: 100
Payment terms to contributors: Free copy of relevant issue, name in issue, biog soon to come
Accept/rejection approx times: Dec/April/August/Oct

NATIONAL OUTREACH For The Housebound, Elderly & Disabled

Outreach is a quarterly magazine for the housebound, elderly, and disabled. It contains articles of relevance and interest to people with a severely limited capacity for movement and travel. The magazine is written by Christians and contains an underlying Christian gospel message. It is produced by volunteers on a non-profitmaking basis. It contains articles on gardening, cooking, healthy living, hobbies and home improvement, plus competitions, quizzes, poems, stories, pen friends, everyday problems and legal matters, which are treated as strictly confidential. Outreach is fun, practical and challenging. Think of it as a kind of Reader's Digest for the housebound, elderly, and disabled. It is one of a few magazines written in LARGE PRINT for the benefit of the elderly and partially sighted. It can also be obtained on cassette for the blind. We welcome anyone who wants to volunteer to help us. Whatever your level of interest, we will have a job for you. You can become an Outreach representative and deliver copies in your area. Or perhaps you have some ideas for articles, or fancy writing for the magazine yourself. You can also help put together our cassette magazine. We are also looking for volunteers for our counselling team, offering legal advice and a care line. National Outreach magazine was founded in 1985 and has a fast growing readership all over the world.

Editor Name(s): Rev J Kirby
Address: 7 Grayson Close, Stocksbridge, Sheffield S36 2BJ
Telephone: 0114 288 5346
Fax: 0114 288 4903
Mag Frequency: Quarterly
Subscription: £3 pa from Jan 1999
Single Issue: 75p
Overseas: £4.40
Payment in: Cheque/PO
Payable to: National Outreach For The Housebound, Elderly & Disabled
Inserts accepted: Yes
Circulation approx: 2,750

NAVIS

Edited by Robert Bush & Bill Morley. Navis is an Arts magazine publishing mainly poetry and artwork, and occasionally short fiction and polemical prose; there is a small section of poetry reviews. Its aims are to publish writing and art of the highest quality by both established and unknown artists; the format, almost square, is designed to give a generous space for the artwork, present the poetry to good advantage and to create a harmonious balance between the two.

Address: 124 Heathwood Gardens, London SE7 8ER
Mag Frequency: 2 a year
Subscription: £6
Single Issue: £3 + 50p p&p
Back Issue: £2 + 50p p&p
Overseas: £9
Payment in: PO/Cheque
Payable to: R Bush
Inserts accepted: Reciprocal only
Circulation approx: 300
Accept/rejection approx times: 2 months

N
NETWORK NEWS

Sinister Beasts, Earth Mysteries, The Occult Shenanigens of the Royal Family, The Occult Symbolism of British Currency, Time Travelling Punk Rockers, Nocturnal Emissions Merchandising and much much more in this occasional journal of guerrilla ontology.

Address: c/o Earthly Delights, PO Box 2, Lostwithiel, Cornwall PL22 0YY.
Email: earthly@planet13.co.uk
Mag Frequency: Quarterly
Subscription: £5
Single Issue: £1.50
Back Issue: £1.50
Overseas: £10
Payment in: Money orders etc.
Payable to: N Ayers
Inserts accepted: No
Circulation approx: 500
Payment terms to contributors: Negotiable.
Accept/rejection approx times: 30 Days

NEVER BURY POETRY

Never Bury Poetry is published quarterly. We are in our 10th year and have a small but thriving subscription list, worldwide. We publish Spring, Summer, Autumn and Winter, cut-off dates for contributions are stated in the current magazine, where the themes for the next several issues are mentioned also. The themes should be interpreted creatively to give a wide scope of poetry; poems may be sent on spec. If she considers them suitable the editor will ask permission to hold them over until a compatible theme arises (sae's or IRC's always please). We are a non-profitmaking concern, relying on selling enough of each issue to publish the next one. Only the printer is paid.

Address: Eilleen Holroyd, 12a Kirkstall Gardens, Radcliffe, Manchester M26 0QS.
Subs to: Bettina Jones, 30 Beryl Avenue, Tottington, Bury, Lancs, BL8 3NF
Mag Frequency: Quarterly
Subscription: £9.50 for 4 issues
Single Issue: £2.50
Back Issue: £1.50
Overseas: £11.50
Payment in: Sterling + sae or IRC for correspondence.
Payable to: Bury Live Lines
Inserts accepted: No
Circulation approx: 150 worldwide
Payment terms to contributors: We are totally non-profitmaking so cannot pay either in cash or kind
Accept/rejection approx times: Within 1 month, usually

NEW LONDON WRITERS

A contemporary fiction and poetry magazine with a metropolitan angle. Prefer work that is fresh and original and that represents the cultural and social diversity of our times. Particularly keen on writers with a sharp ear for dialogue and a healthy sense of absurdity. Also on the lookout for those whose writing reflects a keen awareness of modern-day obsessions.

Editor Name(s): Alice Wickham
Address: c/o 31 Thicket Road, Anerly, London SE20 8DB
Telephone: 0181 7782813
Email: newlonrite@aol.com
Mag Frequency: 3-4 times a year
Subscription: £12
Single Issue: £3
Overseas: Same as UK - sterling only
Payment in: Cheque/PO
Payable to: Alice Wickham
Advertising Rates: £5 per ad (up to 10 lines or 30 words)
Circulation approx: 250
Payment terms to contributors: None
Accept/rejection approx times: 3 months

NEW WELSH REVIEW

Wales's leading literary quarterly in English, New Welsh Review provides a literary/cultural platform for critical articles, poems, short stories and reviews of interest primarily, but by no means exclusively, to a Welsh audience and all with an interest in Wales. It is a place where the best of Welsh writing in English, past and present, is celebrated, discussed and debated but, interpreting its brief very widely, it also takes a keen interest in resonant literary and cultural developments in other parts of the British Isles and much further afield. New Welsh Review is mainly concerned with books but it also covers developments in theatre in Wales (there is a special section) & film and broadcasting, as a natural extension of its literary/cultural brief.

Editor Name(s): Robin Reeves
Address: New Welsh Review, Chapter Arts Centre, Market Road, Cardiff, Wales CF5 1QE
Fax: 01222 665529
Email: robin@nwrc.demon.co.uk
Mag Frequency: Quarterly
Subscription: £16 pa (£30 two years)
Single Issue: £4.50
Back Issue: £3.50
Overseas: Sub cost + £2 surface, £6 airmail
Payment in: Sterling cheque/PO/Visa
Payable to: New Welsh Review Ltd
Inserts accepted: Yes
Terms: £100 per 1000
Advertising Rates: Full page £100/half £60/quarter £25/eigth £15
Circulation approx: 900
Payment terms to contributors: Articles £20 per 1000 words, short stories £50
Accept/rejection approx times: 3 months

N
THE NEW WRITER

The New Writer is a contemporary writing magazine which publishes the best in fact, fiction and poetry. It's different and it's aimed at writers with a serious intent; everyone who wants to develop their writing to meet the high expectations of today's editors. The team at The New Writer are commited to working with their readers to increase the chances of publication. That's why masses of useful market information and plenty of feedback is provided. More than that, we bring you the best in contemporary fiction and cutting-edge poetry backed up by searching articles and in-depth features in every issue. This is a forward-looking magazine with a range of contributors expert in their subjects. Whether you've just started to write or you're a more experienced writer wanting to explore new ideas and techniques, this is essential reading. Also, book reviews, competitions update, news and readers' views.

Editor Name(s): Merric Davidson
Address: PO Box 60, Cranbrook, Kent TN17 2ZR
Telephone: 01580 212626
Mag Frequency: 10 per annum
Subscription: £29.50
Single Issue: £2.95
Back Issue: £2.95
Overseas: £36.50 (Europe)/£42.50 (RoW) - airmail
Payment in: Sterling/Master Card, Visa, Eurocard
Payable to: The New Writer
Inserts accepted: Yes
Terms: £50 per 1000
Advertising Rates: Full page £95/Quarter £40/Back cover £195
Circulation approx: 2000
Payment terms to contributors: £20 per 1000 words non-fiction/£10 per story/£3 per poem
Accept/rejection approx times: 1 month

NIGHT DREAMS

Night Dreams (founded 1994) features poetry, short stories and articles concerning the weird, the frightening and the gruesome. It follows the style of the pulp magazines of the '30s and '40s.

Address: 52 Denman Lane, Huncote, Leicester LE9 3BS
Subs to: 47 Stephens Road, Walmley, Sutton Coldfield, West Midlands B76 2TS
Mag Frequency: Quarterly
Subscription: £10.50 pa
Single Issue: £2.80
Back Issue: £2.50
Overseas: £12.50 pa
Payment in: IMO/Cheque/PO
Payable to: Kirk S King
Inserts accepted: Yes
Terms: £10
Payment terms to contributors: £3 per 1000 words + free copy

$\mathcal{N}$
NINETIES POETRY

Perfect-bound A5 booklet. Containing poems from a variety of writers.

Address: 33 Lansdowne Place, Hove BN3 1HF
Mag Frequency: Quarterly
Single Issue: £4.95 + 38p postage
Overseas: N/A
Payable to: G. Ackroyd
Inserts accepted: No
Circulation approx: 200
Payment terms to contributors: When I have money
Accept/rejection approx times: N/A

NOMAD

Nomad is writing by people with mental health problems, survivors of abuse, addictions or disability. Our aim is to publish high quality, stimulating literary work for the general public. We aim to share insights gained from living at the margins of society, where discoveries are sometimes comic, often painful, never mundane. We publish work by both established and new writers.

Editor Name(s): Gerry Loose
Address: 30 Cranworth Street, Glasgow G12 8AG
Telephone: 0141 357 6838
Fax: 0141 357 6939
Email: SPS@gisp.net
Mag Frequency: 3 a year
Subscription: £6 (includes postage)
Single Issue: £2 (+30p postage)
Payment in: Sterling
Payable to: Survivors' Poetry Scotland
Inserts accepted: Yes
Terms: Contact
Advertising Rates: Contact for rate card
Circulation approx: 1000
Payment terms to contributors: None
Accept/rejection approx times: 6 weeks after submission deadline (end Nov/March/Aug)

N

THE NORTH

The North magazine offers the best of contemporary poetry by new and established writers, as well as critical articles and reviews. Submissions are welcome (up to 6 poems; please enclose SAE).

Address: The Studio, Byram Arcade, Westgate, Huddersfield, HD1 1ND
Fax: 01484 426566
Mag Frequency: Twice a year
Subscription: £10
Single Issue: £5.50
Back Issue: £3
Overseas: £16 (sterling or credit card only)
Payment in: Cheque/PO/Cash in sterling/Visa/Mastercard
Payable to: The Poetry Business Ltd
Inserts accepted: Yes
Terms: Minimum charge £10
Circulation approx: 500
Payment terms to contributors: By arrangement
Accept/rejection approx times: 1 month

N

NORTHWORDS

A magazine for new writing - fiction & poetry. Based in the Highlands of Scotland and aimed at promoting the cultural view from the peripheries and especially the north. Unpublished work only, of high quality.

Editor Name(s): Angus Dunn
Address: Angus Dunn, Editor, The Stable, Long Road, Avoch, Ross-Shire, IV9 8QR
Reviews to: Moira Forsyth, Treetops, 25 Woodlands Road, Dingwall, Ross-Shire IV15 9LJ
Subs to: Neil Urquhart, West Park, Strathpeffer, Ross-Shire IV14 9BT
Mag Frequency: 3 per year
Subscription: £7.50
Single Issue: £2.50
Back Issue: £2
Overseas: £10.50 per 3 issues
Payment in: Sterling
Payable to: NORTHWORDS
Inserts accepted: No
Advertising Rates: £80 full/£50 half/£25 quarter page
Circulation approx: 500
Payment terms to contributors: Modest payment - £3-£50 max
Accept/rejection approx times: 2-3 months

O

OASIS

Oasis aims to present a wide range of excellent writing, concentrating on originality of thought, expression and imagination. In doing this, it tends to veer towards the non-traditional, the experimental, in both poetry and prose. Translations are a strong feature of the magazine. Those intending to submit work should, ideally, purchase a copy or two first to discover the nature of the magazine. Less than about 1% of submissions are accepted.

Address: 12 Stevenage Road, London, SW6 6ES
Mag Frequency: 6 times a year (currently mailed in batches of 2, 3 times a year)
Subscription: £5 for 6 issues
Single Issue: £1.50
Overseas: $20 or sterling equivalent
Payable to: Oasis Books
Inserts accepted: Yes - but occasionally only and then by negotiation
Circulation approx: 350
Payment terms to contributors: Copies
Accept/rejection approx times: 1 month maximum

OBJECT PERMANENCE

Open to most kinds of short stories. Has a definite bias towards experimental/ modernist work. Each issue contains texts from exemplars of the aberrant traditions of the US and the UK, plus a substantial reviews section and as much information as will fit. Featured writers have included Clark Coolidge, Barry Macsweeney, Fiona Templeton and Drew Milne.

Address: Robin Purves, 121 Menock Road, Kingspark, Glasgow G44 5SD
Mag Frequency: 3 issues yearly
Subscription: £7.50 (inc. p & p)
Single Issue: £2.50
Overseas: £9 surface mail/£12 airmail
Payment in: UK Cheque/PO/Overseas Sterling IMO if possible
Payable to: Object Permanence
Inserts accepted: No
Payment terms to contributors: No payment. Contributors get free copies
Accept/rejection approx times: 1 month

0

OBSESSED WITH PIPEWORK

In sequins and silver lycra you look superhuman, supernatural. A shaman, you seem to know how to fly. Candy floss is dropped forgotten among the straw and sawdust as the punters crane and peer to make you out appearing and disappearing up there in the strong lights and shadows under the striped canvas. They gasp and share your joy at transcending danger and the laws of gravity and entropy. That's what I mean when I say Obsessed With Pipework deals in high-wire poems that amaze and delight. Our pantheon includes Allnutt, Harsent, Hart, Koch, Kumin, O'Hara, Olds, Plath, Schuyler, Sexton, Stern. Submissions of around six poems - any length, any style - are welcome, but remember the stamped addressed envelope, unless you submit via fax or e-mail. Nothing predictable, obvious or merely clever, please - let us see your good stuff. The Obsessed criteria are originality, authenticity, creative risk and that 'aha!' feeling. OWP is one of those parties where you don't need breath freshener on the way, and you don't have to leave as the sun comes up on Monday morning. Wear makeup by all means, but as self-expression not concealment. The editor offers suggestions when appropriate.

Editor Name(s): Charles Johnson
Address: Flarestack Publishing, At Redditch Library, 15 Market Place, Redditch B98 8AR
Telephone: 01527 63291(day) 0121 445 2110 (eve)
Fax: 01527 68571
Email: flare.stack@virgin.net
Mag Frequency: Quarterly
Subscription: £12
Single Issue: £3.50
Back Issue: All sold out so far!
Overseas: By arrangement
Payment in: Sterling - cheque/cash/PO
Payable to: Flarestack Publishing
Inserts accepted: Yes
Terms: By agreement
Advertising Rates: By arrangement
Circulation approx: 100+
Payment terms to contributors: 1 free copy
Accept/rejection approx times: 3 weeks maximum

OCULAR

An eclectic and lavishly illustrated magazine. A4 format, 40-44 pages. Surreal/macabre horror; gothic, pagan and occult; fantasy stories, poems and articles, book/music reviews and individual profiles. 'Not just a magazine but a visual hymn to the old gods and to the dreamers of dreams . . . a night summons!'

Editor Name(s): Lesley E Wilkinson
Address: Rosewood Cottage, Langtoft, Driffield, East Yorks YO25 OTQ
Telephone: 01377 267440
Mag Frequency: 2-4 times a year
Subscription: £8
Single Issue: £2.25
Overseas: £10
Payment in: Cheque/PO/UK stamps
Payable to: Lesley Wilkinson
Inserts accepted: Yes
Circulation approx: 200
Payment terms to contributors: Free copy
Accept/rejection approx times: 2-3 weeks max

0

OLD YORKSHIRE

An A5 format magazine printed on glossy paper. We specialise in recording York-shire's past for future generations. Articles ranging from prehistoric times up to circa 1970 will be considered. The only criterion is that they must be solely about Yorkshire and its people, nothing else will be considered. Articles with accompanying photographs or artwork stand a greater chance of acceptance. Features on York-shire's industry, famous or just ordinary people, abbeys, castles, battles, living conditions, customs, are all welcome. The scope is enormous. There is much of interest for the family historian: if you wish to know how your grandparents lived and worked then this is the magazine for you. Preferred article length is between 800-2,500 words. Longer features may be considered for serialisation. We also accept interesting single photographs with captions of up to 300 words. But please no Yorkshire fiction; all material submitted must be factual. A 'guidelines for contributors' leaflet is available on request.

Address: Brian Barker, Production Editor, Northern Line Publications, 111 Wrenbeck Drive, Otley, W Yorks LS21 2BP
Fax: 01943 461211
Mag Frequency: Quarterly at present - may go bi-monthly
Subscription: £9.50 annual (also includes free newsletter Muck & Brass)
Single Issue: £2.50
Overseas: £11.50 Europe
£13.50 USA, Australia (airmail)
Payment in: Sterling Banker's Draft overseas; Cheque/PO- inland
Payable to: Northern Line Publications
Inserts accepted: No
Advertising Rates: On request
Circulation approx: Growing quickly
Payment terms to contributors: £10 per 1000 words pro rata + 1 year's free subscription. Paid on publication.
Accept/rejection approx times: 4 weeks

O

ONE

One is a Christian magazine which offers cheer and friendship. This 32-page magazine is isued quarterly. It contains articles about the bible, news items, letters from readers, financial advice, animal stories and a serial story. Readers may join the cassette and paperback library, write to the 'Befriender' for advice, enter the literary competitions with prizes and have their articles and poems published. There is also a 'Prisoner's Friend' who writes to prisoners. Members may ask for a birthday card. They may advertise free of charge in the magazine. Penfriend club One To One is an active, ongoing sub-section. Why not send for a sample copy of One magazine, and share your faith with other readers?

Editor Name(s): Mrs WK Cardy
Address: Mrs Wendy K Cardy, 48 South Street, Colchester, Essex CO2 7BJ
Telephone: 01206 520156
Fax: 01206 577404 - to att: One magazine
Mag Frequency: Quarterly
Subscription: £4 pa
Single Issue: £1.20
Back Issue: 70p
Overseas: 10 IRCs for sub
Payment in: Cheque/PO/IRCs/stamps/dollars
Payable to: One
Inserts accepted: Yes
Terms: Free
Circulation approx: 200
Payment terms to contributors: 1 extra free copy
Accept/rejection approx times: 4 weeks

O

ORBIS

This is from No 94 (Autumn 94): primarily a poetry magazine, and though we do publish prose titles occasionally, we do not use much in a year (max:1000 words, not formula fiction). We use virtually every kind of poetry, except the more extreme experimental type or poetry in which the message occludes the language. Likely to accept work from new writers, but accept only about 2% of what we receive.

Address: 199 The Long Shoot, Nuneaton, Warks CV11 6JO
Mag Frequency: Quarterly
Subscription: £15
Single Issue: £4
Back Issue: £2
Overseas: US$28
Payable to: Orbis magazine
Inserts accepted: Yes
Terms: £50 per 1000
Circulation approx: 1000
Payment terms to contributors: £5 per acceptance/£50 per issue prizes
Accept/rejection approx times: Return post

OSTINATO

Ostinato publishes poems/articles/interviews/prose relating to jazz/improvised music. The emphasis is on work that enshrines jazz and its practitioners in context; be it spiritual, socio-political or musical. Production values are very high. Original artwork and photographs are used. Review section is lengthy but mostly in-house. Ostinato is currently in limbo due to financial difficulties associated with ill health. Sales of back issues would help kick-start. Details/press package from Editorial Address. SAE please.

Address: PO Box 522, London N8 7SZ
Mag Frequency: Irregular
Subscription: Not currently applicable
Single Issue: Varies usually £2.50
Payment in: Sterling cheques only
Payable to: Ostinato
Inserts accepted: Yes
Terms: Swop with other magazines
Circulation approx: Unknown but reaches a wide audience
Payment terms to contributors: Contributary copy
Accept/rejection approx times: When magazine is active: 2 weeks; longer at other times

0

OTHER POETRY

Other Poetry was published in Leicester from 1979 to 1989, and was revived in Newcastle in 1994. It consists of poetry and reviews. The poetry is judged by a panel of four editors, and is considered on no other grounds than merit.

Address: Evangeline Paterson, 105 Osborne Court, Osborne Avenue, Jesmond, Newcastle upon Tyne NE2 1LE
Reviews to: Michael Standen, 29 Western Hill, Durham DH1 4RL
Mag Frequency: 3 issues per annum
Subscription: £10
Single Issue: £3.50
Back Issue: £2
Overseas: £11 surface mail/£12 airmail
Payment in: Sterling
Payable to: Other Poetry
Inserts accepted: Yes
Terms: £20 per 1000
Circulation approx: Increasing
Payment terms to contributors: £5 per poem
Accept/rejection approx times: 4-6 weeks

O

OUTPOSTS POETRY QUARTERLY

For more than fifty years Outposts has published new poetry by both the established and the yet to be recognised. The magazine has never supported a dogma, nor a coterie: it has been our policy to publish the best from the unsolicited material we receive. Two issues each year are general issues of new poetry plus reviews, one of which will carry an essay on some aspect of poetry such as rhyme technique, or an extended review of an important book or poet. A third issue will look at the work of a contemporary poet, such as James Brockway, Peter Dale, Sylvia Kantaris, Derek Walcott. Our fourth is a larger anthology issue with a translation section. Outposts is one of the few magazines open to new translations. It has been said that Outposts is the place to find tomorrow's poets today. The magazine is part of the Hippopotamus Press, so it is not surprising that some who had their first poems printed in Outposts have gone on to have full collections from the Hippopotamus Press. Recent issues have included new poetry by Peter Abbs, Alan Brownjohn, Ian Caws, William Cookson, Peter Dale, Philip Gross, John Heath-Stubbs, Elizabeth Jennings, Lotte Kramer, Edward Lowbury, Christopher Pilling, Sally Purcell, Peter Russel, Vernon Scannell, Penelope Shuttle and prose from Peter Dale, Anna Martin, William Oxley, Glyn Pursglove, Eddie Wainwright.

Editor Name(s): Roland John
Address: Hippopotamus Press, 22 Whitewell Road, Frome, Somerset BA11 4EL
Telephone: 01373 466653
Fax: 01373 466653
Mag Frequency: Quarterly
Subscription: £14 for 4/£26 for 8
Single Issue: £5
Back Issue: £3 except specials
Overseas: £16 for 4/£29 for 8
Payment in: Sterling or Visa/Master Card
Payable to: Hippopotamus Press
Inserts accepted: Yes
Terms: £90 full list/£60 UK only
Advertising Rates: £60 full/£30 half page
Circulation approx: 1200
Payment terms to contributors: Small: £5 a page, more for commisioned articles
Accept/rejection approx times: 1 week

O

OXFORD POETRY

Since its revival in 1983 Oxford Poetry has attracted a sound readership and many favourable reviews. Tom Paulin has called it one of the best small poetry magazines in the country. The main purpose of the magazine is to be a forum for new poets' work (and we have a talent for spotting poets early!), but each issue also includes reviews, interviews, features, a translation competition and work by famous writers. In 1990 Seamus Heaney established the Richard Ellmann Prize for the best poem in each volume of the magazine.

Address: Robert Macfarlane, Oxford Poetry, Magdalen College, Oxford OX1 4AU
Mag Frequency: 3 times per year (irregular)
Subscription: £9
Single Issue: £3 plus p&p
Back Issue: £1 plus p&p
Overseas: £11
Payment in: Overseas payments by IMO
Payable to: Oxford Poetry
Inserts accepted: No
Circulation approx: 500
Payment terms to contributors: No payment
Accept/rejection approx times: 6 months max

0

OXFORD QUARTERLY REVIEW

The Oxford Quarterly Review is a high-quality literary journal devoted to publishing the finest in contemporary poetry and fiction. Issue one featured new poetry by Les Murray and an essay on film-montage by David Marnet. The second issue featured poetry by eight Pulitzer prize-winning authors, as well as Edwin Morgan, Miles Chapman and first-time translations of top Rumanian and Polish poets. The third issue: new poetry by Adrienne Rich, James Dickey, Donald Justice, Philip Levine, Michael Middleton and Louise Glück. Unsolicited poems, fiction welcome as are reviews of contemporary writing.

Address: Editor, St Catherine's College, Oxford, OX1 3VS
Mag Frequency: Quarterly
Subscription: Institutional £20/Individual £16
Single Issue: £5
Back Issue: £3.50
Overseas: USA $25 or $30 institutional
Payable to: Oxford Quarterly Review
Inserts accepted: Yes
Terms: £100
Circulation approx: 500
Payment terms to contributors: Copy
Accept/rejection approx times: 2 weeks, unless held for consideration

P
PAGES

Pages, in the current second series (the 12 issues), is subtitled 'resources for the linguistic innovative poetries'. It features a selected writer, with 10pp of her or his work, a page essay, a 2 page response to the texts in the issue and a bibliography. The attempt is to raise awareness of a particular question of writers. I am not looking for contributions to this series (but I don't know what a third series might bring). The poets are: Adrian Clarke, Ulli Freer, John Wilkinson, Hazel Smith, Alan Halsey, Rod Menghan. Virginia Firuberg, Ken Edwards, Maggie O` Sullivan, Cris Cheek, Peter Middleton, and Gilbert Adair.

Address: 15 Oakapple Road, Southwick, Sussex BN42 4YL
Mag Frequency: Irregular - several a year
Subscription: £12 for 12 issues (post free)
Single Issue: £3
Overseas: £24 in sterling equivalent
Payable to: Robert Sheppard
Inserts accepted: No
Circulation approx: 100+
Payment terms to contributors: Free copies

PALADIN

Publishes stories, poems, articles on a literary topic, puzzles and jokes accepted too. 28 - 36 pages. We hope to publish twice a year, if possible.

Address: Ken Morgan, 66 Heywood Court, Tenby, Dyfed SA70 8BS
Mag Frequency: Annually at present
Subscription: £1.50 a copy
Single Issue: £1.50
Back Issue: £1
Overseas: £2 a copy
Payable to: Ken Morgan
Inserts accepted: Yes
Terms: Free if smaller than A5 page
Circulation approx: 50-100
Payment terms to contributors: Copies of magazines, occasionally free booklets and pamphlets.
Accept/rejection approx times: Usually within 1 month.

PARATAXIS: Modernism + Modern Writing

Parataxis is devoted to the critical re-thinking of modernism and to the publication and discussion of contemporary writing. It seeks to provide a forum for discussing critical theory and critical issues, in relation to avant-garde literary traditions of various kinds. Parataxis does not publish unsolicited poetry. The journal will publish occasional issues devoted to particular topics and writers. Anyone thinking of writing for Parataxis is advised to discuss it with the editor first.

Address: Drew Milne, School of English and American Studies, University of Sussex, Falmer, Brighton BN1 9QN
Mag Frequency: Twice a year
Subscription: £6/£10 institutions
Single Issue: £3/£5 institutions
Payment in: In sterling
Payable to: Drew Milne
Inserts accepted: Yes
Terms: Free to non-profit organisations
Circulation approx: 250 copies sold per issue
Payment terms to contributors: None - 2 copies of issue in which work appears

PASSION

Poetry, Fiction, Arts, Criticism, Culture.* Each year Crescent Moon is publishing four collections of poetry, fiction, reviews, and essays on fine art, cinema, music, politics, philosophy, the media, feminism and many kinds of criticism drawn from the UK, Europe, Canada and North America.* Many writers are being published for the first time here, while others are established writers who are featured in publications throughout the world.* Well-known poets and artists such as Andrea Dworkin, Richard Long, VS Naipaul, Peter Redgrove, DJ Enright, Penelope Shuttle, Colin Wilson, Ronald Blythe, Edwin Mullins, Geoffrey Ashe, Alan Bold and Jeremy Reed featured in the first issues.* The work ranges from the passionate, erotic and spiritual, to the humorous, polemical and incisive but it is always entertaining.

Address: PO Box 393, Maidstone, Kent ME14 5XU
Mag Frequency: Quarterly
Subscription: £10 indivual/£15 institution
Single Issue: £2.50
Overseas: $22 individual/$30 institution
Payment in: Sterling/US$ to Crescent Moon
Payable to: Crescent Moon
Inserts accepted: Yes
Terms: £30
Circulation approx: 200
Payment terms to contributors: Negotiable
Accept/rejection approx times: 4 months

PDM

PDM is a pc fanzine on pc-format disk. Although it is primarily computing, it does sometimes have articles on science fiction included. Generally PDM contains a mixture of games, reviews, pc help and miscellaneous items (stories, cheats, information etc). Contributions are welcome, but we cannot afford to pay for them as yet. Please send a stamped self-addressed envelope for more details if you require them.

Editor Name(s): Michael Raven
Address: PDM, 17 Melton Fields, Brickyard Lane, North Ferriby, East Yorks HU14 3HE
Telephone: 01482 631496
Mag Frequency: Monthly
Subscription: £12
Single Issue: £1.50
Overseas: UK only
Payment in: Cash/cheque/PO
Payable to: Michael Raven
Inserts accepted: Yes
Terms: Must be single sheeting & printed for distribution. May be rejected.
Advertising Rates: Free for non-commercial/£1 per printed page for trade ads
Payment terms to contributors: As standard, contributors not paid
Accept/rejection approx times: 28 days

PC-FORMAT DISC

PEACE & FREEDOM

Peace & Freedom is a magazine of poetry, prose and art which focuses on humanitarian/environmental issues mainly, but not solely. We are not looking for work which supports the status quo, so pro royalist, conservative tweeness we avoid like the plague. We're looking for challenging, thought-provoking work which shows genuine compassion. Satirical stuff is okay, too. We also run poetry competitions and forms are available for an SAE/IRC. Peace & Freedom was established in 1985 and has issued a number of booklets and books under the Peace & Freedom Press banner. For full details of Peace & Freedom Press please send an SAE/IRC.

Address: 17 Farrow Road, Whaplode Drove, Spalding, Lincs PE12 OTS
Mag Frequency: Twice yearly
Subscription: £7.50 for 4 issues
Single Issue: £1.75
Back Issue: £1
Overseas: $16
Payment in: UK cheque or PO/Overseas IMO or cash
Payable to: Peace & Freedom
Inserts accepted: Yes
Terms: £20/$50. Free to magazines who are willing to exchange circs.
Circulation approx: 500
Payment terms to contributors: Free issue when work is published
Accept/rejection approx times: Less than 3 months

𝒫
PEEPING TOM

Twice winner of the British Fantasy Society Award for Best Small Press. Includes 'big names' and newcomers. No poetry, no articles, no reviews. Strictly fiction only. Stories should be 100-3000 words, the longer stories used if exceptional. If your story falls loosely into the horror/dark fantasy/sf/fantasy categories, please feel free to send it along. I am also keen to receive humorous submissions (I don't get anywhere near enough) so long as the humour evolves naturally out of the characters and the situations they find themselves in. The best way to discover the sort of stories I'm looking for is to read a copy of the mag. Subscription to Peeping Tom brings you not only the mag ('a showcase for uncompromising horror fiction' according to Dementia 13) but also free membership of Midnight Oil writers' forum - a postal critique and support service.

Editor Name(s): David Bell
Address: Yew Tree House, 15 Nottingham Road, Ashby de la Zouche, Leics LE65 1DJ
Subs to: Stuart Hughes 4 Pottery Close, Belper, Derbyshire DE56 0HU
Telephone: 01530 413371
Fax: 01773 880428
Email: StuartHugh@aol.com
Mag Frequency: Quarterly
Subscription: £8
Single Issue: £2.25
Back Issue: £1
Overseas: Europe £9.75/USA $24 ($7 for sample copy)
Payment in: Sterling or US dollars
Payable to: Peeping Tom Magazine
Advertising Rates: £10 full pg/£5 half/plus comp copy
Circulation approx: 300
Payment terms to contributors: £2.50 per thousand words + complimentary copy
Accept/rejection approx times: 3 weeks

PEER POETRY

To cater both for long and short poems, not being restricted to 30 or 40 lines. To provide sufficient space to demonstrate the range of each writer's capabilities. To provide a platform for a wide variety of talent. To give each poet an idea of the effectiveness of their work as seen by fellow practitioners. To keep cost, particularly entry fees down - there is no charge for entry to the Competition for subscribers. To provide room for the work of about 40 poets in each issue - any number of poems within a maximum of approx 200 lines, 2000 words, and a minimum of one full A4 page of work. To find and display poetry with a feeling for natural rhythm, fluent, flowing, having shape and plan; cherishing the sound and beauty of words and ideas. Haiku and senryu sequences being welcome as well as traditional stanzas in classical forms such as sonnets, rondeaus, lays etc, and all modern verse forms. for further details send SAE.

Address: 26 (SG) Arlington House, Bath Street, Bath, NE Somerset BA1 1QN
Mag Frequency: Bi-annual
Subscription: £12
Single Issue: £7 inc p&p
Back Issue: £6 inc p&p
Overseas: £12 + 250g postage
Payment in: Sterling cheque, PO/IRC coupons acceptable @ 40p each
Payable to: Peer Poetry
Inserts accepted: Depends on content
Terms: Reciprocal
Circulation approx: 350
Payment terms to contributors: £10 per two A4 pages (preferred) poems and articles - pro rata for one A4
Accept/rejection approx times: 2/4 weeks - only if accompanied by 2 SAEs (state whether constructive criticism appreciated)

PEN & KEYBOARD (& Newsletter)

P&K has been going for four years now. Although there have been some rough patches, the reception has usually been very good. The published works are eclectic, coming from many sources both in this country and abroad. Having an enquiry from Australia last summer confirmed that this publication has been seen on every continent. The contents are as varied as the people who write them - from science fiction to hidden temples and from religion to weight lifting. The aim is to get people to write. We do get the literary prats - ie those who can spell and punctuate like Oxford grammarians but whose imagination and interest content is just about as flat as they can be. I prefer a writer who is fervent, tries hard and produces something that moves me.

Address: 526 Fulham Palace Road, London SW6 6JE
Fax: Answerphone 0171 736 2887
Mag Frequency: Quarterly
Subscription: £12 pa
Single Issue: £3
Back Issue: £3
Overseas: On application
Payable to: SQR (Publishing) Enterprise
Inserts accepted: Yes
Terms: Free - up to 200
Circulation approx: 200
Accept/rejection approx times: ASAP

PENDRAGON

Pendragon is an Arthurian interest magazine produced by the membership of the Pendragon Society since 1959. It has a wide readership in Britain and around the world. News, reviews, articles, letters, some poetry. All aspects of Arthurian and related interests: archaelogy, history, myth, folklore, legend, literature, the arts and the media. Membership of the society is extended to annual subscribers who are given reduced price advertising rates and priority contribution acceptance.

Editor Name(s): Christopher Lovegrove
Address: 125 York Road, Montpelier, Bristol BS6 5QG
Subs to: 41 Ridge Street, Watford, Herts WD2 5BL
Email: johnford@mcmail.com
Website: www.pendragon.mcmail.com/index.htm
Mag Frequency: 3 per annum
Subscription: £7.50
Single Issue: £2.50
Overseas: £10 (Europe) £12.50 (World)
Payment in: Sterling cheque/PO/IMO/Travellers cheque
Payable to: The Pendragon Society
Inserts accepted: Yes
Terms: Please enquire
Advertising Rates: £40 per page/£50 back page
Circulation approx: 600
Payment terms to contributors: Free copy
Accept/rejection approx times: 2-3 weeks

P

PENINSULAR

A fabulous magazine which is on the up! Well written short stories, preferably with an unusual twist, short articles, sparky letters page including crits on the previous issue; regular comps open to non-subscribers, send SAE for details. Regret we cannot accept unsolicited manuscripts - have over 100 on file at any given time. Essential to study at least one issue and to send for guidelines.

Address: Cherrybite Publications, Linden Cottage, 45 Burton Road, Little Weston, S-Wirral, L64 4AE
Fax: 0151 353 0967
Email: helicon@gglobalnet.co.uk
Mag Frequency: Quarterly
Subscription: £10.50 per 4 issues
Single Issue: £3
Back Issue: £2
Overseas: Send IRC for price list
Payment in: Sterling cheque or IRCs
Payable to: Cherrybite Publications
Inserts accepted: Yes
Terms: Reciprocal
Circulation approx: 300
Payment terms to contributors: £5 per 1000 words, plus free copy or credit notes
Accept/rejection approx times: 1 month

THE PENNILESS PRESS

Penniless Press publishes poetry, fiction, philosophy, comment, criticism, translations and reviews. Prose writers should try to limit their pieces to approx 3,000 words. The magazine is eclectic in nature and has published work on Odysseus Elytis, jazz, modern painting, Saint-Simon, Marx, Adam Smith, Turgot, Isaac Rosenfeld, crime writing, Condorcet, modern Greek poetry, Henry Roth, Ogden Nash, James Hanley, Kenneth Patchen, WS Graham, Alfred Kazin, Herbert Spencer, John MacMurray, Irving Howe, Freud. It has featured work by Jim Burns, Fred Voss, Adrian Mitchell, Geoff Hattersley, Gael Turnbull, Patricia Pogson, Geoffrey Holloway, Philip Callow, Tom Wood, John Lucas, Joan Jobe Smith, Paul Vinit, Nick Toczek, Victor Serge, David Caddy, Andy Croft, Albert Einstein, Jose Watanabe, Pablo Neruda, Alexis Lykiard, Ortega y Gasset, Jose Cerna and more.

Address: 100 Waterloo Road, Ashton, Preston PR2 1EP
Mag Frequency: Quarterly
Subscription: £8.50
Single Issue: £2.50
Back Issue: £2
Overseas: £8.50
Payment in: Sterling cheque/PO
Payable to: Penniless Press
Inserts accepted: Yes
Terms: Will exchange inserts
Circulation approx: 250
Payment terms to contributors: None
Accept/rejection approx times: 2 weeks

P
PENNINE INK

Pennine Ink was founded in the 1980s by Pennine Ink Writers' Workshop, and is administered by members. It is published yearly, featuring poetry, prose and illustrations. It accepts contributions from all over the world. Poems should be no more that 40 lines, prose (short stories and articles) 1200 words maximum. Illustrations should be suitable for an A5 format. Given that Pennine Ink is only published once a year, it is happy to accept small press magazines for review. There is no constraint on topics or style of poems and prose other than their quality. Publication of Pennine Ink 20 is due March 1999.

Address: Pennine Ink c/c Mid Pennine Arts, Yorke Street, Burnley, Lancs BB11 1HD
Subs to: The Secretary, address above
Fax: 01706 831106
Mag Frequency: Annually
Subscription: £2.50
Single Issue: £2.50
Back Issue: £1.50
Overseas: Cost per magazine + suitable postage
Payment in: Cash/cheque/PO/IMO
Payable to: Pennine Ink Writers Workshop
Inserts accepted: Yes
Circulation approx: 500+
Payment terms to contributors: Free copy of magazine
Accept/rejection approx times: 2 months

PENNINE PLATFORM

A magazine whose policy is independent, avoiding all establishments and sects. All contributions welcome but preference for form (not aimless free verse with no ordering) and for poems of awareness, personal, socio-political and religious, but avoiding propaganda and the conventional. Translations welcome. Submit no more than six poems at once, with name and address on every sheet, and SAE. Editorial comments on submissions are rare. Contains reviews, usually by editor or commissioned.

Address: Dr K E Smith, 7 Cockley Hill Lane, Kirkheaton,Huddersfield, W Yorks HD5 0HH
Mag Frequency: Twice a year
Subscription: £8.50 inc post
Single Issue: £4.50 inc post
Overseas: £12 sterling or £17 in currency or £25 non-sterling cheque
Payable to: Pennine Platform
Inserts accepted: No
Circulation approx: 200
Payment terms to contributors: 1 free copy
Accept/rejection approx times: 3 months

THE PEOPLE'S POETRY

A magazine of accessible poetry on any theme but specialising in lyrical poetry and poetry of the romantic school; particularly sympathetic to traditional rhyme and rhythm and traditional poetic forms. A high romantic and spiritual emphasis - poems containing slang and swear words are unlikely to be accepted, poems of the heart rather than the head are favoured.

Address: Peter Geoffrey Paul Thompson, 71 Harrow Crescent, Romford, Essex RM3 7BJ
Mag Frequency: Quarterly
Subscription: £5
Single Issue: £1.50
Overseas: £5 and sufficient IRCs
Payment in: British or foreign currency
Payable to: The People's Poetry
Inserts accepted: No
Circulation approx: 500
Payment terms to contributors: 1 complimentary copy
Accept/rejection approx times: Normally within 4 weeks

PERSPECTIVE

It is often very difficult for new writers to get their work published, as the platform for short fiction has traditionally been limited. Even the magazines aimed at new writers offer few opportunities, being in the main full of helpful articles by established authors. Our magazine provides an opportunity for new writers to see their work in print and to receive feedback. Perspective is a mixture of articles and the work of new writers. It presents new talent to a broad audience. Copies are sent to agents and publishing houses as well as to selected libraries. Material is selected by means of our annual open competition. Readers are given opportunities to air their views and provide feedback for fellow writers. Our aim is to produce a magazine containing useful information about competitions, forthcoming events and getting work published, as well as continuing our present policy of giving general advice and promoting writing workshops. We have expanded our range by publishing a limited number of longer works. Copyright remains with the author. Extracts on internet at http://ourworldCompuServe.com/homepages/authors

Address: PO Box 1352. Glasgow G45 0DS and C15 100127.2304 or 100127.2304@ compuServe.com
Website: http://ourworldCompuServe.com/homepages/authors
Mag Frequency: Irregular soon to be monthly/Also internet pages
Subscription: Distributed to Guild Members
Inserts accepted: Yes
Terms: Variable - free to £50
Payment terms to contributors: Variable, no fee for competition entries but prizes and bursaries awarded.
Accept/rejection approx times: Variable

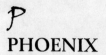

PHOENIX

Phoenix (founded 1996) deals with all aspects of the paranormal/unexplained, including UFOs, hauntings, crytozoology, ESP, strange science, etc. Articles are welcomed on all of the above, together with unusual newsclippings (dated and sourced). Book reviews are also invited (items reviewed must be on relevant subjects).

Address: 60 The Upper Drive, Hove, East Sussex BN3 6NE
Mag Frequency: Bimonthly
Subscription: £14 a year
Single Issue: £2.50
Overseas: $30 USA ($5 for single issue)
Payment in: IMO/PO/sterling cheque/foreign currency
Payable to: Alan Baker
Inserts accepted: No
Circulation approx: Increasing
Payment terms to contributors: Free copy of magazine
Accept/rejection approx times: 1 to 2 weeks (allowing for transit in mail)

PIERS

The journal of the National Piers Society giving news of current developments, historical research items, poems, b&w pictures, engineering articles - anything related to piers.

Editor Name(s): Martin Easdown
Address: 7 Stuart Road, Folkestone CT19 6NL or 33, Littlefield Lane, Grimsby DN31 2AZ
Telephone: 01472 341283 (contact - Soc Chairman)
Fax: 01527 456 561
Email: pjredditch@msn.com
Mag Frequency: Quarterly
Subscription: £5 pa (£10 includes Society membership)
Single Issue: £1+postage
Overseas: £10 (includes Society membership)
Payment in: £sterling
Payable to: National Piers Society
Inserts accepted: Yes, if of benefit & pay postage difference
Advertising Rates: TBA
Circulation approx: 500
Accept/rejection approx times: Issue after next

PLANET - The Welsh Internationalist

A bi-monthly magazine of the arts and current affairs, centred on Wales but in a broader context of Europe and the world beyond. Areas of special interest: poetry, fiction, politics, the environement, science, visual art. Recent contributors include, from Wales: RS Thomas, Emyr Humphreys, Jan Morris, Gillian Clarke, Robert Minhinnick; from abroad: Les Murray, Guy Vanderhaeghe, Jaan Kaplinski, Ian McDonald, Tabish Khair.

Editor Name(s): John Barnie
Address: Planet, PO Box 44, Aberystwyth, Ceredigion SY23 3ZZ
Telephone: 01970 611255
Fax: 01970 611197
Mag Frequency: 6 pa
Subscription: £13
Single Issue: £2.75
Back Issue: Varies
Overseas: £14 surface(US$30)/£23air(US$42)
Payment in: Sterling
Payable to: Planet
Inserts accepted: Yes
Terms: £25
Advertising Rates: Full pg £50/half £25/qtr £12.50
Circulation approx: 1400
Payment terms to contributors: £40 per 1000 wds prose/£25 minimum per poem. Payment on publication
Accept/rejection approx times: 4 weeks

PLUME

Plume is a good quality literary magazine, with a French connection, produced in Brighouse and Nice! We welcome unsolicited manuscripts and are especially keen to receive well-written, original and challenging stories, articles and poetry. We are also interested in receiving monochrome artwork. Two competitions are run annually: one for short stories of between 1500-2000 words and one for poetry of up to forty lines. Critiques are available on request for a small extra fee. Plume also accepts manuscripts in French, to be submitted to Jen Fustec, 42 Av Monplaisir, 06100 Nice, France.

Editor Name(s): Jan Bentley/Jen Fustec
Address: 15 Bolehill Park, Hove Edge, Brighouse HD6 2RS UK or 42 Av Monplaisir 06100 Nice France
Telephone: 01484 717808
Email: plumelit@aol.com
Mag Frequency: 2 issues a year
Subscription: £6.50 UK & Europe
Single Issue: £3.50
Back Issue: £2
Overseas: £7 by IMO
Payment in: Sterling
Payable to: Plume
Inserts accepted: No
Circulation approx: 200
Payment terms to contributors: By negotiation
Accept/rejection approx times: 6 weeks

p

PN REVIEW

For over a quarter of a century, PN Review has pursued poetry in all its forms, in all corners of the world. It has an outstanding record among contemporary literary journals. Six times a year reports, articles, poems, translations and reviews compete for space in Britain's most independent literary magazine. Committed to the traditional and the experimental in poetry, PN Review has remained above contemporary trends in theory and criticism. The emphasis is always on poems before poets, content over personality. From its pugnacious beginnings in the early seventies, to its present distinction as a place of discovery and appraisal, PN Review has been at the cutting edge of intellectual debate. In an age of post-modern relativism and uncertainty, it has taken its bearings from modernism as the crucial foundation of the twentieth century canon. PN Review has carved out a unique niche in the precarious world of literary magazines. While other competitors may fall by the wayside, PN Review will continue. Always breaking new ground. Always questioning. 'Unorthodox and unpredictable, provocative and addictive, an intelligent magazine with a strong sense of purpose.' Dennis O'Driscoll.

Editor Name(s): Michael Schmidt
Address: PN Review, 4th floor, Conavon Court, 12-16 Blackfriars Street, Manchester M3 5BQ
Telephone: 0161 834 8730
Fax: 0161 832 0084
Email: pnr@carcanet.u-net.com
Mag Frequency: Bi-monthly - 6 times a year
Subscription: 1year: £29.50 person/£35 institution
2year: £56.50 person/£68 institution
Single Issue: £4.50
Overseas: EEC £35pers/£41inst; US $55pers/$68inst - all airmail
Payment in: Sterling cheque on Brit bank/Access/Visa
Payable to: PN Review
Inserts accepted: Yes
Terms: £380 for all subscribers (max A5)
Advertising Rates: Full £350/half £200/Quarter £110/Sixth £90. Discount to small orgs 25%, also discounts for run-on ads; contact Penny Jones.
Circulation approx: 1500 individual/500 trade
Payment terms to contributors: Varies - dependent on length of article
Accept/rejection approx times: 4/6 weeks

POETIC HOURS

Poetic Hours (founded 1993) is the newsletter of the Dreamlands Poetry Group whose subscribers write much of the poetry and features within it - although outside contributors are welcomed. The magazine consists of a mixture of articles on famous poetry/poets and readers' poetry. Poets are not paid but all the profits of the magazine are donated to major charities with each issue carrying reports of how money has been spent. This policy generates a positive attitude within the contributors which results in a wide range of diverse material from writers with a real enthusiasm for all aspects of poetry. Poetic Hours welcomes all types of work and subscribers are talented 'amateurs' of all ages from the UK and beyond. The magazine tends to reflect the interests poets have in reading the work of others like themselves; so regular features like 'My Xanadu' - where a subscriber examines his favourite poem - and a 'featured poet' allow people to read about the lives and influences of others. Poetic Hours is not for anyone who takes themselves too seriously, but should be of interest to all those who love poetry and are keen to learn and write their own.

Editor Name(s): Nick Clark
Address: 8 Dale Road, Carlton, Notts NG4 1GT
Mag Frequency: Bi-annually
Subscription: £5 pa
Single Issue: £3
Back Issue: £3 + SAE
Overseas: £7 pa sterling outside EU or $20 US
Payment in: Sterling, cheque (UK/EU only), US dollars
Payable to: Erran Publishing
Inserts accepted: No, unless relating to non-profitmaking organisations
Circulation approx: Increasing
Payment terms to contributors: None
Accept/rejection approx times: -

P

POETIC LICENCE

Poetic Licence publishes new poetry and line drawings. Based in Croydon, Surrey, most of its contributors and readership come from the Croydon/South London area - but good new poetry and line drawing is welcomed from anyone, anywhere. There are three editors for each issue of Poetic Licence, rotating through the varied membership of Poets Anonymous. There is therefore no particular 'house style'.

Editor Name(s): Rotates - contact is Peter Evans
Address: 70 Aveling Close, Purley, Surrey CR8 4DW
Telephone: 0181 645 9956
Mag Frequency: 3 per year
Subscription: £7 pa
Single Issue: £2.50
Overseas: As UK
Payment in: Sterling cheques
Payable to: Poetic Licence
Inserts accepted: No
Circulation approx: 100
Payment terms to contributors: No payment
Accept/rejection approx times: Up to 3 months

POETIC WRITING

New title this year from Poetry Update founder Eric Goldsworthy. All new poetry, all levels - every month. Of interest to struggling first-time poets and others, who want to be published but can't get started. Available by annual subscription. Subscribers can publish a poem every month - so if you want to see your work in print, this is the one to subscribe to!

Editor Name(s): Eric Goldsworthy
Address: Erix Publications, 27 Old Gloucester Street, London WC1N 3XX
Email: editor@writing.co.uk
Mag Frequency: Monthly
Subscription: £50 pa
Single Issue: £5
Overseas: US$100 sub/US$10 single
Payment in: Sterling cheque on a UK bank/credit card
Payable to: Erix Publications
Inserts accepted: Yes
Terms: £100 per 1000
Advertising Rates: Please enquire - reasonable prices!
Circulation approx: 1000
Payment terms to contributors: None

P

POETICAL HISTORIES

Pamphlet series - one poet per issue. Letterpress printing on antique paper, limited edition. 45 isssues published to date. Publishes both senior and novice poets, with no distinction other than a preference for writing of a modernist tendency.

Editor Name(s): Peter Riley
Address: 27 Sturton Street, Cambridge CB1 2QG
Fax: 01223 576 422
Email: priley@dircon.co.uk
Mag Frequency: 3-6 issues per annum
Subscription: Issues billed as published
Single Issue: £3 or £4
Overseas: As UK+postage
Payment in: Sterling only
Payable to: Peter Riley (Books)
Inserts accepted: No
Terms: A5 inserts available w/ book catalogues @£10
Advertising Rates: N/A
Circulation approx: 300
Payment terms to contributors: Copies only
Accept/rejection approx times: 1-2 weeks

POETRY AND AUDIENCE

We do not discriminate against any form of poetry but our own interests bend towards, on the one hand, a more lyrical style, and on the other, language-based experimentation. Having said this, we publish purely on the basis of merit, and obscurity is welcomed. Previous contributors include Carol Ann Duffy, Geoffrey Hill and Tony Harrison, part of an established tradition which provides a forum for unpublished poets to see their work alongside the better known practitioners.

Address: C/O School of English, University of Leeds LS2 9JT
Fax: 0113 233 4774
Email: engpanda@leeds.ac.uk
Mag Frequency: 2 times a year
Subscription: £4 pa
Single Issue: £2
Back Issue: £1.50
Overseas: £6
Payment in: Cheque/PO payable as above
Payable to: The University of Leeds
Inserts accepted: Yes
Circulation approx: 200
Payment terms to contributors: Free copy of issue
Accept/rejection approx times: 10 weeks at most

P
THE POETRY CHURCH

The Poetry Church is an Anglo-American Christian poetry quarterly with a church music supplement. It publishes subscribers' poetry privately in the Feather Books Poetry Series and also members' hymns/music. Each year it compiles over 200 pages of new poetry and prayer in an anthology. Many of our poets are nationally known; others newcomers; some handicapped. We publish any Christian poetry we feel comes from the heart. Our poets range from academics to prisoners writing from condemned cells on death row. We feel we are encouragers of new Christian writers, as well as experienced ones. Not only does The Poetry Church encourage poets, it supports art and music with Christian themes. This year our magazine sponsored the Russian Orthodox choir, Nova Chora Russicum, from St Petersburg, on their British tour. The Poetry Church is used as a resource in preaching/teaching, and is increasingly bought by parishes as a supplement to the parish magazine.

Editor Name(s): Rev John Waddington-Feather/sub-editor Paul Evans
Address: Fair View, Old Coppice, Lyth Bank, Shrewsbury SY3 0BW
Telephone: 01743 872177
Fax: 01743 872177
Email: john@feather.icom-web.com
Website: \\www.feather.icom-web.com
Mag Frequency: Quarterly
Subscription: £7
Single Issue: £4
Overseas: $15
Payment in: Cheque/PO. Overseas US dollar bills or sterling cheque
Payable to: Feather Books
Inserts accepted: No
Advertising Rates: Negotiable
Circulation approx: 1000
Payment terms to contributors: None
Accept/rejection approx times: 1 week

POETRY IRELAND REVIEW

Poetry Ireland Review was first published in 1981 and is the de facto journal of record for contemporary poetry in Ireland. We publish the best of contemporary poetry from Ireland and overseas. We also review every collection of poetry published in Ireland each year. The editor is appointed for 4 issues (1 year) with occasional special issues. Recent contributors: Seamus Heaney, Fleur Adcock, Michael Longley and Eavan Boland.

Editor Name(s): Catherine Phil MacCarthy (present - changes)
Address: Poetry Ireland Review, Bermingham Tower, Dublin Castle, Dublin 2 Ireland
Telephone: 671 4632
Fax: 6714634
Email: poetry@iol.ie
Mag Frequency: Quarterly
Subscription: Ireland & UK £24/£20 conc
Single Issue: £6
Overseas: £32 surface/£44 airmail
Payment in: Irish £/Dollars/Sterling
Payable to: Poetry Ireland Ltd
Inserts accepted: Yes
Terms: Exchange or £100 per 1000
Circulation approx: 1100
Payment terms to contributors: 1year sub or £10
Accept/rejection approx times: 4 months

P

POETRY LIFE

Poetry Life was launched on the 15th April 1994 and is now fairly established as one of the UK's leading poetry magazines. The founding principle behind the magazine is to explore the booming and rich poetry scene in the UK and worldwide. To publish real interviews with poets both famous and great, produce quality articles on poetry publishers, getting work published, festivals, performance poetry, style, reviews and the politics of poetry. Poetry Life has included interviews with Carol Ann Duffy, Joolz, Michael Donaghy, Les Murray, John Cooper Clarke, Benjamin Zephaniah, James Fenton, William Sieghart, Michael Longley, Brian Patten and Kamau Brathwaite. We have published quality articles by Richard Tyrrell, Paul Hyland, Peter Finch and AA Gill, plus articles on poetry in Zimbabwe, performance poets in Liverpool, the RAB assessment services, Poems on the Underground - the poetry success story, Swansea - the UK Year of Literature, the European Association for the Promotion of Poetry, the Nuyoricans, the Sarajevo Poetry Festival, Poets of the Machine, Poetry on the Internet and 'Fifteen Years in Jail for a Poem' - the true story of the poet Ali Idrissi Kaitouni by Amnesty International. All this and the Poetry Life Open Poetry Competitions, now established as one of the premier national competitions, bringing talented poets to wider public attention.

Editor Name(s): Adrian Bishop
Address: 1 Blue Ball Corner, Water Lane, Winchester, Hampshire SW23 0ER
Email: adrian.abishop@virgin-net
Mag Frequency: 3 issues a year
Subscription: £9 pa
Single Issue: £3
Payable to: Poetry Life
Inserts accepted: Yes
Circulation approx: 800
Payment terms to contributors: We only pay for articles

POETRY LONDON NEWSLETTER

New poems, features and reviews from the brightest names, whether new or established, plus information and listings of poetry events, groups and resources.

Editor Name(s): Peter Daniels/Katherine Gallagher/Kevan Johnson/Pascale Petit/ Scott Verner
Address: PLN Poetry Editor, 26 Clacton Road, London E17 8AR
Subs to: PLN Subscriptions, 35 Benthal Road, London N16 7AR
Telephone: 0181 8066121 (Peter Daniels)
Fax: 0171 502 1407
Email: pdaniels@easynet.co.uk
Mag Frequency: 3 per year
Subscription: £9 one yr/£17 two yr
Single Issue: £3.50
Back Issue: £1
Overseas: £13(sur)/£16(air) - one yr; £24(sur)/£30(air) - two yr
Payment in: £sterling - if not add £8 equiv for costs
Payable to: Poetry London Newsletter
Inserts accepted: Yes
Terms: £60 for 600
Advertising Rates: £120 full/£60 half/£30 qtr/page
Circulation approx: 800
Payment terms to contributors: Poetry £20 min p poem/Reviews £30 p 1000 wds
Accept/rejection approx times: 1 week-2 months

P
POETRY MANCHESTER

Bi-annual poetry magazine/review: as many international poets and subscribers as national (India, Australia, USA., Germany, Denmark, Rep. of Ireland); translations of European writers.

Address: 13 Napier Street, Swinton, Manchester M27 0JQ
Mag Frequency: Biannual
Subscription: £3.50 pa
Single Issue: £2
Overseas: As UK
Payment in: By cheque to the editorial address
Payable to: Sean Boustead
Inserts accepted: No
Circulation approx: 940 (growing)
Payment terms to contributors: 2 copies of the relevant issue
Accept/rejection approx times: Up to 1 month

POETRY MONTHLY

Poetry Monthly is a friendly, informal and democratic magazine run for those with a lively and open minded interest in poetry and to publish diverse poems, both free verse and formed, by new and experienced poets alike with open pages for articles, general comment, friendly helpful suggestions or even praise on the poems by poets for poets. It is an independent publication run by the editor for the love of it, relying purely on the generosity of subscribers and the small profit from Poetry Monthly Press for its existence. Non-subscribers' submissions require a stamped and self addressed envelope or 2 Internation Reply Coupons for a reply. Replies to subscribers' submissions will be returned with their postal copy of Poetry Monthly. Comments and queries by email welcome. Email poetry submissions by subscribers only. Deadline for comments on the previous issue: 8th of the month. Publication date: 20th of the month.

Editor Name(s): Martin Holroyd
Address: 39 Cavendish Road, Long Eaton, Nottingham NG10 4HY
Telephone: 0115 9461267
Email: martinholroyd@compuserve. com
Internet web page: http://ourworld.compuserve.com/homepages/martinholroyd
Mag Frequency: Monthly
Subscription: £12 per year or £8 per six months UK/EU
Single Issue: £1.50
Overseas: £30 sterling ($40 US)
Payable to: Poetry Monthly
Inserts accepted: No
Payment terms to contributors: 1 copy of Poetry Monthly in which an author's work appears

POETRY NOTTINGHAM INTERNATIONAL

44-plus pages - poems, letters, short reviews, short (500 word) articles on issues in poetry, features. Any style of poetry that is well-written and - if in a set form - technically correct. Unpublished poetry only. I particularly look for originality of subject matter, poems that appeal to the emotions but are not sentimental, and upbeat poems/subtle humour to contrast with the serious poems.

Editor Name(s): Cathy Grinrod
Address: 71 Saxton Avenue, Heanor Derbyshire DE75 7PZ
Mag Frequency: Quarterly
Subscription: £9 per annum
Single Issue: £2.25
Back Issue: £1.25 inc p&p
Overseas: £15 sterling
Payable to: Poetry Nottingham International
Inserts accepted: Yes
Terms: Will exchange with other magazine
Circulation approx: 275
Payment terms to contributors: Complimentary copy
Accept/rejection approx times: 2 months max - often sooner

POETRY NOW MAGAZINE

Poetry Now Magazine tries to publish a selection of poetry covering the broadest range of poetry the magazine's readers are writing. We aim to give enjoyment to, and answer the needs of, our readers. Every letter, poem and article that comes into the office makes a difference to the shape and direction of the magazine. This is the reason why it continues to change and grow. We hope that you will become a part of the driving force. Sections include: * Poems on a theme * Competition news, views & events * Poetry workshop * Articles of interest to poets * Poet profiles.

Editor Name(s): Andrew Head
Address: 1-2 Wainman Road, Woodston, Peterborough PE2 7BU
Telephone: 01733 230746
Fax: 01733 230751
Email: pete@forwardpress.co.uk
Website: www.forwardpress.co.uk
Mag Frequency: Quarterly
Subscription: UK £14
Single Issue: £3.50
Overseas: £18
Payment in: PO/Cheque/Credit card
Payable to: Forward Press
Inserts accepted: Yes
Terms: Reciprocal
Circulation approx: 2000
Payment terms to contributors: Poems £5 - £10. Other payments negotiated
Accept/rejection approx times: 12-16 weeks

POETRY REVIEW

Poetry Review publishes new poems, reviews and features on contemporary poetry. Each issue has a theme illuminating tendencies and controversies. Work by the leading poets of today is published alongside the most promising new poets.

Address: The Poetry Society, 22 Betterton Street, London WC2H 9BU
Mag Frequency: Quarterly
Subscription: £23
Single Issue: £5.95
Back Issue: Varies
Overseas: £31/US$56
Payment in: Sterling $ US Dollar only/Eurocheque/Visa/Mastercard
Payable to: The Poetry Society
Inserts accepted: Yes
Terms: £100 per 1000
Circulation approx: 5000

POETRY SCOTLAND

Poetry Scotland is a broadsheet quarterly dedicated entirely to new poetry. Subtitled Forty Poems By Twenty Poets, it includes Scottish and international writing in English, Scots and Gaelic. Available in over 100 outlets Scotland-wide, or post free from the publishers. Its quick response time makes it a favourite with the poets, and its generous educational discount and open format make it ideal for schools. Good trade terms to booksellers etc.

Editor Name(s): Sally Evans
Address: Diehard Publishers, 3 Spittal Street, Edinburgh EH3 9DY
Mag Frequency: Quarterly
Subscription: £5 for 5 issues
Single Issue: £1 post free
Overseas: £5 for 5 post free worldwide
Payment in: Sterling/sterling cheques
Payable to: Diehard Publishers
Inserts accepted: No
Advertising Rates: None
Circulation approx: 748 (at issue 5)
Payment terms to contributors: 8 copies of publication
Accept/rejection approx times: 1 week

P
POETRY WALES

Poetry Wales aims to bring its readers the best of poetry from Wales and the world, with an emphasis on new talent. Founded in 1965 to provide a forum for Welsh poets writing in English, it has an international outlook, featuring poets from the US, Australia and elsewhere alongside established and new poets from Wales. The current issue (Oct '98) celebrates writers as diverse as William Wantling (Korean War veteran, poet and drug addict), Joseph Brodsky, Lynette Roberts (Wales-based Argentinian-born poet), Gillian Clarke, and young talents Frances Williams and Owen Sheers. Contributors should send up to six poems directly to the editor, enclosing an SAE for reply. Long and prose poems welcome.

Editor Name(s): Robert Minhinnick
Address: Robert Minhinnick, 11 Park Avenue, Porthcawl CF36 3EP
Reviews to: Amy Wack, 20 Denton Road, Canton, Cardiff, CF5 1TE
Telephone: 01656 767834
Mag Frequency: Quarterly
Subscription: £12 a year/£22 two years
Single Issue: £3.00
Overseas: £18 pa
Payment in: Sterling - IMO or credit card (Visa, Mastercard)
Payable to: Poetry Wales Press
Inserts accepted: Yes
Terms: £50 plus VAT for 800
Advertising Rates: £60 half pg(160x100mm), £30 quarter pg (70x100mm)
Circulation approx: 850
Payment terms to contributors: By arrangement
Accept/rejection approx times: 1 month

PQR (Poetry Quarterly Review)

PQR was launched in Autumn 1995. It is a broadsheet (A4) magazine providing in-depth reviews of both mainstream and small press poetry publishing. Features include:* Reviews of poetry books and collections* Work from a Featured Poet in each issue* Articles and essays on related topics* Listings: analysis of current poetry magazines* Editorial comment on the poetry scene* New Voices: promising list collections* Front Page: major new books

Address: Coleridge Cottage, Nether Stowey, Somerset TA5 1NQ
Mag Frequency: 4 times a year
Subscription: £6
Single Issue: £1.75
Back Issue: £1.50
Overseas: Europe £8, USA £10 (airmail)
Payment in: Sterling only
Payable to: Odyssey Poets
Inserts accepted: Yes
Terms: Exchange basis
Advertising Rates: Reasonable - £3-£40
Circulation approx: 500
Payment terms to contributors: Free copy to reviewers/agreed fee to Feature Poet
Accept/rejection approx times: 4 weeks

PRACTICE MAKES PERVERT

An A4, 24-page 'sketchpad' zine photocopied onto (100% recycled) beautiful coloured sugar paper. Includes drawings, doodles, poems, found images, sketchpad pages, collage, cartoons (by Dr Steg), etc. Exists in a constant state of flux, with new pages replacing old ones as better material is discovered/sent in.

Address: I Think X Productions, c/o 43 Ewart Street, Brighton, East Sussex BN2 2UP
Mag Frequency: N/A
Subscription: Send SAE for details
Single Issue: £2 (incl postage)
Back Issue: £1 (for Nearly Got Sprung)
Overseas: £2.50 Eur/£3RoW
Payment in: Sterling - cash/cheque/PO/UK stamps
Payable to: V I Pollard
Inserts accepted: Yes
Payment terms to contributors: Free copy of issue work in
Accept/rejection approx times: 1 week (send SAE)

PREMONITIONS

The magazine anthology of science fictional horror stories, poetry and art; Premonitions publishes original stories, genre poetry, and artwork - in the form of unique 'graphic poems'. Premonitions covers an exceptionally broad range of themes: from futuristic urban shockers and mature 'space adventure', to 'mood' fiction, dark satire, psychological terrors and surrealistic tales. Premonitions is quality in quantity with a dozen short stories in each issue!

Address: Tony Lee, Pigasus Press, 13 Hazely Combe, Arreton. Isle of Wight, PO30 3AJ
Mag Frequency: Annual
Subscription: £10 (UK only) for 4 issues
Single Issue: £2.50 (UK only)
Overseas: Send SAE/IRC for details
Payment in: Pay by IMO in sterling
Payable to: Tony Lee
Inserts accepted: No
Terms: N/A
Circulation approx: Unknown
Payment terms to contributors: None
Accept/rejection approx times: Approx. one month

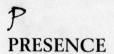

PRESENCE

Presence is a haiku magazine publishing haiku, senryu, tanka, renga and related forms in English. Other short poetry is accepted, if compatible. We also use artwork for black/white copying. Books for review and announcements of publications or events of haiku interest are welcome. We publish articles on all aspects of haiku, whether relating to the Japanese tradition or contemporary practice in English.

Editor Name(s): Martin Lucas
Address: 12 Grovehall Avenue, Leeds LS11 7EX
Mag Frequency: 2 issues per year
Subscription: £5/2 issues
Single Issue: £2.50
Overseas: £5 or $10 (US) per 2 issues
Payment in: Cash or cheque/overseas cash only
Payable to: Haiku Presence
Inserts accepted: Yes
Circulation approx: 130+
Payment terms to contributors: Free issue of magazine
Accept/rejection approx times: Within 1 month

PROP

Prop is a magazine of new poetry and short fiction, plus related essays, interviews and book reviews; we also review other small press magazines of a poetry or short fiction bias. As well as purely 'literary' essays, we also like essays which fuse literature with other genres - for example we recently published essays on the short story's relationship with film. We are open to all kinds of poetry and short fiction, from the 'traditional' to the 'experimental'. Writers we have published include Charles Simic, Sophie Hannah, David Constantine, Nina Cassian, Roy Fisher, Douglas Oliver, Elizabeth Bartlett, Tom Paulin.

Editor Name(s): Steven Blyth/Chris Hart
Address: 31 Central Avenue, Farnworth, Bolton BL4 0AU
Mag Frequency: 3 times a year
Subscription: £10 for 4 issues
Single Issue: £3
Overseas: $15
Payment in: Cheque/IMO
Payable to: Prop
Inserts accepted: Yes
Terms: Reciprocal arrangements
Advertising Rates: By arrangement
Circulation approx: 250
Payment terms to contributors: Free copy of magazine
Accept/rejection approx times: 1 month

P

PSYCHOPOETICA

We prefer short, experimental, unrhymed poetry - preferably under 30 lines. But since we also like to compile a large varied selection of poetry (traditional, rhymed and unrhymed, light verse, haiku, visual poems, etc), we will read and consider any style and format. We're not too keen on self-indulgent, therapeutic poetry (unless it's very good and original), nor sweetly inspirational 'fluffy' stuff. We like poetry that has some (or all) of the following: humour, vivid imagery, powerful feelings, guts and substance, originality, creative style, boundary-shifting, punch or twist, word-play, craftsmanship . . . etc . . . Relevant artwork and graphics are frequently used; contributors are invited to experiment with various fonts and presentational effects. All submissions should be legible, typed or printed and ideally in clean, camera ready format (preferably titled in capitals with author's name at the bottom plus hometown in brackets beneath). If preferred, authors may send camera ready work after acceptance. Good, clean photocopies are OK. All submissions should include self-addressed stamped envelope or IRCs for foreign mail.

Address: Geoff Lowe, Department of Psychology, University of Hull, Hull HU6 7RX or Trevor Millum, Fern House, High Street, Barrow on Humber DN19 7AA
Subs to: Subs to Geoff Lowe
Mag Frequency: 2 big issues per year and occasional 'theme' anthologies
Subscription: £12 (inc p&p) for 4 issues
Single Issue: £3 plus p&p
Back Issue: £2.50
Overseas: $24 for 4 issues
Payment in: Dollar notes or sterling
Payable to: G Lowe
Inserts accepted: Yes
Terms: £60 per 300 (or exchange deal)
Circulation approx: 300+
Payment terms to contributors: Under negotiation/contributor's copy
Accept/rejection approx times: Normally within 1 month

PSYCHOTROPE

Psychotrope is an illustrated magazine of psychological horror, mad love and surreal short stories from new and established small press writers. Psychotrope attempts to explore the dark and disturbing underworlds of madness, obsession, secrecy and the subconscious with a unique mix of traditional and experimental prose. I am always on the lookout for good, inventive new stories for publication, but tend to avoid tales of gothic horror, the supernatural, all-out science fiction or 'dwarf and wizard' fantasy. The emphasis is on harsh, modern settings although occasionally I don't mind bending the rules for something surprising and fresh, assuming it fits somewhere under the banner of 'psychological horror, mad love and surrealism'. Submissions of manuscripts of between 500 and 5000 words should always be accompanied by an SAE - sorry but no SAE no reply. Slightly shorter or longer pieces will always be considered if exceptional. All submissions will be replied to within 2 months and rejections are accompanied by helpful and constructive criticism. Alas, Psychotrope is not able to pay contributors in money, although they will receive a complimentary copy of the magazine. A free small ad section is available for books and magazines dealing with horror/sci fi/fantasy/slipstream, and ads of up to 150 words should be sent to the editorial address.

Address: Flat 6, 10 Ombersley Road, Worcester WR3 7ET
Mag Frequency: Semi-annually (approx)
Subscription: £7.50 for 4 ($20)
Single Issue: £2.10 ($5.50)
Back Issue: £1.50 ($4.25)
Overseas: See above
Payable to: Psychotrope
Inserts accepted: Yes
Terms: £60 per 300 (or exchange deal)
Circulation approx: 300+
Payment terms to contributors: Contributor's copy of magazine only
Accept/rejection approx times: 1-2 months

PULSAR

Pulsar - and Ligden Poetry Society (LPS) - were formed by Ligden Publishers in December 1994 with the aim of encouraging the writing of poetry for pleasure and possible publication in Pulsar (published quarterly). We seek interesting and stimulating work - thoughts, comments and observations; genial or sharp. LPS is non-profitmaking; funds received help cover the cost of printing, distribution etc. LPS/Pulsar are run by poetry enthusiasts for poetry enthusiasts - are not a business or corporate concern. Pulsar is supported by the Burmah Castrol Arts Awards in partnership with Swindon Arts Foundation. Published poets include Gerald England, Lewis Hosegood, Joy Martin, Hardiman Scott . . . For further information send A5 addressed return envelope containing 31p postage to the Editor.

Address: David Pike, 34 Lineacre, Grange Park, Swindon, Wiltshire SN5 6DA
Email: david.pike@virgin.net
Mag Frequency: Quarterly
Subscription: £10
Single Issue: £2.50
Overseas: Europe £10 equivalent/USA $30
Payment in: By cheque - £ sterling preferred
Payable to: Ligden Poetry Society
Inserts accepted: Yes
Terms: 200/£15
Circulation approx: 250
Payment terms to contributors: Free copy of magazine
Accept/rejection approx times: Up to 4 weeks

PURPLE PATCH

Established in 1976, Purple Patch has a home-produced feel, yet maintains a high standard of poetry. Its gossip column laughs at and along with current news and trends in the poetry world (and cries a little sometimes). Short prose fiction and essays are welcome but their acceptance is limited by space. Purple Patch is holding a National Small Press Poets' Convention in the West Midlands in June 1999. Details available now.

Editor Name(s): Geoff Stevens
Address: 25 Griffiths Road, West Bromwich B71 2EH
Telephone: 0121 588 6642
Mag Frequency: 3 a year
Subscription: £3.50
Single Issue: £1.25
Overseas: £6 sterling cheques or $15 cash
Payable to: Purple Patch
Inserts accepted: Yes
Terms: By negotiation
Advertising Rates: By negotiation
Circulation approx: 200
Payment terms to contributors: UK contributors - 1 copy
Accept/rejection approx times: 1 month

P
PUSSY POETRY

Pussy Poetry is a small press publication originally set up to increase confidence and awareness of women's poetry. It is about attitude, anger, emotion and not hiding our feelings away. Contributors have the option of doing their own artwork/page illustration to accompany their poems. There is a maximum of 25 lines due to the small format of the publication. Poems can be on any subject, but the contributors must be women.

Editor Name(s): Erica
Address: c/o 6 Rookery Close, Keddington Park, Louth, Lincolnshire LN11 0GF
Mag Frequency: Yearly
Single Issue: 50p & A6 SAE
Overseas: $1 + 2IRCs
Payment in: Cash (sterling or US dollars)/PO/cheque/UK postage stamps
Payable to: Erica
Circulation approx: 300
Payment terms to contributors: None
Accept/rejection approx times: 1-2 months

QUANTUM LEAP

Poetry of all types, including rhyme. Plus, letters page, competitions, pen friends, (SAE with all submissions please). We want Quantum Leap to be a 'user friendly' magazine which encourages its contributors and readers, and gives opportunities for publication to both established poets and those yet to find their way into print (we remember what that feels like!). Will have a 'Five by . . .' feature in each issue showcasing the work of a particular poet. (Write with stamped addressed envelope, for guidelines.)

Address: Alan Carter, Editor, 81 Breval Crescent, Hardgate, Clydebank, G81 6LS
Mag Frequency: Quarterly
Subscription: £12 (UK&EU); £14 (rest of Europe); £16/$32 (RoW)
Single Issue: £3.50 (UK&EU); £4 (rest of Europe); £4.50/$9 (RoW)
Back Issue: £2.50/$5 US
Overseas: See above
Payment in: PO/cheque
Payable to: A Carter
Inserts accepted: Yes
Terms: Ask!
Circulation approx: 100 but growing!
Payment terms to contributors: £2 per poem
Accept/rejection approx times: 2-4 weeks (Publication will usually be in the next issue, but may be held over occasionally)

Q

QUEER WORDS

Queer Words is a quarterly magazine publishing both new and established lesbian and gay writers. Most writers come to us through our annual short story competition with a first prize of £1000. Write for details.

Address: P.O. Box 23, Aberstwyth, Wales SY23 1AA
Fax: 01970 617942
Email: queer@consti.demon.co.uk
Mag Frequency: Quarterly
Subscription: £17.95 per 4 issues
Single Issue: £5.95
Back Issue: £2.50
Overseas: As UK + £5 Europe £10 RoW
Payment in: Cheque/ Visa/Mastercard
Payable to: Queer Words
Inserts accepted: Yes
Terms: £50
Circulation approx: 1000+
Payment terms to contributors: Negotiable but usually complimentary copies
Accept/rejection approx times: 3-6 months

QWF

QWF aims to provide a platform for new women writers and to present a showcase of first class fiction for the discerning reader. A5 magazine around 80-90 pages with a glossy cover publishes about 12 short stories per issue plus articles and a lively readers' letter page and editorial. Looking for original short stories which are vibrant, whacky, off-beat or address women's issues. A thought-provoking read is essential. Accepts stories of less than 4000 words with covering letter. Stories must be previously unpublished. Runs an annual short story competition, open to all (inc male writers). Cash prizes (£300 for winner). Winners published in a separate anthology. Closes July 16 1999.

Address: 71 Bucknill Crescent, Hillmorton, Rugby CV21 4HE
Mag Frequency: Bi-monthly
Subscription: £22.50 for 6 issues
Single Issue: £3.95
Back Issue: £2
Overseas: £26 Europe/£32 RoW - subs
£4.50 Europe/£5 RoW - single iss
£2.75 Europe/£3 RoW - back iss
Payment in: Cheque only
Payable to: J M Good
Inserts accepted: Yes
Terms: Prefer a swap, or £30
Circulation approx: 300 subscribers and rising (1800 copies sold per year)
Payment terms to contributors: £10 short story/£5 article/or 6-month free sub.
Accept/rejection approx times: 1 month - potential contributors must send 2x1st class stamps for guidelines first

R
RAINBOW BRIDGE

Rainbow Bridge (founded Summer 1996) is a compilation of information received by editor, and singer songwriter, Tricia Frances after a Near Death Experience in 1991. This information led to the founding of the Sayana Wolf Trust, an organisation working with familes and children. The magazine features articles on world events, stories, poems, self awareness, healing, Native American interests, Wolf Wisdom, and other related subjects. Each edition features a guest poem or story. A donation from the magazine goes towards the work of the Sayana Wolf Trust.

Address: P.O. Box 136, Norwich, Norfolk NR3 3NJ
Fax: 01603 440940
Email: rainbowbr1@aol.com
Mag Frequency: Quarterly
Subscription: £6 pa
Single Issue: £2
Back Issue: £1.50
Overseas: £10
Payment in: Cheque or PO
Payable to: Rainbow Bridge
Inserts accepted: Yes
Terms: A5 sheet £20
Circulation approx: 1500+
Payment terms to contributors: Free magazine & ad space
Accept/rejection approx times: Immediate

RAVEN NEWS

A4 Magazine printed in A5 format. Pagan/wiccan orientated with news of events, dates for your diary, advice, humorous letters, reviews, poems. We always include information on spell-working or magical practice. The tone is generally light, but we will tackle serious subjects such as the harrassment of witches by the press. Raven is also a mail order company, supplying weird and wonderful magical stuff, and folks who order from us will get a year's subscription to the magazine free! Send 2 first class stamps for catalogue.

Address: Raven, 17 Melton Fields, Brickyard Lane, North Ferriby, East Yorks HU14 3HE
Fax: 01482 631 496
Mag Frequency: 5 times a year
Subscription: £2
Single Issue: 50p
Overseas: £5
Payment in: Sterling only
Payable to: Raven
Inserts accepted: Yes
Terms: £5
Circulation approx: 1200
Payment terms to contributors: Our love and kisses

ℛ
RAW EDGE MAGAZINE

Raw Edge Magazine seeks to publish the best new writing from the West Midlands, plus news and comment of use to readers and writers in the area. Work from both established and new writers is considered on its own merits. Contributions are welcomed from all sections of the community, in any style of writing and on any subject. If you feel that you are not being represented by the writing, or cannot identify with it, send your own writing, or encourage those whose writing you do identify with to submit their work. Manuscripts received will normally be considered for the issue that is currently under preparation. Only in exceptional circumstances will any be carried over to future issues. Copies of the magazine will be reserved for all persons published in that issue. The Editor's decision is final. Raw Edge Magazine is published by Birmingham Readers and Writers' Festival Ltd and is funded by West Midland Arts.

Editor Name(s): Dave Reeves
Address: PO Box 48567, Birmingham B3 3HD
Mag Frequency: Twice a year
Subscription: £2 pa
Single Issue: Free
Back Issue: £1
Overseas: No overseas subs
Payable to: Birmingham Readers and Writers' Festival
Inserts accepted: No
Circulation approx: 16500
Payment terms to contributors: Only pay commissioned articles - negotiable
Accept/rejection approx times: Up to 6 months

RAW NERVE

Raw Nerve, published by Razor Blade Press, is an A4 magazine with a full colour front and back cover, on average 36 pages. We publish horror/dark fantasy short stories between 50 and 5000 words. The stories we like are nasty, well written, with a clear beginning, middle and end. (But not necessarily in that order!) We also publish interviews with established writers (Clive Barker, Ian Banks in part issues) and book reviews. Each issue contains a graphic story, and we are always on the lookout for comic strip writers/artists as well as illustrators. We have started to publish books, after the success of our anthology Razor Blades last year. In October we are publishing Faith In The Flesh by Tim Lebbow, and The Dreaming Pool by Gary Greenwood.

Address: Darren Floyd, 186 Railway Street, Splott, Cardiff CF2 2NH
Reviews to: Linsey Southard, 115 Pearl Street, Cardiff
Email: darren.floyd@virgin.net
Website: htpp://freespace.virgin.net/darren.floyd/musite.htm
Mag Frequency: Quarterly
Subscription: £15 (seven issues free P&P)
Single Issue: £2.50
Overseas: On request
Payment in: Cheque/PO
Payable to: Razor Blade Press
Inserts accepted: Yes
Terms: £10 per 1000
Circulation approx: 700 + growing!
Payment terms to contributors: Copy of relevant issue
Accept/rejection approx times: 1½ months

R
REACH POETRY MAGAZINE

A high quality magazine at 40 pages, A5 format, card cover. Lively letters page and a £50 prize each month for 'Readers' Vote' going to the most popular poet in the previous issue. Essential to send SAE for guidelines before submitting work.

Editor Name(s): Shelagh Nugent
Address: Linden Cottage, 45 Burton Road, Little Neston, S. Wirral L64 4AE
Telephone: 0151 353 0967
Fax: 0151 353 0967
Email: helicon@globalnet.co.uk
Mag Frequency: Monthly
Subscription: £10 for 6 issues
Single Issue: £2
Back Issue: £1
Overseas: Send IRC for price list
Payment in: Sterling cheques/IRCs
Payable to: Cherrybite Publications
Inserts accepted: Yes
Terms: Reciprocal
Advertising Rates: Reciprocal
Circulation approx: 200
Payment terms to contributors: No payment
Accept/rejection approx times: 2 weeks

THE REATER

Strictly no flowers just blunt chiselled poetry, contains poems by Charles Bukowski, Fred Voss, Gerry Locklin, Shane Rhodes, Joan Jobe Smith also short stories, photographs and interviews.

Address: 18 Church Street, North Cave, Brough, East Yorkshire HU15 2LW
Mag Frequency: Once yearly
Subscription: £9 pa
Single Issue: £8+£1.50p&p
Overseas: £13 pa
Payment in: Cheque/PO
Payable to: Wrecking Ball Press
Circulation approx: 850-1000
Accept/rejection approx times: 1-3 months

R
RED HERRING

Red Herring is a fold poetry sheet which welcomes new poetry of all kinds. It is distributed free through Northumberland Libraries thereby getting into the hands of a wide readership, many of whom would not otherwise pick up new poetry.

Editor Name(s): Nicholas Baumfield/Jean Baker
Address: Red Herring, MidNAG, East View, Stakeford, Choppington, Northumberland NE62 5TR
Telephone: 01670 510512
Fax: 0160 520457
Mag Frequency: 2-3 times a year
Subscription: £1 per issue
Single Issue: £1
Overseas: £1
Payment in: IMO/PO/sterling cheque
Payable to: Mid Northumberland Arts Group
Inserts accepted: No
Circulation approx: 3000
Payment terms to contributors: 6 copies
Accept/rejection approx times: 6 months

REFLECTIONS

Mainly poetry, some short pieces of prose, regular black & white photography and art work. Reflections provides an outlet for those interested in using the creative arts to share positive ideas and emotions. Many contributors choose to do this by offering appreciations of beauty, work which has a healing influence, or communicates aspects of their spiritual life, in the broadest sense of this term. Much of the poetry in Reflections adopts a traditional stance towards rhyme, rhythm and melody, although the editorial team welcomes both formal verse and free verse. Potential contributors should keep in mind that whatever its merits, work which focuses on the mundane, or has an overall negative tone is likely to fall outside of Reflections' remit. Reflections is not aligned to any political, social or religious movements. Work can only be returned if accompanied by suitable SAE; work may be offered anonymously.

Address: PO Box 178, Sunderland, SR1 1DU
Mag Frequency: Quarterly
Subscription: £5 annually (inc p&p)
Single Issue: 95p plus 30p p&p
Back Issue: 50p plus 30p (subject to availability)
Overseas: Europe £6.20 (inc p&p)/other on application
Payment in: Sterling only
Payable to: Reflections
Inserts accepted: No
Circulation approx: 200
Payment terms to contributors: Free copy
Accept/rejection approx times: Up to 2 months

RELAPSE

Currently on its kick-ass 6th issue, this little magazine is everything you could ever need - music, poetry, humour, and a twist of madness. Essential reading . . .

Editor Name(s): Krystian Taylor 01275 856647
Address: 102 Old Church Road, Nailsea, Bristol BS48 4ND
Mag Frequency: Quarterly
Subscription: £4 (includes postage)
Single Issue: £1
Back Issue: £1.50
Overseas: £7
Payment in: Cheque/PO/Cash
Payable to: Krystian Taylor
Inserts accepted: Yes
Terms: £25 for 1000/£15 for 500
Advertising Rates: £20 for full page A5
Circulation approx: 1000
Payment terms to contributors: Free copy

RETFORD WRITERS

Retford Writers is a quarterly publication consisting of work by members and postal subscribers. Short pieces of poetry, short stories or factual accounts.

Address: 3 Welham Road, Retford, Notts DN22 6TN
Mag Frequency: 4 per annum
Subscription: £5
Single Issue: £1.25
Back Issue: £1
Payable to: Retford Writers
Inserts accepted: No
Circulation approx: 25
Payment terms to contributors: Nil

R
RETORT

Retort publishes new work by established and emerging poets. There is no house style as to style, form or subject matter. The majority of the pages are filled with poems, but there are also articles, reviews and readers' letters. Articles can be on any subject but there are three series under way: *Key Poets - An in-depth appreciation of the so-called 'key poets' prescribed for study at key stages 3 and 4; *Neglected Poets - A brief examination of a poet who is either unjustly neglected or whose critical standing has fallen; *Critiques - An analysis/appreciation of a particular poem. Retort also runs a bi-annual poetry competition with cash prizes. The three prize-winning and five commended poems are published in the magazine format: A5, perfect bound. Copyright is retained by contributors.

Address: Editor, 7 Dolonside Court, Nutfield Road, Merstham, Surrey RH1 3EL
Subs to: Competition secretary, 9A Craddocks Parade, Ashtead, Surrey KT21 1QL
Mag Frequency: Quarterly
Subscription: £19 (individuals)/£15 (entrants in competitions)
Single Issue: £4.95
Overseas: Available on request
Payment in: Sterling cheques/drafts drawn on a UK bank
Payable to: Market Cross Publishing
Inserts accepted: Yes
Terms: Negotiable
Circulation approx: 400
Payment terms to contributors: Compimentary copies
Accept/rejection approx times: 3 months

THE RIALTO

The Rialto publishes work by new poets established poets and famous poets. You are very welcome to send your poems (with SAE). Recent issues have carried articles by poets but The Rialto is first and foremost a poem-centred magazine.

Editor Name(s): Michael Mackmin
Address: PO Box 309, Aylsham, Norwich, Norfolk NR11 6LN
Mag Frequency: 3 issues pa
Subscription: £10 pa (£8 if on low income)
Single Issue: £3.90
Back Issue: Limited number available: please inquire
Overseas: Europe £12; USA £16; Australia/Japan £17
Payment in: Sterling only
Payable to: The Rialto
Inserts accepted: No
Advertising Rates: No ads carried
Circulation approx: 1500 print run
Payment terms to contributors: £20 per poem on publication
Accept/rejection approx times: 10 weeks

_R_
A RIOT OF EMOTIONS

*Artwork: B&W illustrations only. *Size: Maximum finished area should not exceed 14 x 20 cm/5.5 x 8 inches. For aesthetic reasons all full page pieces must be portrait - no landscape. Smaller pieces of any size are acceptable. All artwork should be camera ready (as you would wish to see it printed) including any photographic work which must be screened or photocopied. Submissions of words and art combined, eg comic strips, illustrated poems/text are also acceptable.*Written work: All text must be typed or neatly hand-written, and punctuated as you would wish to see it appear in print. All hand-written submissions will be typed by the editor unless it alters the presentation of the work. I am mainly interested in publishing poetry and short pieces of prose/fiction. I will consider short stories also, maximum 2000 words. *Subject matter: There are no real restrictions (*), but I favour the bizarre/weird/ esoteric/imaginative and experimental. Selection of work is made purely on the basis of what I personally like. I do not judge whether contributions are 'good' or 'bad' according to any literary criteria or artistic rules. I am not interested in publishing anything racist, sexist, homophobic or otherwise of discriminatory nature; apart from these few restrictions, an editorial policy of no censorship means that I do sometimes publish work of a shocking or confrontational nature, and pieces which contain strong language or 'swearing' provided it is for reasons of self expression and not merely gratuitous offence. Anyone easily offended should consider this fair warning. Opinions expressed by the contributors are not necessarily shared by the editor. *Reviews: Reviews of small press publications - zines, books, pamphlets, mail art projects, etc - are included in every issue.

Address: PO Box WK31, Leeds, West Yorkshire LS11 9XN
Mag Frequency: Once yearly
Subscription: No subs yet
Single Issue: £1.20 post paid
Back Issue: 90 pence post paid
Overseas: $2 per issue Europe/$3 RoW
Payment in: Overseas - cash only US dollars
Payable to: Andrew Cocker
Inserts accepted: No
Circulation approx: 500
Payment terms to contributors: 1 free copy to all contributors
Accept/rejection approx times: Usually 2 weeks - 1 month

RUBBERNECK

Rubberneck was founded in 1985 by its editor/publisher Chris Blackford. The magazine's principal interest is international experimental musics; in particular, improvised music, free jazz, and avant-garde rock. Recent issues have included the likes of Simon H Fell, Hugh Davies, Biota, Michel Doneda, Max Eastley, Hans Reichel, Lol Coxhill and Pierre Favre. Contents consist of interviews, essays (usually written by leading musicians involved in experimental musics) and relevant CD and book reviews. Occasionally, an issue devoted to previously unpublished experimental fiction (up to 1500 words per item) is published. Prospective contributors to Rubberneck are advised to check out a copy of the magazine before submitting their work, accompanied by a SAE or IRC. There is no subscription to Rubberneck. The most recent issue of the magazine can be obtained by sending a large 40p SAE (UK), or a large self-addressed envelope with 2 IRCs (EC countries) or 3 IRCs (other countries).

Editor Name(s): Chris Blackford
Address: Rubberneck, 21 Denham Drive, Basingstoke, Hampshire RG22 6LT
Mag Frequency: 2 per year (occasionally 3)
Subscription: N/A
Single Issue: See details in description
Back Issue: £1.75 (UK) £2.50 (Overseas)
Payment in: Sterling only
Payable to: Rubberneck
Inserts accepted: Yes
Terms: £35 per 1000
Circulation approx: 1500
Payment terms to contributors: Free copy of magazine
Accept/rejection approx times: 2 weeks

ℛ
RUSTIC RUB

Poetry and art magazine - includes interviews. Emphasis on international flavour/networking sometimes includes reports on what's going on. No reviews. Always good value for money. Open to long poems and prose poems.

Address: Jay Woodman, 33 Meadow Walk, Fleet, Hampshire GU13 8BA
Mag Frequency: Biannual
Subscription: £7.50
Single Issue: £4
Overseas: £9 (Single £5)
Payment in: Cheques in sterling only
Payable to: J Woodman
Inserts accepted: Yes
Terms: By special arrangement only
Circulation approx: 300-400
Payment terms to contributors: Complimentary copy
Accept/rejection approx times: Usually straight away - longer if undecided

SACCADE

Saccade publishes quality horror, science fiction and fantasy fiction, but also considers other related genres such as crime etc. Although primarily a fiction magazine we also publish interviews, reviews and articles on subjects that will be of interest to the readers. Such subjects as psychology and folklore have previously appeared. We also feature illustrations and artist profiles.

Address: 93 Green Lane, Dronfield, Sheffield S18 6FG
Mag Frequency: Three times a year
Subscription: £6 for 4 issues.
Single Issue: £1.75
Overseas: £8
Payment in: Cash/Cheque/PO/IMO
Payable to: R Gill
Inserts accepted: Yes
Terms: No charge
Circulation approx: 100 - 150
Payment terms to contributors: Free copy of magazine in which they appear.
Accept/rejection approx times: Fortnight

S

SALOPOET

Salopoet, founded in 1976, publishes poetry of members only.* Current membership is around 150. The magazine is published quarterly, the poems published being chosen by a panel of six committee members from poetry submitted by members. The Society runs two competitions per year - an open competition and one for members only.* The winning poems of the open competition are published each year in our Christmas Edition. Poetry reading evenings are held monthly at various members' homes.

Address: Mrs I P Hoult, Magazine Secretary, 5 Squires Close, Madeley, Shropshire TF7 5RU
Reviews to: Mr. Allister Fraser MBE, President, 5 Cordingley Way, Donnington, Shropshire, TF2 7LW
Mag Frequency: Quarterly
Subscription: £10
Single Issue: £2.50
Back Issue: £1.50
Overseas: £10 plus additional postage (eg $20 USA)
Payment in: Annual in advance - cheque/PO/IMO
Payable to: Salopian Poetry Society
Inserts accepted: Yes
Terms: No charge currently
Circulation approx: 150
Payment terms to contributors: No payments made
Accept/rejection approx times: 2 months

SAMHAIN

Britain's longest-running horror film magazine includes features, interviews, reviews etc, relating to the world of horror films and fiction. We are always on the lookout for new contributors, especially reviewers and feature writers. In October we celebrated our twelth anniversary with issue 70.

Address: 77 Exeter Road, Topsham, Exeter, Devon EX3 OLX
Email: samhain@bta.com
Mag Frequency: Bi-monthly
Subscription: £9/$20 (5 issues)
Single Issue: £2.50 (cover price)
Back Issue: £2.50 each or full set (1-69) for £55
Overseas: £10 (Europe) $20 (US)
Payment in: US cash only - no US cheques
Payable to: Samhain
Inserts accepted: Yes
Circulation approx: Increasing
Payment terms to contributors: Free issues of the magazine

S

SCAR TISSUE

Scar Tissue publishes horror/dark-fantasy short fiction and poetry, sick-joke cartoons and weird illus (artwork must be ink/b&w only), plus reviews of genre-related books, zines, films etc. Say anything in 500 words or less. We want sharply written prose and criticism. Mss must be single-spaced/camera-ready for Scar Tissue's no-budget, cheap 'n' cheerful, cut 'n' paste format. Advert swaps or contributors' guidelines from small press editors/independent publishers welcome. If in doubt send it anyway! NB: SAE/IRC essential for reply.

Editor Name(s): Tony Lee
Address: Pigasus Press, 13 Hazely Combe, Arreton, Isle of Wight PO30 3AJ
Telephone: 01983 865668
Mag Frequency: Irregular
Single Issue: Free for SAE/IRC
Overseas: 1 IRC per issue
Inserts accepted: Yes
Terms: Flyer swaps by arrangement
Advertising Rates: Adverts swaps welcome
Circulation approx: 200-300
Payment terms to contributors: Copy only
Accept/rejection approx times: 4-8 weeks

SCARED TO DEATH

Since 1992 Scared To Death has been bringing you the very best modern horror fiction. We've published work by Ramsey Campbell, Peter James, Mark Morris, Steve Harris, Stephen Gallagher, Guy Smith, Shaun Hutson, plus many more top names and exciting newcomers. STD is illustrated by top genre artist Desmond Knight and also features articles, interviews, reports, news, letters and full colour photographs. You shouldn't miss this terror-packed journal, popular in the UK and USA, and described by Ramsey Campbell as 'scandalous and entertaining'! We accept powerful, memorable horror fiction of up to 4000 words, with cover letter, writer's biog and SAE. All letters/enquiries are very welcome. Don't miss out! Get Scared To Death.

Editor Name(s): Editor Joe Rattigan/Asst Editor Dave Toast
Address: STD Publishing, 1 Hill Farm Close, Oldham, Greater Manchester, OL8 2LL
Telephone: 0160 6241497
Mag Frequency: Quarterly (March/June/Sep/Dec)
Subscription: £9 (discounts for readers)
Single Issue: £2.50
Back Issue: Not available
Overseas: £12
Payment in: UK currency/cheque/PO
Payable to: Joe Rattigan
Inserts accepted: Yes
Terms: £5 (or free sample)
Advertising Rates: Full pg A5 £10/half pg £5
Circulation approx: 400
Payment terms to contributors: Complimentary copy
Accept/rejection approx times: 2-4 weeks

S

SCENES FROM THE INSIDE

A 150-page anthology of independent comic art from around the world, ranging from satire, art-brut, post modern noir, slice-of-life, all put together with a view to being a good-looking, design-led, fun read . . . phew! . . . It's easier to describe what we're not . . . we don't do superhero stories, we're not into that quaint English cod surrealism that permeates much of the British comic scene, and we're not like Viz - to be in Scenes, a strip must be driven by either a strong intelligent narrative or a dynamic sense of design or a playfully forward thinking sense of humour (think Day-To-Day, Robert Altman) or just be good and new in some strange way . . . Scenes aims to represent the point on the graph where subculture chafes against culture, burning off the slag of pretension, leaving ingots of comic purity . . . hmmm . . .

Address: Box 63, 82 Colston Street, Bristol BS1 5BB
Mag Frequency: 1-2 times a year
Subscription: £19 for 4 issues (+1 free back issue) inc p&p
Single Issue: £4.95
Back Issue: #2-6 - £2.75/#7 onwards - £4.95
Overseas: £20 for 4 issues (+2 free back issues) inc p&p
Payment in: Concealed cash/Cheque/PO
Payable to: Drat 'N' Blast Books
Inserts accepted: Yes
Terms: Free
Circulation approx: 3000
Payment terms to contributors: We don't pay contributions - we don't pay ourselves either - Scenes exists as a showcase
Accept/rejection approx times: 4-6 weeks

5

SCHEHERAZADE

Scheherazade is an A5 black and white illustrated magazine specialising in fantasy and science fiction with the emphasis on plot and character rather than technical effects. We also publish author interviews and other features. We do not publish poetry reviews. The magazine was originally started in response to the prevalence of 'cyberpunk' and other hard/masculine SF in most other British magazines. We wanted to provide an alternative for writers of short story fantasy and the 'softer' more human aspects of science fiction.

Address: 14 Queen's Park Rise, Brighton, East Sussex BN2 2ZF
Email: shez@mistral.co.uk (but no email submissions)
Mag Frequency: 2-3 times a year
Subscription: £8.50 (UK) £10.50 (overseas) - 4 issues
Single Issue: £2.50 (UK) £3.50 (overseas)
Back Issue: £2
Overseas: £10.50 (sterling only)
Payment in: Sterling only. Cheques payable to Scheherazade.
Payable to: Scheherazade
Inserts accepted: No
Advertising Rates: Advert exchanges welcome
Circulation approx: 300
Payment terms to contributors: Small payment plus copy of magazine
Accept/rejection approx times: 3-4 months

The complete guide to poetry & small press magazines   299

S

SCI-FRIGHT

To debut February 1999. Sci-fi/fantasy/horror/thriller. We will publish short poems, under 40 lines. Any length fiction - no serials. Prose - no word count. Reviews of sci-fi books/zines etc. Articles and features also welcome. Please send submissions camera-ready - any fingerprints/pen marks will show and therefore cannot be accepted. Artwork- weird and wonderful - will be considered. All contributions/orders are welcome now.

Editor Name(s): Sian Ross
Address: Springbeach Press, 11 Vernon Close, Eastbourne Sussex BN23 6AN
Mag Frequency: Bi-monthly
Subscription: £9.50
Single Issue: £2
Overseas: SAE/IRC for details
Payment in: Cheque/PO
Payable to: S Ross
Inserts accepted: Yes
Terms: Exchange only
Advertising Rates: £5 full A5 page/smaller exchange only
Circulation approx: ?
Payment terms to contributors: Free copy
Accept/rejection approx times: Under 1 week

SCIENCE OF THOUGHT REVIEW

Based on the teaching of English Christian mystic Henry Thomas Hamblin, the Review has been in existence since 1921. It is devoted to the spiritual life and applied right thinking. First-hand experiences are popular that give a positive note to the reader looking for uplift, inspiration and solace. We cover meditation, complementary medicine and self development - but no more poetry please. As we are a charity, an SAE would be appreciated.

Address: Stephanie Sorrell, Science of Thought Review, Bosham House, Bosham, Chichester, W. Sussex PO18 8PJ
Fax: 01243 572109
Email: scienceofthought@mistral.co.uk
Website:
Mag Frequency: Bi-monthly
Subscription: £7 annually (minimum)
Single Issue: £1.25
Back Issue: 50p (including postage)
Overseas: £9 Australia/NZ; $26 USA $24 Canada
Payment in: Cheque; Visa/Delta/Mastercard etc
Payable to: Science of Thought Press
Inserts accepted: No
Circulation approx: 2,500 (including 200 abroad)
Payment terms to contributors: Copy of magazine
Accept/rejection approx times: 2-4 weeks

S

SCOTTISH STUDIES

Scottish Studies is the Journal of the School of Scottish Studies of the University of Edinburgh. It publishes research on Scottish traditional life and cultural history. Contributions are made by both the staff of the school and by other scholars in the field and take the form of full-scale articles, shorter notes and book reviews. Notes include first-hand reports of field work and research and transcriptions from the School's manuscripts and tape-recorded archives. Occasionally includes bibliographies.

Address: Alexander Fenton & Ian Fraser, School of Scottish Studies, 27 George Square, Edinburgh EH8 9LD
Subs to: Mrs R F Beckett at above address
Fax: 0131 650 4163
Mag Frequency: Annual
Subscription: £12
Single Issue: Current £10 (Vol 31)
Back Issue: £7
Overseas: US$25
Payable to: Scottish Studies
Inserts accepted: No
Circulation approx: 750

SCRATCH

Scratch publishes poetry and criticism of new poetry; it uses work by both new and established writers, and tends to writing which is engaged but not dogmatic, accessible but not simplistic, expansive in form but not pointlessly experimental; it leans to the left, and is keen to publish long poems, and sequences.

Address: 9 Chestnut Road, Eaglescliffe, Stockon on Tees TS16 0BA
Mag Frequency: 2 a year
Subscription: £7
Single Issue: £4
Back Issue: £2
Overseas: £15
Payable to: Scratch
Inserts accepted: Yes
Terms: £25
Payment terms to contributors: By negotiation - usually 2 free copies
Accept/rejection approx times: 6 weeks

S
SCRIPTOR

Scriptor is a new magazine of writing from the South-East (Kent, Surrey, Sussex, Essex and London). Published by The Providence Press (Whitstable), it aims to provide a new opportunity for writers of poetry, short stories and essays. Scriptor Two was published in October 1998 and contained the work of over 50 regional writers, including that of its editors. Scriptor Three will appear at the end of October 2000, and the last date for submissions is April 30th 2000. Contributors' guidelines are available directly from the publishers from 1 October 1999 (please enclose SAE). Only work from writers living/working in the South-East, as indicated above, will be considered. Scriptor's content is intentionally diverse, reflecting the nature of the work of its contributors. All submissions are given careful consideration. The magazine is not merely sold back to successful contributors, but marketed extensively through small press outlets such as book fairs, mail-order etc. Scriptor is supported by the National Lottery through the Arts Council of England.

Address: Scriptor, The Providence Press Whitstable, 22 Plough Lane, Swalecliffe, Whitstable, Kent CT5 2NZ
Mag Frequency: Every two years (from 1996)
Single Issue: £3.50 + 50p p&p
Back Issue: £1.99 (post free)
Payable to: Scriptor
Inserts accepted: No
Circulation approx: (Issue 2) 200+
Payment terms to contributors: Currently under review. Every successful contributor will receive a complimentary copy of the magazine and the opportunity to purchase further copies at a substantial discount.
Accept/rejection approx times: Approx 6-8 weeks

SEAM

Lively new poetry from a wide range of writers, established and aspiring. Under new editorship. Funded by Eastern Arts.

Editor Name(s): Maggie Freeman/Frank Dullaghan
Address: PO Box 3684, Danbury, Chelmsford, Essex CM3 4DJ
Mag Frequency: 2 yearly
Subscription: £6
Single Issue: £3
Overseas: £10
Payable to: Seam
Inserts accepted: Yes
Terms: Free, by reciprocal agreement
Advertising Rates: Please ask
Circulation approx: 250
Payment terms to contributors: 1 free copy
Accept/rejection approx times: 2-4 weeks

S

SEPIA

No rhymes - avoid strict metre, avoid clichés - believe in the poem or story; poems normally up to 80 lines; stories normally up to 2500 words, reviews; artwork.

Address: Sepia - Kawabata Press, Knill Cross House, Nr Anderton Road, Millbrook, Torpoint, Cornwall, PL10 1DX
Mag Frequency: 3 Times a year
Subscription: £2
Single Issue: 75p
Back Issue: 75p
Overseas: $5 (USA)
Payment in: Overseas: $ bills or sterling cheque - no US checks!
Payable to: Kawabata Press
Inserts accepted: Yes
Terms: Usually do as a swap
Circulation approx: 100
Payment terms to contributors: None - only free copy
Accept/rejection approx times: 2 weeks

SHEARSMAN

Shearsman is a magazine that is dedicated to poetry in English and foreign poetry in translation, though occasional short review notices also appear. The magazine specialises in what, for want of a better term, is often described as post-modernist poetry. Speculative contributions are welcome from any source, but the potential contributor should be aware that 95% of all such contributions are turned down. The editor would like to increase the 5%, but finds that the low success rate is usually caused by wishful contributors not knowing the nature of the magazine or of its regular contents. Potential contributors are therefore encouraged to see a copy of the magazine in advance. Translations should be accompanied by the appropriate copyright clearance if applicable.

Editor Name(s): Tony Frazer
Address: 47 Dayton Close, Plymouth PL6 5DX
Email: tfrazer@dfl.telmex.net.mx
Mag Frequency: 4 times a year
Subscription: £5
Single Issue: £1.50
Overseas: US$10 pa/$3 single
Payment in: £sterling or US$: Check with editor if wishing to pay in other currencies
Payable to: Shearman Books if sterling/Anthony Frazer if other currencies
Inserts accepted: No
Advertising Rates: Ads only carried on exchange basis
Circulation approx: 200
Payment terms to contributors: 4 copies of mag in which work appears
Accept/rejection approx times: 1 month

S

SHEFFIELD THURSDAY

Sheffield Thursday is a literary and arts magazine, edited by EA Markham from the School of Cultural Studies, Sheffield Hallam University. This international publication, appearing twice a year 'manages to be lively, informative and entertaining'. Poetry, art, essays, fiction and reviews give a feel of what's contemporary in the arts, and the interview with a major artist/arts worker is a prominent feature. Interviewees have included Margaret Drabble, Michelle Roberts, Malcolm Bradbury, Alastair Niven and (in the form of a questionnaire) assorted short story writers. As well as a forum for local and regional talent the magazine allows generous space in its 150-200 pages to work from the widest possible field: The first issue features quatrains from Iranian-born poet, Mimi Khalvati; an article on the challenge of finding a notation for performance or 'dub' poetry, by West Indian poet and critic Mervyn Morris; and Greek poet Alexis Lykiard playfully urging us to eat meat. Other issues have maintained the international thrust with work from Europe, the Americas, Asia . . .

Address: School of Cultural Studies, Sheffield, Hallam University, 36 Collegiate Crescent, Sheffield SI0 2BP
Mag Frequency: Twice a year
Subscription: £7 pa. (+£1 p&p)
Single Issue: £3.50 (+48p p&p)
Back Issue: £3.50 (+48p p&p)
Overseas: £10 pa
Payment in: Sterling - Cheque/PO
Payable to: Sheffield Hallam University
Inserts accepted: Yes
Terms: By negotiation
Advertising Rates:
Circulation approx: 750
Payment terms to contributors: By negotiation
Accept/rejection approx times: 3 months and getting better

SHRIKE

Shrike publishes poets who do not take their environment and its tradition at face value but view its elements and realign them according to their own needs.

Address: 13 Primrose Way, Alperton, Middlesex HA0 1DS
Mag Frequency: Bi-annual
Subscription: £10 for 3 issues
Single Issue: £4
Back Issue: £2
Overseas: £15
Payment in: Cash/cheque
Payable to: Paul Wright or Jo Mariner
Inserts accepted: Yes
Circulation approx: 150
Payment terms to contributors: 1 copy

S

SIERRA HEAVEN

Sierra Heaven is a magazine of fantasy, horror, and science fiction for the layman! We make no outlandish claims of pushing forward any boundaries, cutting-edge experimental fiction, or suchlike, but we do promise good, quality fiction (up to 20,000 words) accompanied by excellent illustrations from a superb collection of artists. Our artists regularly produce story-specific material for the magazine, both full and half-page work, and are proud to be associated with the format. Similarly, this is one of the attractions for a great many would-be contributors. Sierra Heaven rarely publishes poetry, but is in constant need of potential features, articles, interviews etc - whether they be about favourite artists, authors, perhaps a favourite trilogy of books, or a superbly realised alien/fantasy world, etc. The editorial policy of the magazine is thin to say the least, but basically the editor will publish genre material which he personally finds interesting, humorous, rather novel, or otherwise intriguing. Our 'Shorts inc' section comprises genre material from over 15 different authors; these short shorts have a maximum wordage of just 250 and are incredibly popular with author and readers alike, as well as being devilishly difficult to write. Sierra Heaven is 50 + A4 pages of solid reading, although at time of going to press we're considering an increase to 64-72 pages due to the wealth of the material regularly received. The editor respectfully believes the magazine can best be described as a black & white version of two excellent US fiction magazines: Science Fiction Age and Realms Of Fantasy; and is constantly striving to achieve such a status within the UK! Amen.

Address: c/o 13 Stanley Road, Bulphan, Essex RM14 3RX
Mag Frequency: 1-2 a year
Subscription: £14/4 issues
Single Issue: £2.95 + 55p postage (or A4 SAE)
Back Issue: £3.50 (inc. p&p)
Overseas: £4.50 Europe; $8 US
Payment in: Overseas payment should be in UK funds or $ cash
Payable to: Alex Bardy
Inserts accepted: Yes
Terms: £15/500
Circulation approx: 450
Payment terms to contributors: Complimentary copy for material/artwork published (excludes letters and short pieces)
Accept/rejection approx times: We are very proud of a turnaround time of approx 28 days

SKALD

Skald is an old Norse word for a poet, but this magazine features all forms of creative writing. It is based in North Wales and aims to reflect that area to some extent. To that end, a proportion of the writing is in Welsh, though fresh and original writing from elsewhere is always welcome. Artwork is also published if it is easily reproducible, and need not necessarily be illustration to accompany text.

Address: 2 Greenfield Terrace, Menai Bridge, Anglesey N Wales LL59 5AY
Mag Frequency: Bi-annual
Subscription: £3 (for 2 issues) (inc postage)
Single Issue: £1.50 (inc postage)
Back Issue: £1
Overseas: £6
Payment in: Cheque in sterling/PO
Payable to: Skald Community Magazine
Circulation approx: 300
Payment terms to contributors: Free copy of magazine
Accept/rejection approx times: 6 weeks

S

SKELETON GIRLS

Skeleton Girls is dedicated to real-life Gothic goddesses and contains poetry, prose, artwork and photography by the goddesses and similar work dedicated to them by their admirers. Details of other titles from the same address.

Address: Ty Fraen, The Park, Blaenavon, Torfaen NP4 9AG
Email: dolya@aol.com
Mag Frequency: Sporadic
Subscription: No subs
Single Issue: £2 or $4
Payment in: Any currency
Payable to: Ms Lindsay Brewis
Inserts accepted: Yes
Circulation approx: 300+
Accept/rejection approx times: 2 weeks

SLIPSTREAM

Slipstream offers the reader poetry, prose and articles. We publish a diverse and eclectic mix of quality writing - work that shows the writer is open to experimentation, taking risks and pays attention to detail.
In each issue we seek to publish at least two pieces of prose, a mix of poets, and at least one article. We do not publish 'how to write' articles. Instead, we invite a writer to explore his/her work, providing a commentary to a poem or prose piece/story. Articles are usually commissioned. We occasionally produce themed issues. A theme will be announced in previous issues and writers will be invited to submit work by a given deadline. Submissions are welcome. Poetry: up to 6 poems. Prose: up to 3000 words. Illustrations and artwork also sought. Please send SAE with all submissions. Detailed guidelines available - send SAE. We strongly recommend reading the magazine before submitting.

Editor Name(s): Cathy Cullis/Helen Knibb
Address: 4 Crossways, Crookham Village, Fleet, Hants GU13 0TA
Email: cathy@cullis.demon.co.uk
Mag Frequency: 3 x year
Subscription: £6
Single Issue: £3
Overseas: £8
Payment in: Cheque/PO - sterling only
Payable to: Slipstream
Inserts accepted: Yes
Terms: Exchanges welcome or donation negotiable
Circulation approx: Approx 200
Payment terms to contributors: One complimentary copy
Accept/rejection approx times: 3 months

S
SMILE

Basically an educational forum for hard science (chiefly physics, astronomy and mathematics), history, philosophy and politics, with occasional arts pieces, mainly classical music; we have also featured Chinese and Vietnamese cultural studies, martial arts and Doctor Who! We adopt no political or religious stance and demand only that contributions are properly researched, intelligent and informative. Bad grammar, swearing and shoddy craftmanship are not generally tolerated. The backlash against 'pop' trash starts here.

Address: Box 4, 136 Kingsland High Street, London E8
Mag Frequency: Usually 3 issues per year.
Single Issue: £2
Back Issue: £2.50
Payment in: No cheques - cash or POs (uncrossed) only
Payable to: Andy Martin
Inserts accepted: No
Circulation approx: 2000
Payment terms to contributors: 20 copies per contributor of magazine or negotiable
Accept/rejection approx times: Three weeks reply from receipt of submission

SMITHS KNOLL

Founded in 1992 and named after the North Sea lightship, it aims at readability. Particularly attractive to would-be contributors are its two-week turnaround time for submissions and the editors' willingness to offer constructive criticism when they are interested in a poem. It showcases a wide range of poetry from different kinds of writers - established, up and coming, and complete first timers. It prints only previously unpublished new poetry, well-presented and perfect bound.

Address: 49 Church Road, Little Glemham, Woodbridge, Suffolk, IP13 0BJ
Mag Frequency: 3 issues per year
Subscription: £10 for 3 issues
Single Issue: £3.50
Back Issue: £2-£3.50
Overseas: £12
Payment in: Sterling only
Payable to: Smiths Knoll
Inserts accepted: Sometimes, by previous arrangement
Terms: Depends on postage cost
Circulation approx: 500
Payment terms to contributors: £5 + complimentary copy
Accept/rejection approx times: Less than 2 weeks

S
SMOKE

New writing, poetry and graphics by some of the best established names, alongside new work from Merseyside, from all over the country and all over the world. Contributors have included Simon Armitage, David Constantine, Carol Anne Duffy, Douglas Dunn, Miroslav Holub, Jackie Kay, Roger McGough, Adrian Mitchell and Jo Shapcott.

Editor Name(s): Dave Calder/Dave Ward
Address: The Windows Project, First Floor, Liver House, 96 Bold Street, Liverpool L1 4KY
Telephone: 0151 709 3688
Mag Frequency: Twice yearly
Subscription: £3 for 4 issues
Single Issue: 50p + post
Overseas: £5 for 4 issues
Payable to: Windows Project
Inserts accepted: Yes
Terms: Exchange
Advertising Rates: N/A
Circulation approx: 1000
Payment terms to contributors: 1 copy
Accept/rejection approx times: 2 weeks

SNAPSHOTS HAIKU MAGAZINE

Snapshots is an internationally acclaimed haiku magazine featuring high quality contemporary English-languge haiku and senryu by both new and world-famous haiku poets, each usually being represented by a number of poems. It is the only UK journal devoted exclusively to haiku and senryu. Contributors include Janice Bostok, Randy M Brooks, David Cobb, Caroline Gourlay, Martin Lucas and Michel Dylan Welch. Snapshots is perfect-bound with a full-colour glossy card cover, and also features brief biographies of its contributors and a Best-Of-Issue Award as voted for by subscribers. Submissions of up to 20 individual haiku and/or senryu are welcome. These must be original, unpublished, not under consideration elsewhere and accompanied by a covering letter and an sae (+ 2 IRCs internationally). Tanka may be submitted to our new tanka journal Tangled Hair. Poems included in the magazine may also be published on the Snapshots website which also includes reviews and details of Snapshot Press books, etc. Snapshots also sponsors an annual competition for unpublished collections of haiku, senryu and/or tanka. In addition to a cash prize the winning author's collection is published by Snapshot Press. (Send sae for details. Closing date 31 July.)

Editor Name(s): John Barlow
Address: Snapshot Press, PO Box 35, Sefton Park, Liverpool L17 3EG
Email: snapshotpress@hotmail.com (comments and enquiries only, submissions must be by post)
Website: www.mccoy.co.uk/snapshots
Mag Frequency: Quarterly
Subscription: £16
Single Issue: £4.50
Back Issue: Singles £4/1998 box set £15
Overseas: Subs £18 Eur/£20 (US$34) RoW; Singles £5 Eur/£5.50 (US$10) RoW; 1998 box set £16 Eur/£17 (US$29) RoW
Payment in: Cheque/PO/IMO/Sterling Bank Drafts/US bills - for US checks add $4 bank charge
Payable to: Snapshot Press
Inserts accepted: Yes
Terms: £10 or exchange. Must be haiku related
Advertising Rates: N/A
Circulation approx: Increasing. Current print run 200
Payment terms to contributors: None. £15 Best-Of-Issue Award
Accept/rejection approx times: Usually 1-4 weeks

S

SOL MAGAZINE

Sol is chiefly a poetry magazine, tied to no particular school of writing, preferring instead simply to publish the best poems that it receives from its contributors. Since it was established in 1969 it has published work by Roger McGough, David Halliwell, Thomas Land, Andrew Darlilngton, Frederic Vanson, Susan Fromberg Schaeffer, Margot K Juby, Michael Daugherty, David Jaffin, John Whitworth, Gavin Ewart, Ian McMillan, and many others. We also publish articles about literature, philosophy and politics, and short stories, up to 5000 words.

Address: 24 Fowler Close, Southchurch, Southend-on-Sea, Essex SS1 2RD
Mag Frequency: Twice yearly
Subscription: 2/£3.50; 4/£6.50
Single Issue: £1.80
Back Issue: £1
Overseas: US: 2/$10; 4/$20
Payment in: Sterling/cash equiv - no foreign cheques
Payable to: Sol Publications
Inserts accepted: Yes
Terms: 35p per 100g
Circulation approx: 250
Payment terms to contributors: £1 per page
Accept/rejection approx times: 3 months

SOUTH

In April 1997 South was launched as a new poetry magazine. It is a merging of Doors, concerned with the relationship between poetry in the country and the world beyond, and South, a regional magazine covering Sussex, Hampshire, Dorset, Isle of Wight and Berkshire. Poets from outside the region are welcome to contribute, but poems should bear some relationship with this part of the country. Each issue is divided into three sections: *1. A critical profile of a poet associated with the South, followed by a selection of their poems. *2. This section will include South Services, In My View, articles on poets associated with the South, review and letters from readers. *3. A collection of poetry chosen from material submitted by poets.

Poets published will be invited to read at a celebration to launch each issue, giving poets an opportunity to hear each others' work and meet over a drink. Please send no more than 6 poems (with C5 sae). Poems should preferably be typed on A4 paper (one side only) with the poet's name and address clearly shown on each poem. We also welcome prose articles (about 800 words) on poets and topics of interest to readers and writers in the Southern counties. Any details of poetry events taking place in the region would be gratefully recieved, along with letters and publications to be reviewed.

Address: Wanda Publications, (South Magazine), 61 West Borough, Wimborne, Dorset BH21 1LX
Fax: 01202 881 061
Email: wanda@wanda.demon.co.uk
Mag Frequency: Twice yearly
Subscription: £6 one yr/£11 two yr
Single Issue: £3.50
Back Issue: Issues 1-14 £2, issues 15 onwards £3
Overseas: As UK+p&p
Payment in: Cheque/PO
Payable to: Wanda Publications
Inserts accepted: No
Circulation approx: 400
Payment terms to contributors: 1 complimentary copy

S

SOUTHFIELDS

A cultural review with emphasis on the cultures of Scotland, publishing poetry of a wide range of styles and commitments. Southfields has an interest in aesthetics, social criticism and pleasure. Would-be contributors should read an issue before submitting work.

Editor Name(s): Raymond Friel/David Kinlock/Richard Price
Address: R.Price, 8 Richmond Road,Staines TW18 2AB
Mag Frequency: 2 per year
Subscription: £6
Single Issue: £3
Back Issue: £4
Overseas: £10
Payment in: PO/cheque/cash/sterling only
Payable to: Southfields Press
Inserts accepted: Yes
Terms: Negotiable
Circulation approx: Varies, but under 500
Payment terms to contributors: Complimentary copy
Accept/rejection approx times: 3 months

SPANNER

Art and literary magazine usually dedicated to one artist or poet or group. Includes interviews or working documents. Presentation is rough and ready and almost instant. No unsolicited manuscripts.

Address: 14 Hopton Road, Hereford HR1 1BE
Mag Frequency: Irregular
Subscription: £12 Sterling
Single Issue: £5
Overseas: Surface mail - sterling only as above
Payable to: Spanner
Inserts accepted: No
Circulation approx: Varies, under 500 copies
Payment terms to contributors: Negotiated
Accept/rejection approx times: N/A

S

SPECTACULAR DISEASES

The press specialises in highly irregular experimental writing. Its house journal is very irregular, but books and pamphlets are released at a rate of 4-6 per year.

Address: 83b London Road, Peterborough, Cambs PE2 9BO
Email: booksend@learning-centre.demon.co.uk
Mag Frequency: Irregular
Subscription: No subs
Single Issue: £4
Back Issue: Various
Payment in: Cheque drawn on British bank
Payable to: Paul Green
Circulation approx: Variable
Payment terms to contributors: Copies
Accept/rejection approx times: 1 month

SPECTRUM

Founded 1990 by Stuart A Paterson (poet), its editor. Recently began to receive SAC subsidy after braving the financial storms of an independent publication's lot for 6 years. Main emphasis is on publishing poetry and short stories by new and established writers, the promotion of the former being of utmost importance. Poetry accepted varies in form, though there's, if anything, a slight bias towards formal verse. Work accepted from all over. Pleased (but not proud) to be Scottish, but not parochial. Average issue: 68 pages, A5, laminated cover, 8-12 line-drawn illustrations, 2-3 short stories, editorial, news, few reviews, but more writing.

Address: c/o Stuart A. Paterson, 2A Leslie Road, Kilmarnock, Ayrshire KA3 7RR
Subs to: Amanda Fergusson, 1 Hemphill, Moscow, By Galston, Ayrshire KA4 8PS
Mag Frequency: Twice yearly
Subscription: £6 incl p & p
Single Issue: £3 incl p & p £2.50 otherwise
Back Issue: £2.50 incl p & p
Overseas: £8
Payment in: Cheque/PO/IMO
Payable to: Spectrum
Inserts accepted: Yes
Terms: Varies - usually on a 'swap' basis though (or goodwill)
Circulation approx: 300-600 (subscribers/public sales)
Payment terms to contributors: 1 contributor's copy
Accept/rejection approx times: Up to 8 weeks - but usually much quicker if poss!

S

THE SPICE-BOX

This magazine was founded in 1997 and replaced Wire Poetry Magazine which ran from 1989 to 1997. The Spice-Box includes poetry taken from works published in its associated booklet series as well as special features on how authors can publish their own work. Please sample a copy of the magazine before sending your manuscript.

Editor Name(s): Malcolm Napier
Address: 1 Alanbrooke Close, Knaphill, Woking, Surrey GU21 2RU.
Mag Frequency: Annually
Subscription: N/A
Single Issue: £2.75
Back Issue: £2.25
Overseas: £4.25 inc p&p
Payment in: Cheque/PO
Payable to: Aramby Publishing
Inserts accepted: No
Advertising Rates: £25 per page (A5)
Circulation approx: 1000+
Payment terms to contributors: 2 free copies
Accept/rejection approx times: 6 months

THE SPINSTER'S ALMANACK

The Spinster's Almanack, for textile enthusiasts, is published four times a year in January, April, July and October. It is edited by Rowena Edlin-White and Dee Duke who aim to produce a friendly but useful magazine with instructional articles, letters and reviews, Guild news, patterns and recipes. We research our material thoroughly but try not to take ourselves too seriously and we find that it is this approach which has made readers world-wide, in Great Britain, Eire, America, Australia, Canada and beyond and this makes for a good cross-fertilisation of ideas. New writers: we have a number of regular contributors but are always interested in new ones. If you would like to offer an article, send for our Guidelines for Contributors from the address below, enclosing a stamped addressed envelope, please.

Editor Name(s): Rowena Edlin-White/Dee Duke
Address: The Spinster's Almanack, Willow House, 11 Frederick Avenue, Carlton, Nottingham NG4 1HP
Telephone: 0115 9873135
Subs to: Dee Duke, 23 Vaughan Avenue, Papplewick Lane, Hucknall, Nottingham, NG15 8BT
Telephone: 0115 9635538
Mag Frequency: 4 times a year (Jan/April/July/October)
Subscription: £7.60
Single Issue: £1.60
Back Issue: Various - half price
Overseas: £8.50 surface/£11 airmail
Payment in: Sterling or US bills
Payable to: The Spinster's Almanack
Inserts accepted: Yes
Terms: For 250, £15
Circulation approx: 250 (subs) but reaches many more through spinsters & weavers' guilds.
Payment terms to contributors: £5 per article + complimentary copy; we do not pay for reviews, recipes, letters
Accept/rejection approx times: 3 - 4 weeks

S

SPLIZZ

Splizz was founded in 1993. It features poetry, prose and pictures alongside extensive reviews of contemporary music. Splizz started off as a bi-monthly publication, but now appears quarterly, and in the last few years has become extremely successful both in the UK and further afield. Our aim is to provide new writers with an opportunity for their work to be published. We are always seeking a helping hand, and welcome your contributions at any time. 1998 has seen the launch of an offshoot publication called Splizz Stories, a collection of short stories from writers throughout the world; originally planned as a one-off, it has proved so successful that another one is already in the pipeline for 1999. Contributiions would be most welcome.

Editor Name(s): Amanda Morgan
Address: 4 St Mary's Rise, Burry Port, Carmarthenshire SA16 OSH
Mag Frequency: Quarterly
Subscription: £5
Single Issue: £1.30
Overseas: 5 IRCs per issue
Payment in: Sterling cheque/PO/IRC/cash
Payable to: Amanda Morgan
Inserts accepted: Yes
Terms: Negotiable
Advertising Rates: A5 ads-£3.50/centre pages or back cover-£5
Circulation approx: Worldwide, and still increasing
Payment terms to contributors: N/A
Accept/rejection approx times: 2-3 weeks

THE SPOTTED RHUBARB ZINE

Currently on issue 25, The Spotted Rhubarb Zine is a superb publication. It features art, poetry, tonnes of reviews, interviews with bands, articles and lots of stupidity. Writers include the infamous 'Lord Testicle' and Krystian Taylor. A great read - you'll be screaming out for more. Utter madness.

Address: Krystian Taylor, 102 Old Church Road, Nailsea, Bristol BS19 2ND
Mag Frequency: Bi-monthly
Subscription: £6
Single Issue: £1
Back Issue: £1.50
Overseas: £8
Payment in: Cheque/PO/well concealed cash etc
Payable to: Krystian Taylor
Inserts accepted: Yes
Terms: £10 - Also for the same price you can have an A5 advert printed
Circulation approx: 1000
Payment terms to contributors: None, but we're happy to print any good poetry/art

S

SPYDRA

The zine is dedicated to and about Princess Spider, the notorious Hungarian sadist. It contains work by the princess and work dedicated to her by her various slaves, sycophants and admirers.

Editor Name(s): Lindsay Brewis
Address: Spydra, TY Fraen, The Park, Blaenavon, Gwent, UK, NP4 9AG
Email: dolya@aol.com
Mag Frequency: Fitful
Subscription: No subscriptions
Single Issue: £2
Overseas: $4
Payment in: Cash only
Payable to: No cheques or POs
Circulation approx: 250
Payment terms to contributors: None
Accept/rejection approx times: Undefined

STAND MAGAZINE

Stand is a literary magazine that avoids the academic. Its first concern is with new unpublished poetry, fiction, translation, reviews. It has a regular critical column by the poet and critic William Scammell, and publishes readers' letters, if they are informed and incisive. Above all, let the work be fresh and original. It alternates a poetry/prose competition; thus 1998 - poetry competition, and 1999 - short story competition. Send SAE or IRCs for details.

Address: Stand Magazine, 179 Wingrove Road, Newcastle on Tyne NE4 9DA
Fax: 0191 273 3280
Mag Frequency: Quarterly
Subscription: £11.95
Single Issue: £3.95
Overseas: £13.50/$25 US Dollars
Payment in: Cheque/Credit Card
Payable to: Stand Magazine
Inserts accepted: Yes
Terms: 4500 = £250 + VAT
Circulation approx: 4500
Payment terms to contributors: £25 a poem unless under 20 lines
Accept/rejection approx times: 1-2 months

S
STAPLE

The magazine is entirely open, and sets little or no store by reputation - or lack of one. The editors try not to have preconceptions and, other things being equal, will favour writers whose work they don't know over those they do. Staple does not carry work over from one issue to the next, so, in spite of the fact that the quantity of work received vastly exceeds that which can be used, material is always needed for the next issue. The disadvantage is that the editors' decision may be quick or slow depending on when the typescript was sent. The most effective times to send to Staple are normally: March (for July publication); early September (for December publication); November (for March publication). The poetry is 'mainstream' - ie Staple will consider poems which are either free in form or written in not-too-obvious traditional modes. The fiction is non-genre. There are exceptions to every rule, but in general Staple is unlikely to take detective stories, sci-fi, gothic etc - or parodies thereof. The work published tends to have a bias towards the documentary. The magazine was established in 1982. The Staple Open Poetry competition followed in 1986; from 1999 it will run every year.

Address: Bob Windsor, Gilderoy East, Upperwood Road, Matlock Bath, Derbyshire DE4 3PD
Subs to: Donald Measham, Tor Cottage, 81 Cavendish Road, Matlock, Derbys DE4 3HD
Mag Frequency: 3 issues, & First Editions (collection) supplement
Subscription: Annually £12
Single Issue: £3.50
Back Issue: Two for £3
Overseas: Eur £14; RoW£17.50 surface/£20 air
Payable to: STAPLE
Inserts accepted: Yes on exchange or payment basis
Terms: £20 per 500
Circulation approx: 500 - special issues 750+
Payment terms to contributors: £5 per poem/£10 per story
Accept/rejection approx times: See above for optimum submission times

S

STEPPING OUT

Stepping Out is a small 20-page magazine which offers support to people who are agoraphobic or who suffer from nervous illness. It sympathises with them and encourages them to think positively. Readers are invited to send in letters, articles, and poems to encourage others. It also has features, news items, notes about psychiatrists, and stories. Members receive a birthday card and may ask for information, have advice from a 'Befriender', and advertise their names and addresses and crafts for sale. They may also join the penfriend club One To One at £5 for life, £2 pa, or free if they are on a low income. The magazine Stepping Out also offers literary competitions with prizes. This magazine is of great value to housebound people.

Editor Name(s): Mrs WK Cardy
Address: 48 South Street, Colchester CO2 7BJ
Telephone: 01206 520150
Fax: 01206 577404 for att: One magazine
Mag Frequency: Quarterly
Subscription: £5
Single Issue: £1.20
Back Issue: 70p
Payment in: Cheque/PO/stamps
Payable to: Stepping Out
Inserts accepted: Yes
Terms: Free
Circulation approx: 50
Payment terms to contributors: 1 extra copy free
Accept/rejection approx times: 4 weeks

S

STONE SOUP

Stone Soup (founded 1994) is an international magazine for new writing, publishing mainly poetry, theory and interview. It aims 'to provide a fluent dialogue between small and established national literatures,' and first two issues are printed bilingually in English and the languages of former Yugoslavia. Edited by British poet Ken Smith and Bosnian poet Igor Klikovac, Stone Soup is 'the effective combination of poetry, fiction, philosophical and political writing,' favouring writing concerned with the problems of modern European society, problems of language and exile. The first three issues include the exclusive materials by Umberto Eco, Jean Baudrillard, Alain Bosquet, Noam Chomsky, Slavoj Zizek, Hanif Kureishi, Juan Goytisolo, Arseny Tarkovsky and Janos Pillinszky. The magazine works largely on a commission basis; unsolicited mss must have an sae supplied.

Address: 37 Chesterfield Road, London W4 3HQ
Mag Frequency: Quarterly
Subscription: £15 a year
Single Issue: £7
Back Issue: £5
Overseas: Europe £18/RoW £21
Payment in: Cheques/postal orders in sterling
Payable to: Stone Soup
Inserts accepted: Yes
Terms: £1
Circulation approx: 3000
Payment terms to contributors: Payment by arrangement
Accept/rejection approx times: 60 days

THE STORY OF . . .

The Story Of . . . A set of two trilogies showcasing the authoress Mhairian Trevelyan; in the Sci Fi/Dark Fantasy/Cyberpunk genres.

Address: Akasha Inc, 99 Van Dyke Street, Toxteth, Liverpool L8 0RS
Mag Frequency: Once a year
Subscription: £5.50 to join info service
Single Issue: £3.50
Overseas: Add £1 for EU/add £2 for RoW
Payment in: Cheque/PO/IMO/IRC
Payable to: S McCarthy.
Inserts accepted: Yes (up to A4)
Circulation approx: Varies - Up to 1000.
Payment terms to contributors: N/A

S

STRANGE STATION

Rising from the rubble of Kyles Klub UK, Strange Station continues to present small press zines packed with the best short stories, poetry and articles but now with a thoroughly queer slant. The intensely personal Rubber Stones which surfaced mid-1997 heralded the end of the angst-ridden material previously championed and led to a lengthy break in output. Now comes Little Girl, a once-yearly queerzine, each issue to incorporate one extended short story, a featured poet, a featured artist and various contributor pieces. Potential contributors are advised to send sae for submission guidelines before sending work. Issue One of Little Girl is due December 1998 priced £1, which also includes a further title from the back catalogue free.

Editor Name(s): Michael Coleman (future guest editors TBA)
Address: c/o 18 Sunningdale Avenue, Sale, Chesire M33 2PH
Mag Frequency: Once a year
Single Issue: £1
Overseas: 3 IRCs per copy
Payment in: Cheque/PO/IRCs/trade
Payable to: Michael Coleman
Inserts accepted: No
Advertising Rates: N/A
Circulation approx: 100
Payment terms to contributors: Copy of mag
Accept/rejection approx times: 2 weeks

STRIDE

An occasional arts magazine, featuring literature, music, visual arts alongside reviews and new writing. Recent issues have included Sun Ra, William Burroughs, Jeremy Reed, Grail Marcus, Brian Eno, King Crimson, Biba Kopf etc. 'Perversely eclectic, well written and highly impressive' (Ramroid Extraordinaire) 'Informed and accessible writing well worth investigating' (Rubberneck).

Address: Stride, 11 Sylvan Road, Exeter, Devon EX4 6EW
Mag Frequency: Occasional
Subscription: N/A
Single Issue: Last issue £5.95
Back Issue: £3.95
Overseas: $10 bill only
Payable to: Stride
Inserts accepted: No
Circulation approx: 2000
Payment terms to contributors: Free copy
Accept/rejection approx times: 1 week

S

STRIX

Strix is run by authors Anna Franklin and Sue Phillips. It is a fully independent fantasy and horror magazine featuring some of the brightest writers and artists around. We aim for at least five stories in every issue, usually far more, and try to balance the dark and the light, though we do especially appreciate dark humour. Genres include traditional horror, all kinds of fantasy and speculative fiction, slipstream, black comedy, comic fantasy and a limited quantity of poetry. Bloodcurdling gore is not generally in evidence, and pornography is not welcomed. Past contributors have included Angela Black, Anna Franklin, Ceri Jordan, DF Lewis, Gary Harrison, Joe Rattigan, John B Ford, John Light, Michael Pendragon, Michael Sosner, Paul Finch, Sean Russell Friend, Simon Bestwick, and Sue Phillips. We are proud of our monochrome artwork which is of a particularly high standard and has included illustrations from the likes of Helen Field, Gerald Gaubert, Desmond Knight, Anna Franklin, and Rebecca Jeavons. In addition, we welcome articles on source material for writers and reviews of books, films, CD rom, and music related to the style of the magazine. A major and very popular feature of the magazine is our letters page, which has become a forum for the news and views of our readers and contributors and often tends towards the humorous.

Address: Strix, PO Box 12, Earl Shilton, Leics LE9 7ZZ
Email: Raginohart@aol.com
Mag Frequency: Quarterly
Subscription: £7.50 for 4/£11.50 for 6 (incudes postage)
Single Issue: £2
Overseas: USA 1 @ $5 and 4 @ $20
Payment in: Cheque/IMO/US dollars cash
Payable to: Anna Franklin
Inserts accepted: Yes (A5/A6). But adverts preferred
Advertising Rates: Page £22/half pg £11/quarter pg £6/eighth pg £4. Line ads 5p per word. Box no 75p; contacts, events etc free.
Circulation approx: 500
Payment terms to contributors: Contibutor's copy
Accept/rejection approx times: 21 days

SUB-SCRIBE

Sub-scribe is the quarterly creative writing and arts journal produced by Denude Studio in Manchester. It is dedicated to showcasing previously unpublished poetry, prose, artwork from young people in the North West. It provides a forum for young artists and writers currently under-represented. By liasing with the region's schools, colleges, youth and community projects, Sub-Scribe aims to expose, nurture and promote new creative talent. All submissions are carefully considered and we welcome all forms of artistic expression - poetry, short stories, art, photography, as well as thoughts and opinions. Original work and manuscripts are automatically reproduced and the innovative layouts and designs highlight each submission's respective individuality. All prospective contributors should write, in the first instance, with covering letter and SAE.

Address: PO Box 72 Manchester M14 5SD
Mag Frequency: Seasonal
Subscription: £8
Single Issue: £2
Overseas: £10
Payment in: Cheque/PO/Secured sterling
Payable to: Denude Studio
Inserts accepted: Yes - with mail orders
Terms: Free
Circulation approx: 1000
Payment terms to contributors: Free issue
Accept/rejection approx times: Immediate response with SAE

S
SUFFER THIS

Rumoured to be cursed, Suffer This is an almost unreadable piece of postal poetry art. Serious migraine material. Featuring the best new and established writers. Suffer This is an intense reaction and a perfect antidote to moronically lame-looking zines, it is recommended that perspective contributors check out a back issue befoe the submission of material. Please include a SAE. The backlash starts here.

Address: Denude Studio (Suffer This), PO Box 72, Manchester M14 5AD
Mag Frequency: Seasonal
Subscription: No subs
Single Issue: £1 plus postage
Payment in: Secured sterling/cheque/PO
Payable to: M McNamara
Inserts accepted: Yes
Terms: Free
Circulation approx: 200
Payment terms to contributors: 1 issue
Accept/rejection approx times: Immediate response with SAE

SUMMER BULLETIN

32-page booklet with details of meetings, news of members, general information about the Yorkshire Dialect Society, prose and verse from members, new writers being encouraged to submit their work for consideration. We accept dialect from all corners of the vast, old county of Yorkshire.

Address: Summer Bulletin, 3 Northdale Mount, Bradford BD5 9AP
Subs to: Yorkshire Dialect Society 'Rambles' 61 Moor Lane, Carnaby, Bridlington YO16 4UT
Mag Frequency: Annually
Subscription: £7 for subs to Summer Bulletin & Transactions of the Yorkshire Dialect Society, plus membership of the Society
Single Issue: £2
Back Issue: £1
Overseas: £7 Europe/£10 rest of world
Payment in: Sterling UK £
Payable to: Yorkshire Dialect Society
Payment terms to contributors: None

S

SUPER TROUPER

Hello, and welcome to our page! Super Trouper is a little different from most other magazines in that we do not appear in printed form, but instead are recorded onto cassette. So you get to hear our mag rather than read it! Usually, we last for 60 minutes, but sometimes manage 90, depending on how much good stuff you send us. We like songs, poetry, instrumental music, comedy sketches and very short (5 minutes max) short stories. There's also lots of small press news, reviews and interviews. What a great show!

Address: Andy Savage, 35 Kearsley Road, Sheffield S2 4TE
Mag Frequency: Up to 4 per year
Subscription: £12 post paid for 4 issues
Single Issue: £3.50 post paid
Overseas: $20
Payment in: Cheque/PO
Payable to: Andrew Savage
Circulation approx: Around 100 per issue
Payment terms to contributors: A free copy
Accept/rejection approx times: 4 weeks maximum

SWAGMAG

The magazine of Swansea's writers and artists. Edited by Peter Thabit Jones, it publishes poetry, prose, features, interviews and reviews. Cartoons/photos/artwork. Includes work in the Welsh language too. Recent issues include interview with Adrian Mitchell, features on Paul Peter Piech, international artist, and anglo-welsh poet Harri Webb.

Address: c/o Dan-y-bryn, 74 Cwm Level Road, Brynhyfryd, Swansea, SA5 9DY
Mag Frequency: Twice yearly
Subscription: £5 + 50p postage
Single Issue: £2.50 + postage
Back Issue: £1.50 + postage
Overseas: On request
Payable to: SWAG, Swansea Writers' and Artists' Group
Inserts accepted: Yes
Terms: On request
Circulation approx: Increasing
Payment terms to contributors: Free copy of magazine
Accept/rejection approx times: 3 months

S

THE SWANSEA REVIEW

A journal of poetry, criticism and prose (including fiction). Occasional musical scores. Features including interviews (eg Helen Vendlar, Les A Murray, Denise Levertov), poetry (eg John Heath-Stubbs, Charles Tomlinson, Mimi Khalvati, John Greening) and critical essays (eg Nicholas Potter, M Wynn Thomas, Fred Beake).

Address: Glyn Pursglove, Dept. of English, University of Wales, Swansea, Singleton Park, Swansea SA2 8PP
Telephone: 01792 205678 X4308
Email: g.pursglove@swansea.ac.uk
Mag Frequency: Twice yearly
Subscription: £5
Single Issue: £2.50
Back Issue: £2
Overseas: £6
Payment in: Cheque preferred, sterling if possible
Payable to: The Swansea Review
Inserts accepted: No
Circulation approx: 500
Payment terms to contributors: 2 free copies
Accept/rejection approx times: 6 months

THE SWEDENBORG SOCIETY MAGAZINE

The magazine publishes articles about or relating to the writings, life and thought of Emanuel Swedenborg.

Editor Name(s): Stephen McNeilly
Address: Swedenborg House, 20/21 Bloomsbury Way, London WC1A 2TH
Telephone: 0171 405 7986
Email: swed.soc@netmatters.co.uk
Mag Frequency: Once a year
Subscription: Free to members
Single Issue: Free to members, £1 to non-members
Back Issue: £1
Overseas: N/A
Payable to: The Swedenborg Society
Inserts accepted: No
Circulation approx: 1000
Payment terms to contributors: No payment

T

THE TABLA BOOK OF NEW VERSE

The Tabla Book Of New Verse is the successor to Tabla poetry magazine. Since its foundation in 1991, Tabla has pursued a policy of combining work commissioned from well-known poets with selected entries from a tie-in competition. Writers new to Tabla are requested to approach us through the competition in the first instance: please send an sae. Those accepted for publication are then invited to offer work for future issues and to have a collection reviewed. A recognition that poets and poems, however accomplished, find their readers slowly has helped to shape Tabla's editorial policy; so, too, has the belief that it is preferable to publish too little than too much. Hence, only one slim volume of Tabla has appeared every twelve months since 1992. In that time, we have published new work by some of the most prominent names in contemporary verse, including Seamus Heaney, Carol Rumens, Peter Redgrove, Charles Simic, Ruth Padel, Paul Muldoon, Jane Duran, Tobias Hill, Pauline Stainer and Medbh McGuckian. Tabla has been widely praised in the poetry press for its contents and its elegant design. It has also twice enjoyed the distinction of publishing poems which have then been shortlisted for the Best Individual Poem Of The Year category of the Forward Poetry Awards.

Editor Name(s): Stephen James
Address: Stephen James, Dept of English, University of Bristol, 315 Woodland Road, Bristol BS8 1TB
Fax: 0117 928 8860
Mag Frequency: Annual
Subscription: N/A
Single Issue: TBA
Back Issue: £5 (1998)
Overseas: Add UK£10 equivalent to price to cover bank charge & post
Payment in: Sterling
Payable to: Tabla
Inserts accepted: Yes
Terms: Exchange or by arrangement
Circulation approx: 500+
Payment terms to contributors: Competition prizes/complimentary copies
Accept/rejection approx times: 2 mos from competition closing date

TAK TAK TAK

Formed in 1986 Tak Tak Tak is a publishing house and label dedicated to the experimental in writing, music and other media. Publications have taken various forms. We are not currently accepting unsolicited contributions.

Address: BCM Tak, London WC1N 3XX
Mag Frequency: Occasional
Subscription: Variable
Single Issue: Variable
Back Issue: Variable
Overseas: Variable
Payment in: Cheque/IMO/PO/registered cash
Payable to: Tak Tak Tak
Inserts accepted: No
Circulation approx: Variable
Payment terms to contributors: Copies or royalty by negotiation

T
TANGLED HAIR

Tangled Hair is the first journal published in the UK to be devoted exclusively to tanka. Its aim is to present high quality contemporary English-language tanka by both new and internationally established poets in an attractive journal. Tangled Hair is perfect-bound with a glossy card cover and each poem is printed on its own page for maximum effect. It also features brief biographies of its contributors and a Best-Of-Issue Award as voted for by subscribers. Submissions of up to 12 tanka are welcome. These must be original, unpublished, not under consideration elsewhere and accompanied by a covering letter and an sae (+ 2 IRCs internationally). Haiku and senryu may be submitted to our haiku magazine Snapshots. Tanka featured in Tangled Hair may also be published on the Snapshots website.

Editor Name(s): John Barlow
Address: Snapshot Press, PO Box 35, Sefton Park, Liverpool L17 3EG
Email: snapshotpress@hotmail.com
Website: www.mccoy.co.uk/snapshots
Mag Frequency: Quarterly
Subscription: £14
Single Issue: £4
Overseas: Subs £16 Eur/£18 or US$30 RoW; singles £.50 Eur/£5 or US$9 RoW
Payment in: Cheque/PO/IMO/Sterling Bank Draft/US bills - for US checks add $4 bank charge
Payable to: Snapshot Press
Inserts accepted: Yes
Terms: £10 or exchange. Must be tanka or haiku related
Advertising Rates: N/A
Payment terms to contributors: None. £15 Best-Of-Issue Award
Accept/rejection approx times: Usually 1-4 weeks

T

TANJEN NOVELLAS

Founded 1996 - specialising in sci-fi, fantasy and horror of between 20,000 to 60,000 words. We distribute to shops as well as through mail order. Each issue perfect bound, colour cover and over 100 A5 pages.

Address: 52 Denman Lane, Huncote, Leicester LE9 3BS
Mag Frequency: 6 yearly
Subscription: £3 (for 8)
Single Issue: £4.99
Overseas: £46
Payment in: IMO/cheque/PO
Payable to: Tanjen Ltd
Inserts accepted: Yes
Terms: £10
Circulation approx: 2000
Payment terms to contributors: 5% royalties
Accept/rejection approx times: About 1 in 20

T
TEARS IN THE FENCE

An international literary magazine that combines new writing with criticism and reviews, Tears In The Fence is one of the leading poetry publishers in the UK. Recent contributors include Edward Field, Barry MacSweeney, Lee Harwood, Fred Voss, John Freeman, Mary Maher, KV Skene, Donna Hilbert, Karen Rosenberg, Mandy Pannett, Gillian Allnutt, David Hart, Jay Ramsay, KM Dersley, Martin Stannard, Barbara Ellis et al.

Editor Name(s): David Caddy
Address: 38 Hod View, Stourpaine, Blandford Forum, Dorset DT11 8TN
Telephone: 01258 456803
Mag Frequency: 2/3 issues annually
Subscription: £10 for 3
Single Issue: £4
Overseas: £15 sterling/US$15 cash
Payment in: IMO/sterling cheques/US dollars cash
Payable to: Tears In The Fence
Inserts accepted: Yes
Terms: £10 per 1000
Advertising Rates: Available upon request
Circulation approx: 1800
Payment terms to contributors: 1 copy of magazine
Accept/rejection approx times: 2/3 weeks

TEARS OF ARIEL

Tears Of Ariel features collections of authors (no poetry) and artists in the following genres: sci fi, (dark) fantasy, cyberpunk, (gothic) horror, suspense and surreal. Free story editing (postage must be paid) by editor who is Master's level tutor. Submissions guidelines available with SAE/IRC.

Address: Akasha Inc, 99 Van Dyke Street, Toxteth, Liverpool L8 0RS
Mag Frequency: Twice a year
Subscription: £5.50 to join info service
Single Issue: £6.50 (£5.50 info service members MIRAGE)
Overseas: To join info service - £9(EU)/£11 RoW; single copies add 2 IRC EU/4 IRC RoW
Payment in: Cheque/PO/IMO/IRC
Payable to: S McCarthy
Inserts accepted: Yes
Circulation approx: Varies - up to 1000
Payment terms to contributors: Free copy of volume they appear in but, must send 50p sae
Accept/rejection approx times: 4 weeks

T

TERRIBLE WORK

Poery. Text. Reviews. Art. The poetry is an oblique cross-section of left-field poetics: as likely to publish a new young poet as yet uninfluenced by mainstream stifleism as it is the latest work from experienced innovators (Andrew Duncan, Aaron Williamson, Bruce Andrews). Not interested in bed-sit bores or performance posers however, and not interested in knitted anecdote or crocheted cliché either. Only the terrible is beautiful. Carries huge polemical and analytical review section.

Editor Name(s): Tim Allen/Josephine Ebert/Steve Spence
Address: 21 Overton Gardens, Mannamead, Plymouth PL3 5BX
Mag Frequency: Twice a year
Subscription: £9 for 3
Single Issue: £3.50
Back Issue: £2
Overseas: USA $7.50/$20
Payment in: Cheque/PO
Payable to: Terrible Work
Inserts accepted: No
Circulation approx: 400
Payment terms to contributors: Comp copies
Accept/rejection approx times: From ROP to 3 months

T

THE THIRD ALTERNATIVE

TTA is a multi-award-winning magazine of 60 glossy A4 pages and colour cover which is heralded as one of the best, most innovative fiction magazines in the world. It publishes extraordinary new stories - these can be modern, literary SF/fantasy/ horror, or just as often not of any particular genre, blurring the borders between the outré and the mainstream. We publish many well-known authors but just as many newcomers, often giving writers their first ever credit. The magazine has an unrivalled record of honorable mentions and reprints in various anthologies, from The Year's Best Fantasy And Horror in the USA to The Time Out Book Of New Writing. We also publish in-depth reviews, profiles and interviews, as well as regular provocative comment columns - all complemented by stunning artwork. Submissions are welcome as long as they follow standard ms format and are accompanied by SAE and covering letter. We also recommend Zene for continued updates and news. Please study several issues of TTA before submitting - not a requirement, just a recommendation!

Address: Andy Cox, TTA Press, 5 Martins Lane, Witcham, Ely, Cambs CB6 2LB
Telephone: 01353 777931
Email: ttapress@aol.com
Website: http://purl.oclc.org/net/ttaonline/
Mag Frequency: Quarterly
Subscription: £11 (4 issues)
Single Issue: £3
Back Issue: Sold out
Overseas: Europe £3.50/£13
USA & Canada US$6/$22
RoW £4/£15
Payment in: Cheque/PO etc. Foreign currency cheques acceptable at rates equivalent to above (preferred to foreign cash).
Payable to: TTA Press
Inserts accepted: Yes
Terms: Negotiable
Advertising Rates: Ad space available
Circulation approx: 20000
Payment terms to contributors: Contracts issued upon acceptance, payment on publication.
Accept/rejection approx times: 4-6 weeks

T
THE THIRD HALF (LITERARY MAGAZINE)

The Third Half will, in future, vary per issue, but will showcase the work of 4-6 writers each time. Sets/mini-books of 12-20 pages need to be sent for appraisal (open subjects, but no obscenity wanted).

Editor Name(s): Kevin Troop
Address: 16 Fane Close, Stamford, Lincolnshire PE9 1HG
Telephone: 01780 754193
Mag Frequency: Occasional
Single Issue: £3 includes post
Back Issue: £5.50 includes post
Payment in: Pounds sterling/Eurocheques overseas
Payable to: KT Publications
Inserts accepted: No
Circulation approx: Worldwide - print run varies
Payment terms to contributors: By arrangement (copies with individual issues)
Accept/rejection approx times: 1 week

THOMAS HARDY JOURNAL

The Thomas Hardy Journal is published by the Thomas Hardy Society thrice yearly and has two main objects: to provide information about the Society's activities and to be a forum for the publication of letters, reviews and articles about Hardy's writings, his life and his background. Literary contributions are welcomed but will not be returned unless accompanied by the necessary postage. No payment is made for articles but writers have the satisfaction of publication in a periodical of authority and repute, and they will be given four complimentary copies of the issue in which their article appears. Articles should be typed in double spacing on one side of the paper only, and should be as brief as possible. 4,000 words should normally be regarded as the maximum. Please include a short entry (up to 10 lines) for the notes on contributors. The Editor reserves the right to shorten letters. Book reviews are usually invited but may be volunteered. They should normally be between 200 and 800 words. Any other items, such as relevant and reproducible illustrations, news cuttings, book excerpts and other miscellanea which might be of interest to our readers, will be gratefully received.

Address: 25 Hawthorn Grove, Heaton Moor, Stockport SK4 4HZ
Subs to: Thomas Hardy Society, PO Box 1438, Dorchester, Dorset DT1 1YH
Mag Frequency: 3 times a year
Subscription: £12
Single Issue: £4
Payable to: Thomas Hardy Society
Inserts accepted: Yes
Terms: £100
Advertising Rates: Full page £79/half page £35
Circulation approx: 1500
Payment terms to contributors: No payment, 4 copies

T
THUMBSCREW

Thumbscrew is an independent poetry journal publishing work by internationally renowned writers, alongside exciting new poets and critics. Important contributions include Ted Hughes on Sylvia Plath, recently-discovered stories by Louis MacNeice, and Charles Simic on the art of invective - as well as work from Paul Muldoon, Fleur Adcock, Craig Raine, Seamus Heaney and others. Thumbscrew also sets out to provoke critical debate with a series of essays re-evaluating the reputations of several 'major' contemporary poets.

Address: PO Box 657, Oxford OX2 6PH
Mag Frequency: 3 issues annually
Subscription: £10 pa
Single Issue: £3.50
Overseas: Europe £12.50/USA $27
Payment in: Cheque/PO
Payable to: Thumbscrew
Inserts accepted: Yes
Terms: £50 per 1000
Circulation approx: 580
Payment terms to contributors: 2 free copies
Accept/rejection approx times: 1-2 months

THUNDERBOX

Small press journal with strong ties to science fiction fandom, but not exclusively sf-oriented. Personal, anecdotal essays; literary/music/cinema criticism. Potential contributors are urged to contact us first. (No fiction, no poetry, no non-commissioned artwork.)

Address: Steve & Ann Green 33 Scott Road, Olton, Solihull B92 7LQ
Email: ghost.words@virgin.net
Mag Frequency: 3/year
Subscription: No subs
Single Issue: Self-addressed A4 envelope, plus 2 x 1st class stamp (UK only)
Back Issue: Not available
Inserts accepted: No
Circulation approx: 200+
Payment terms to contributors: Complimentary copy of issue
Accept/rejection approx times: 3 months

T

TIME BETWEEN TIMES

General interest, multi-path occult. Contains news and views, history, stories, handicrafts and contacts. Available on solstices and equinoxes. Article length up to 1000 words. Longer material by arrangement. Artwork b/w line drawings only please.

Editor Name(s): Llew
Address: Time Between Times, 41 Forest Road, Hinkley, Leics LE11 1HA
Email: tbt@oakapple.force9.net
Mag Frequency: Quarterly
Subscription: £6
Single Issue: £1.75
Back Issue: £2
Overseas: £7 Europe/$15 USA, Canada
Payment in: Cheque/crossed PO
Payable to: R Lapworth
Inserts accepted: Yes
Terms: Negotiable
Advertising Rates: On application
Circulation approx: 300
Payment terms to contributors: Free issue of magazine
Accept/rejection approx times: 6 weeks

T

TIME HAIKU

Time Haiku is a magazine (founded 1995) which publishes haiku, tanka and short poems in English. Short essays are published and there are articles on various aspects of haiku. The main intention of the magazine is to make haiku more accessible and popular and to provide a place where all types of haiku can be found. Works by new writers are just as welcome as those of established haiku writers. The magazine is intended to appeal both to experts and those just curious about haiku. A newsletter is also published twice a year to give information about haiku and other poetry events. Past contributors have been Gavin Ewart, John Light, Chris Sykes, Douglas Johnson, Dan Pugh and so on!

Editor Name(s): Erica Facey
Address: 105 Kings Head Hill, London E4 7JG
Telephone: 0181 529 6498
Mag Frequency: Twice yearly
Subscription: £5.50 pa including two newsletters
Single Issue: £2.50
Overseas: £7 Europe/£10 other
Payment in: Sterling cheques; foreign currency must allow for commission
Payable to: Time Haiku Group
Inserts accepted: Yes
Terms: £1 per 1000
Advertising Rates: £50 per page
Circulation approx: Increasing
Accept/rejection approx times: About 1 in 5 acceptances

T
TOCHER

Tocher - the name was chosen because of its fairly common use in both Scots and Gaelic, meaning dowry - contains some of the riches stored in the archives of the School of Scottish Studies. That archive now contains about 10,000 tapes, as well as a large number of video recordings. Transcriptions of some of those have been issued in Tocher since 1971. There are stories and legends, songs, items on customs, children's rhymes, proverbs, riddles, the occasional recipe, and reminiscences of daily life from Shetland to the Borders. Items in Gaelic are translated into English, and glossaries are added to Scots items when that is thought appropriate. The production of the magazine is entirely done by the staff of the School of Scottish Studies, and it is printed in the University of Edinburgh. No 53 (summer 1998) includes Orkney Ba' Game reminiscences, Rob Roy stories (Gaelic), strong man anecdotes, Peter Hall appreciation, songs and reviews of CDs and books. A double issue, 54&55 is in preparation. It contains an article on potato harvesting in East Lothian and other agricultural themes, including songs. The Rev Norman MacDonald, a tradition-bearer from Skye, is also featured, with songs and stories.

Editor Name(s): Miss Morag MacLeod
Address: Miss Morag MacLeod, School of Scottish Studies, 27 George Square, Edinburgh EH8 9LD
Subs to: Mrs Fran Beckett same address
Telephone: 0131 650 4150
Mag Frequency: Bi-annual
Subscription: £6 for 2 issues
Single Issue: £3.50
Back Issue: Issues 2-24 £1/26-43 £1.50/44-on £2
Overseas: $18 for 2
Payable to: Tocher
Inserts accepted: No
Advertising Rates: Full pg £100/half pg £50/quarter pg £25 (A5)
Circulation approx: 800
Payment terms to contributors: N/A
Accept/rejection approx times: N/A

TOUCHPAPER

The science fiction newsletter of polemics and review. Touchpaper is an irregular newsletter of commentary, review and other matters of interest to anybody concerned with the science fiction genre. Readers, writers, critics, academics and publicists are all welcome to send us their opinions and views (relevant or irrelevant) about science fiction. Please study our guidelines for contributors (available for SAE/IRC) before submitting nonfiction writings. Like many other (similar or not) genre publications of today, the contents of Touchpaper may be subject to editorial vagaries and whim. There isn't a fixed policy or schedule. All writings will be considered, so long as the material fits in with the newsletter's basic theme. Contributors have free rein to say whatever they want but libellous stuff will go straight in the rubbish bin. Publishes nonfiction up to 500 words.

Editor Name(s): Tony Lee
Address: Pigasus Press, 13 Hazely Coombe, Arreton, Isle of Wight PO30 3AJ
Telephone: 01983 865668
Mag Frequency: Quarterly
Subscription: £2 for 5 issues
Single Issue: Free for SAE/IRC
Overseas: 1 IRC per issue
Payable to: Tony Lee
Inserts accepted: Yes
Terms: Available on request for SAE/IRC
Advertising Rates: Available on request for SAE/IRC
Circulation approx: Unknown
Payment terms to contributors: Pays in copy only
Accept/rejection approx times: 4-6 weeks

T
TRANSACTIONS OF THE YORKSHIRE DIALECT SOCIETY

Transactions reflects the work and interests of the Yokshire Dialect Society, founded in 1897 to study and promote the varied dialect of Yorkshire. Articles range from academic linguistics and folklore to original prose verse in Yorkshire dialect.

Editor Name(s): Dr Arnold Kellett
Address: 22 Aspin Oval, Knaresborough, North Yorks HG5 8EL
Mag Frequency: Annually
Single Issue: £4
Payable to: Yorkshire Dialect Society, c/o 61 Moor Lane, Carnaby, Bridlington YO16 4UT
Inserts accepted: No
Circulation approx: 550
Payment terms to contributors: None
Accept/rejection approx times: 6 months

TREE SPIRIT

T

The magazine of Tree Spirit, charity 801511, includes news and views on all matters related to trees: poems, drawings, stories and articles which are tree orientated. Tree Spirit's aims are to protect trees and woodlands, to create new woods, to promote a greater understanding, awareness and affection for trees, woods and the natural environment.

Address: Hawkbatch Farm, Arley, Nr. Bewdley, Worcs DY12 3AH
Subs to: Emma & Liam Dowline, 82 Kingston Road, Earlsdon, Coventry CV5 6LR
Mag Frequency: 3/4 annually
Subscription: £12 waged/£7.50 unwaged
Single Issue: £1.50
Back Issue: £1
Overseas: £20
Payment in: Cheque/PO/foreign currency
Payable to: Tree Spirit
Inserts accepted: No
Circulation approx: 350-500
Payment terms to contributors: Free copy of magazine
Accept/rejection approx times: 1 month from receipt

U
UDOLPHO

Founded 1990 for the amusement of those who delight in morbid, macabre and black-hued themes, both ancient and modern Gothick! Publishes high-quality paperbacks on related subjects, and four large-format illustrated magazines yearly together with a quarterly newsletter. Some scope for original and imaginative fiction, but main preference is for history, biography and intelligent but amusing essays on the arts. Members have a definite advantage over writers outside the Society.

Address: Chatham House, Gosshill Road, Chislehurst, Kent BR7 5NS
Mag Frequency: Quarterly - March/June/Sept/Dec
Subscription: £22.50
Single Issue: £6.50 (inc p+p)
Back Issue: £2.50 - £6.50
Overseas: £26
Payment in: Cheque/PO
Payable to: The Gothic Society
Inserts accepted: Yes
Terms: £15 per 100 + VAT
Circulation approx: 900
Payment terms to contributors: None
Accept/rejection approx times: Few weeks

UK ACTION

Readers have recently described it as 'a jounal of informed comment', a 'meaty read' and 'fun'. It's a family magazine with a serious slant, for the UKA is an organisation dealing with alcohol and drug abuse. We are interested in thoughtful articles of community interest. We also like literary features, recipes, poems and news of interesting organisations. Sample copies/guidelines sent on request. Regretfully there is no payment, but six voucher copies are sent to each contributor. There is an annual literary competition - either short story or poetry - with cash prizes. Query first though - sample copy gives idea of lengths.

Editor Name(s): Daphne Ayles
Address: United Kingdom Alliance, 176 Blackfriars Road, London SW1 8ET
Mag Frequency: Quarterly
Subscription: £2.50
Single Issue: 25p + postage
Back Issue: 2nd class postage stamp
Overseas: Send IRCs
Payment in: Cheque/PO/Stamps in small denom
Payable to: United Kingdom Alliance
Payment terms to contributors: 6 voucher copies

u
ULTIMATE CULT VIDEO GUIDE (1st Edition)

A guide to all videocassettes released before 1983 (in the UK) and within the sci-fi, horror or cult cinema genres. The guide has a dual rating system showing both quality of film on cassette (ie - how good film is) and also how rare tape itself has become! It will be updated annually (for accuracy).

Address: The Cottage, Smithy Brae, Kilmacolm, Renfrewshire, Scotland PA13 4EN
Mag Frequency: Annually
Subscription: No subs
Single Issue: £5 (UK)/$10 (Others)
Payable to: G N Houston
Inserts accepted: No
Circulation approx: Not known
Payment terms to contributors: No contributions accepted

UNDERSTANDING MAGAZINE

Understanding Magazine includes poems, short stories, parts of plays, book reviews and articles. Understanding Magazine was founded by Denise Smith in 1989.

Editor Name(s): Editor Denise Smith/Assoc Ed Thom Nairn
Address: 20A Montgomery St. Edinburgh EH7 5JS
Fax: 0131 4782572
Mag Frequency: 2 yearly or one double issue
Subscription: £7 for 2 issues
Single Issue: £3.50
Back Issue: £2.50
Overseas: £8
Payment in: Cash/cheque in sterling
Payable to: Dionysia Press Ltd
Inserts accepted: Yes
Advertising Rates: £100 full page/flyer £25/25p per word
Circulation approx: 500 increasing
Payment terms to contributors: Free copy
Accept/rejection approx times: 6 months

𝓊
UNICORN

We are a bridge between the religious and the secular, as we may feature testimonies of lives changed by Jesus Christ, and focus upon spiritual issues through our 'Angelwing' section. We will continue to encourage new blood while promoting popular poets of the day. We are eclectic and not afraid to experiment with ideas. We will endeavour to find creative ways of presenting the Gospel to a changing society.

Editor Name(s): Alex Warner
Address: 12 Milton Avenue, Millbrook, Stalybridge, Cheshire SK15 3HB
Telephone: 0161 303 2152
Mag Frequency: When possible
Subscription: No subscriptions
Single Issue: £2
Payable to: Alex Warner
Inserts accepted: Yes occasionally
Advertising Rates: Discuss with editor
Payment terms to contributors: Free copy if your work accepted
Accept/rejection approx times: Varies: we try to reply within 3 weeks

U

THE UNIVERSAL MIND

The Universal Mind is a magazine which seeks to explore the unusual in all its forms, with stories of horror, sf and fantasy. Short stories, poetry, illustrations and anything else you can think of will be considered.

Editor Name(s): Carl Thomas
Address: 4 Baptist Street, Rhos, Wrexham LL14 1RH
Telephone: 07970 316 772 (mobile)
Mag Frequency: Annual
Subscription: £4.50
Single Issue: £2.50
Back Issue: None available
Overseas: £5 EU/$10 USA
Payment in: Cash/cheques/PO/swaps etc. Foreign currencies must allow for exchange
Payable to: Carl Thomas
Inserts accepted: Yes
Advertising Rates: Write for details
Payment terms to contributors: Copy of magazine

u
URGES

Urges is a small press magazine which publishes erotic tales of fantasy and horror. We don't want any more 'I've taken a vampire home' stories or 'Sex with an alien' stories. Also includes poetry and illustrations.

Address: Ian Hunter, Huntiegoulse Press, 32 Caneluk Avenue, Carluke M28 4LZ
Mag Frequency: Quarterly
Subscription: £9 for 4 issues
Single Issue: £2.50
Overseas: $20 for 4 issues
Payment in: Cheque/PO payable to Ian Hunter
Payable to: Ian Hunter
Inserts accepted: Yes
Circulation approx: 100
Payment terms to contributors: £3 per 1000 words/£3 per poem/£5 for illustrations
Accept/rejection approx times: 12-14 weeks

U

URTHONA

Urthona (founded 1992) is dedicated to exploring the arts from a spiritual perspective. We see beauty in its widest sense as a tool for change - both personal and social. Urthona publishes contemporary poetry, short stories, reviews and indepth articles on artists (modern and 'old masters') whose work exhibits a dynamic spiritual vision. We are particularly inspired by the Buddhist tradition of the east and by the work of William Blake - Urthona is his archetypal spirit of the Imagination.

Editor Name(s): Rathegarbha/Shantigarbha
Address: 3 Coral Park, Henley Road, Cambridge CB1 3EA
Telephone: 01223 566567
Fax: 01223 566568
Website: Search under Urthona
Mag Frequency: 2 a year
Subscription: £6.50 pa
Single Issue: £3.50
Overseas: £11.50 pa (airmail)
Payment in: Sterling only
Payable to: Urthona
Inserts accepted: Yes
Terms: POA
Advertising Rates: Page £65/third £40/qtr £325/6x6.8 box £18
Circulation approx: 900
Payment terms to contributors: Free copy of mag
Accept/rejection approx times: 2 months

V

VARIOUS ARTISTS

Various Artists Bristol's premier poetry magazine. We also accept good graphics. Recent issues have included work by RL Cook, Sophie Hannah and Mary Maher. We like good, well-written poems up to 40 lines. No misogynist, racist or anti-minority stuff please.

Address: 65 Springfield Avenue Bristol BS7 9QS
Mag Frequency: 1 annually
Subscription: £3
Single Issue: £1
Overseas: $5
Payment in: Cash
Payable to: A Lewis Jones
Inserts accepted: Yes
Circulation approx: 300
Payment terms to contributors: 1 complimentary copy
Accept/rejection approx times: 10 days-2 weeks

THE VELVET VAMPYRE

Vampyre-based A5 glossy black/white spot colour magazine. With news, reviews on books, films, occasional music. Stories fiction, horror, vampyre, romantic gothic. Illustrations, photos, articles on Vampyre Society events. Fashion, accessories, product information. Small ads. Hoping to expand to include more lifestyle and home interest. Published by The Vampyre Society (founded in 1987 by Carole Bohanan).

Address: PO Box 68, Keighley, West Yorkshire BD22 6RW
Mag Frequency: 3 or 4 times a year
Subscription: £16
Single Issue: £2.60
Overseas: £24
Payment in: Sterling cheque/PO
Payable to: The Vampyre Society
Inserts accepted: Yes
Terms: £80
Circulation approx: 700-1000
Payment terms to contributors: None - free copy of magazine
Accept/rejection approx times: 6 months

ν

VIGIL

Exploration of relationship through poetry and fiction from writers around the world. An international journey into what it means to be human amidst daily threats to freedom from political oppression, the tyranny of hunger and poverty or the chains of technological control systems. Affirmation of the sanctity of the human spirit through the beauty of heart and soul expression in poems and stories of highest endeavour. Above all fellowship in the craft of words to promote greater consciousness of our humanity rejoicing in our cultural diversity yet coming together in the common cause of our inspiration.

Address: Vigil Publications, 12 Priory Mead, Bruton, Somerset BA10 0DZ
Mag Frequency: 2 pa
Subscription: £8 for 3 issues
Single Issue: £3
Back Issue: £1.20 - £2.80
Overseas: £10 for 3 issues
Payment in: Cheque/PO in sterling
Payable to: Vigil Publications
Inserts accepted: Yes
Terms: £25
Circulation approx: 250
Payment terms to contributors: 1 free copy
Accept/rejection approx times: 6 weeks

VISIONARY TONGUE

Dark fantasy fiction magazine, aimed at newcomers to the field. Our team of consultant editors are all professional writers, who work on a one-to-one basis with our contributors, passing on their knowledge and experience of the genre. Editors include Storm Constantine, Christopher Fowler, Brian Stableford and Freda Warrington. We've been nominated and short-listed for the British Fantasy Society Award three years in succession.

Editor Name(s): Eloise Coquio
Address: 6 St Leonard's Avenue, Stafford ST17 4LT
Email: vtongue@compuserve.com
Mag Frequency: Thrice yearly
Subscription: £8.60 for 4 issues
Single Issue: £2.40
Overseas: £13
Payment in: UK:PO/Cheque; **Overseas:**IMO/Sterling equiv
Payable to: Visionary Tongue
Inserts accepted: Yes
Terms: Write for details
Advertising Rates: Wriite for details
Circulation approx: 600
Payment terms to contributors: Complimentary issue
Accept/rejection approx times: 4-6 weeks

V

VISIONS

Visions is a non-profit magazine dedicated to bringing you the best in sf/fantasy/ horror fiction. I aim to include a wide range of styles/tastes in each issue. All forms of sf/fantasy/horror are more than welcome of any length (up to 10,000 words) - but stories over 2000 words are especially welcomed on disk! Printed manuscripts and disks (IBM 720k or Amiga 880k only) accepted - both if possible. Artists are also welcome to get in touch - write for details.

Editor Name(s): Sean Kennedy
Address: 116 Long Lane, Carlton-In-Lindrick, Worksop, Notts, S81 9AT
Email: visions@excite.co.uk
Website: www.bigfoot.com/~visions_mag
Mag Frequency: Bi-Monthly
Subscription: £7.50 (6 issues)
Single Issue: £1.50
Overseas: Subs: US$20 (Europe)/US$25 (RoW); Single: US$4 (Europe)/US$5 (RoW)
Payment in: US$/Francs/DM/Sterling
Payable to: S Kennedy
Inserts accepted: Yes
Terms: Ask
Advertising Rates: Ask
Circulation approx: 120+
Payment terms to contributors: Free copy
Accept/rejection approx times: 2 weeks - 2 months

VOICES FROM CORNWALL

Poems, short stories, black & white graphics (A5) by local writers (on all themes) or people exiled from Cornwall living elsewhere - and also poems about Cornwall by people from elsewhere. Reviews and listings of other journals welcomed by way of information for readers/contributing writers. All kinds of styles of poetry - on all kinds of themes - welcomed. Enclose SAE/IRC for reply.

Address: David Allen Stringer, 5, Newtown, Fowey, Cornwall PL23 1JY
Mag Frequency: Quarterly
Subscription: £5 pa
Single Issue: £1.25
Back Issue: £1
Overseas: £6.50 Europe/£8 RoW
Payment in: Currency notes (overseas)/UK or US cash/cheque
Payable to: David Allan Stringer
Inserts accepted: Yes
Circulation approx: 200
Payment terms to contributors: Free copy
Accept/rejection approx times: 1 month

W

WASAFIRI

Wasafiri is Britain's only international magazine for black British, Asian, Caribbean, African and diasporic writing in English. Taking its name from the Kiswahili word for 'traveller', Wasafiri promotes 'cultural travelling' through literature. It provides an internationally-renowned and accessible creative space for cross-cultural reading and debates, and publishes a mixture of critical articles, poetry, fiction, interviews and a substantial reviews section. Founded in 1984, it has built a worldwide reputation for the innovative publishing of new literary talents and for breaking down the borders of narrowly defined national literatures.

Editor Name(s): Ed Susheila Nasta/Managing Ed Richard Dyer
Address: Dept of English & Drama, Queen Mary & Westfield College, University of London, Mile End Road, London E1 4NS
Telephone: 0171 775 3120
Fax: 0181 980 6200
Email: Wasafiri@qmw.ac.uk
Mag Frequency: 2 issues a year
Subscription: £14/£20/£26 - individual 1/2/3 year subs; £24/£32/£36 - institution 1/2/3 year subs
Single Issue: £7(UK)/£9 (Overseas)
Back Issue: £5(UK)/£6(Overseas)
Overseas: £18/£26/£34 individual 1/2/3 year subs; £30/£42/£50 institution 1/2/3 year subs
Payment in: UK sterling
Payable to: Wasafiri
Inserts accepted: Yes
Advertising Rates: £175 full page/£100 half/£50 qtr/ £250 inside back cover
Circulation approx: 1000
Payment terms to contributors: Only to commissioned authors - on publication

W

WEARWOLF

Wearwolf, of diverse content and sporadical publication, voted Monster Raving Looney at the last election, which'll probably give you some idea. Send SAE for details. Wolf's Head Press also coordinates the Random Premier League, possibly the UK's first fantasy football league for zines, small presses and allied trades. 2x20p stamps for a newsletter/further info.

Address: Wolfs Head Press, P.O. Box 77, Sunderland SR1 1EB
Mag Frequency: Sporadic
Subscription: £3 for 5 issues
Single Issue: 2 x 26p stamps
Overseas: On request
Payment in: Strictly CWO
Payable to: Wolf's Head Press
Inserts accepted: Yes
Terms: Reciprocal exchanges preferred
Circulation approx: Variable
Payment terms to contributors: Extremely unlikely
Accept/rejection approx times: By year 2000, if submitted immediately

WEST COAST MAGAZINE

West Coast Magazine consists of short fiction, poetry, articles, essays and reviews. Our aim is always to be a platform for mainly new and up and coming, as well as the established writers. The editors of West Coast Magazine demand a high quality in the standard of work we publish. We like to see works from writers who enjoy a challenge - the quirky and offbeat usually sit well with us. As ever space is a deciding factor when selecting material and for that reason we like to try and keep things to around 3,500 words. We will, though, publish bigger pieces if we like them enough, but they would need to be quite special. We like sequences of poems, or groups of poems that complement each other, though that is not strictly necessary. Single poems are welcome also. As for articles, we will publish anything of interest, preferably literary interest, but not necessarily so - in the past we have published articles on football, music, French cinema, public sector housing and contemporary art among others. Please always send SAE with contributions or no reply, and don't overload the envelope - 2 or 3 short stories max and 5-6 poems (unless, and only if, they are a larger sequence). Like most mags cash is in short supply, but we do always try to pay a small fee.

Address: Top Floor, 15 Hope Street, Glasgow G2 6AB
Mag Frequency: 3 per year
Subscription: £10 (four issues)
Single Issue: £2.50 includes post and package
Overseas: £15 in sterling or £20 equivalent
Payable to: West Coast Magazine
Inserts accepted: Yes
Terms: £50 for 1000
Circulation approx: 850
Payment terms to contributors: Small fee when we can, usually after publication.
Accept/rejection approx times: Please allow 8 weeks for reply

w

WEYFARERS

An independent magazine founded in 1972 which now travels world-wide. Poetry serious and humorous, rhymed/metred and free verse. Three issues per year: different editors take turns, giving variety. Payment for contributors is a free copy and good company of new and established poets, and widely read. Copyright remains with poet. Linked to annual competition with prizes. News pages tell of poetry events, other mags, books etc. Our accepted poems are largely mainstream/modern. See a copy before sending poems.

Editor Name(s): Stella Stocker/Martin Jones/Jeffrey Wheatley
Address: 1 Mountside, Guildford, Surrey GU2 5JD
Subs to: 9 White Rose Lane, Woking, Surrey GU22 7JA
Mag Frequency: 3 times a year
Subscription: £5
Single Issue: £2
Back Issue: £1
Overseas: £6 (sterling)
Payment in: If in foreign draft add £6 equivalent
Payable to: Guildford Poets Press
Inserts accepted: Yes but very limited by prior arrangement
Circulation approx: 300
Payment terms to contributors: 1 free copy only
Accept/rejection approx times: Up to 4 months depending on when received, deadlines end May/September/January

W
WINDLESORA

Windlesora is the local history journal for the town of Windsor and its surrounding villages. Articles should only be submitted if they have been written following research into original sources or are memories of people who have lived in the town. We do not want re-hashes of already published work or articles about the Castle or Eton College. Most contributions come from local people but we are particularly interested in contacting experts on various topics who can write about the Windsor aspect of their interest. In this way we have already published an article on some of Windsor's historic pillar boxes. We are also interested in family historians who have traced their family back to Windsor. We review appropriate books, museums and exhibitions. Articles of 2500 words are required down to 100 word fillers. We print black & white photographs and drawings.

Address: 256 Dedworth Road, Windsor SL4 4JR
Mag Frequency: Annually
Single Issue: £2.75
Back Issue: £2 + p & p 35p
Payable to: Windsor Local History Publications Group
Inserts accepted: No
Circulation approx: 500
Payment terms to contributors: Free copy
Accept/rejection approx times: 4 weeks

W

THE WORD

The Word magazine is the seasonal publication of Partners In Poetry, an organisation started by poets to advise, inspire and reward a new genesis of lost writer. The poets who founded this organisation believe poetry to be an art form and medium of expression rather than an exercise in the technicalities of grammatical English. 'Poetry is without debate the greatest writing medium that is available to a writer, so should not be harnessed, or stifled, by Westernised preconditioning, or any such inhibitor. As free are we to think and create, so should we be, as versatile and unconstricted - to convey and communicate.' Ian Deal, 1997. Co-editor Brian Palin believes that 'A void exists in the world of poetry at present, because of which poetry and the world of English literature literally screams for direction. A direction crucial to the development of all mankind for the next millennium and beyond. We are at a point similar to the Lake Poets in the 1880's. Just as Wordsworth and Coleridge strived for the Romantic Renaissance, so shall we strive for the 'Spiritual Re-awakening of Romance' Renaissance.' As well as the magazine, Partners In Poetry also runs over ten competitions a year.

Editor Name(s): Ian Deal/Brian Palin
Address: Partners In Poetry, 289 Elmwood Avenue, Feltham, Middx TW13 7QB
Telephone: Approach in writing to either editor
Mag Frequency: Seasonal - 4 per year
Subscription: Available shortly
Single Issue: £3.50
Overseas: £3.50 - include IRCs for return
Payment in: Sterling only - Cheque/PO
Payable to: Partners In Poetry
Inserts accepted: Yes
Terms: £50 per 1000 or by negotiation
Advertising Rates: Approx £55 full pg/£35 qtr; pg size148mm x 211mm
Circulation approx: Unknown - reaches over 12 countries
Payment terms to contributors: Articles & poetry - at least a free copy
Accept/rejection approx times: Up to 2 weeks

W
WORDS

Words sets out to bring new material by both published and previously unpublished authors before a wider audience consisting of all ages and abilties, with the result that the standard of writing is very high indeed ! Compiled from entries to our competitions, it is a quarterly magazine specialising in short stories which is sold in aid of the Winnicott Baby Unit (charity Reg No 292668). Before submitting any work authors are advised to study loosely a back issue (available free on receipt of a 31p stamp or overseas 3 IRC's). As the readership is very wide-ranging no work of a possibly offensive nature will be published and all material is strictly edited.

Editor Name(s): Shaun Peare
Address: PO Box 13574, London, W9 3FX
Telephone: 0585 399602
Email: wordsmag@ad.com
Mag Frequency: Quarterly
Subscription: £8
Single Issue: £2
Back Issue: 1 free then £1.25
Overseas: £11 Europe/£15 RoW
Payment in: Sterling only
Payable to: Words
Inserts accepted: Yes
Terms: £20 per 1000
Advertising Rates: one sixth pg £5/other rates POA
Circulation approx: 1000+
Payment terms to contributors: 2 free copies of the issue their work appears in
Accept/rejection approx times: No unsolicited mss accepted

W

WORDS WORTH (Journal of Language Arts)

Editor: Alaric Sumner. Various Guest Editors incl Paul Buck, Richard Tabor. Founded 1977. Publishes innovative work related to language including: visual, found and performance texts, text sound compositions, linguistically innovative work. Writers/artists have included Susan Hiller, Ernst Jandl (TRS Michael Hamburger), Bernard Noel, Mac Wellman, Richard Kostelanetz, Dom Sylvester Houedard (DSH), Carlyle Reedy, Cris Cheek, Henri Chopin. Building a reputation despite erratic publication history. Editors seek work that surprises and amazes them by its unconventional content and form.

Editor Name(s): Alaric Sumner
Address: BM Box 4515, London WC1N 3XX
Mag Frequency: Irregular
Subscription: For 3 issues:Individual £12/Institution £20
Single Issue: Individual £4.50/Institution £8
Overseas: Same as above but £3.50 p& p to USA
Payment in: Sterling or double total price to cover bank charges
Payable to: Words Worth Books
Inserts accepted: Yes
Advertising Rates: (Rates: available)
Circulation approx: Print run 300 at present
Payment terms to contributors: 2 copies of magazine
Accept/rejection approx times: Various - definite rejection often by return!

W
WORDSHARE

Creative writing magazine Wordshare welcomes contributions from disabled people, and people past retirement age. It is an A4 format magazine funded by the Eastern Arts Board.

Address: John Wilkinson, 8 Bodmin Moor Close, North Hykham, Lincoln LN6 9BB
Mag Frequency: As and when sufficient suitable writing comes in
Subscription: Nil
Single Issue: N/A
Inserts accepted: No
Circulation approx: 4000
Payment terms to contributors: No payment. One copy for every submission; two copies for those accepted

W

WORKING TITLES

Working Titles does not accept any work which is racist, misogynistic or any other anti-minority material.

Address: 5 Hillside, Clifton Wood, Bristol BS8 4TD
Mag Frequency: Annual
Subscription: £4.50 for 3
Single Issue: £1.50
Overseas: $8 or equivalent
Payment in: Cash
Payable to: C Williamson
Inserts accepted: Yes
Circulation approx: 250
Payment terms to contributors: 1 magazine
Accept/rejection approx times: 1 month

W
WORKS

I prefer stories that are slightly off-tilt, but they should have some form of logic or foundation. I favour stories that are really different, but don't try to be different for its own sake. I don't want stories of over 5000 words. Subjects preferred are sf, surreal, speculative, and will occasionally consider horror. Ideally you should get a copy of Works as that is the real way you'll get any idea of what I like. I like poetry with strong imagery, in an industrial isolation - deserted landscapes, etc. If you mange to get any of these icons in your prose you're halfway there. No more than 50 lines. Non-fiction articles from 500-4000 words. As long as they're related to sf, publishing small press etc, if you have any ideas send a synopsis to me and we can maybe see it through. I'm open to any ideas. I'm always interested in artwork. I usually forward the artist a story to illustrate. If you're an artist, send me a few pages of your work and we'll take it from there. All stories, poetry, artwork and articles should have your name on each page. I prefer stories to be double spaced. I really insist on a covering letter though, because if you can't be bothered to talk to me, how do you expect me to talk to you? An SAE should be enclosed for the return of acceptance/rejection or ms. Finally whilst I do take care over manuscripts I can't be held responsible once Postman Pat has them, so NEVER send originals.

Address: 12 Blakestones Road, Slaithwaite, Huddersfield HD7 5UQ
Mag Frequency: 1 or 2 per year
Subscription: £5 x two issues
Single Issue: £2.50
Back Issue: Sold out
Payable to: Works
Inserts accepted: Negotiable
Circulation approx: 4000
Payment terms to contributors: Complimentary copy
Accept/rejection approx times: 1-3 weeks

W

WRITE ANGLES

Bi-monthly magazine for writers or anyone interested in literature. Features include news, festivals, new regional publications, competitions and events listings.

Address: Jill Leahy, YHA, 21 Bond Street, Dewsbury WF13 1AX
Fax: 01924 466522
Email: jill.leahy.yha@artsfb.org.uk
Mag Frequency: Bi-monthly
Subscription: Nil
Single Issue: Nil
Inserts accepted: No
Circulation approx: 1500

WRITERS NEWS & WRITING MAGAZINE

The news magazine that no writer can afford to miss, Writers News is the very home of writing. With its associated Writing Magazine, automatically sent to members, its coverage of everything the writer needs to know, its practical help and inspiration, and indeed its sheer depth and variety, it is in a class entirely of its own; and not surprisingly, its readership is more than twice that of all other titles for writers put together. Ingredients include: News of market and other opportunities, events, legislation and trends affecting the writer; its own extensive range of competitions plus full coverage of other people's; reference features such as listings of writers' circles, and a monthly diary of events; personal helpline answering individual questions; in-depth interviews and profiles with practical tips for writers; coverage of all the main genres of writing; regular columns, letters, book reviews and much more; the most complete advertising service for writers. Writers News is only available by direct subscription. Writing Magazine is available from all good newsagents.

Address: Writers News Ltd, PO Box 4, Nairn IV12 4HU
Fax: 01667 454441
Mag Frequency: Writers News - Monthly/ Writing Magazine - Bi-monthly
Subscription: £43.90/ £37.90 by DD
Single Issue: Writing Magazine price £2.25
Back Issue: £3.50
Overseas: Europe £48.90/£43.90 by DD; RoW £53.90/£48.90 by DD
Payable to: Writers News Ltd
Inserts accepted: Yes
Terms: £35 loose/£50 bound-in per 1000
Circulation approx: Writers News - 21,000
Writing Magazine - 45,500

WRITERS OWN MAGAZINE

Includes short stories (max 1,500 words), articles (max 800 words), poetry (max 32 lines) - on most subjects, but must be in good taste. Market information and competitions, letters pages, a quarterly competition with small money prizes and booklet, plus critique/score points. Now in its 17th year of publication. No payment except in copy of the magazine in which work appears, or extension of subscription.

Address: 121 Highbury Grove, Clapham, Bedford MK41 6DU
Mag Frequency: Quarterly
Subscription: £8 per year inc postage
Single Issue: £2 inc postage
Back Issue: £1.75 inc postage
Overseas: £2.75 Single/£11 per year inc postage
Payment in: Cheque/PO in sterling (Overseas - IMO)
Payable to: Mrs EM Pickering
Inserts accepted: Yes
Terms: £3 per 100
Circulation approx: 200
Payment terms to contributors: Copy of magazine
Accept/rejection approx times: 2 weeks

WRITERS' BULLETIN

Markets and news information newsletter, 24 A5 pages and 4-page competitions news insert. Includes markets for non-fiction, fiction, poetry, photographs, cartoons, artwork and more . . . resources, courses, competitions, book reviews (books about writing), editors' moves, publishing news, advice and tips on writing and selling. All markets verified with the editors - no guesswork or second-hand information. Up-to-date news, reliable information.

Editor Name(s): Chriss McCallum
Address: Chriss McCallum, Writers' Bulletin, PO Box 96, Altrincham WA14 2LN
Telephone: 0161 928 9711
Fax: 0161 928 9711
Email: Mcbulletin@aol.com
Mag Frequency: Bi-monthly
Subscription: £2 x no of issues required
Single Issue: £2
Overseas: £2.40 (EU)/£3 (RoW) x no of issues required
Payment in: Sterling cheque/PO
Payable to: Writers' Bulletin
Inserts accepted: Yes
Terms: Usually reciprocal, otherwise £5 per 100
Advertising Rates: Lineage 20p per word (15p subscribers) Display from £6 (eighth page)
Circulation approx: 500
Payment terms to contributors: N/A
Accept/rejection approx times: N/A

WRITERS' CAULDRON

Writers' Cauldron was originally the Writers' Brew created as a showcase for the Transatlantic Critique Club on America Online. The magazine was well received and after a name change is now available on subscription. The magazine is generously laid out with larger than average print size for easy reading. Stories of all types from both new and established authors are featured. Three poets per issue are featured in Poets' Gallery. Unsolicited material welcomed and always replied to providing an sae is enclosed. Note, standard rejections never given. We also run three competitions a year - two categories under 16's and adult. Prizes are publication & % of entry fees.

Editor Name(s): Amanda Gillies
Address: Suite 2, 39 Heathhill Industrial Estate, Dawley, Shropshire TF4 2RH
Telephone: 01952 275290
Email: Writers.Cauldron@writers.brew.clara.net/club/
Website: http://www.writers.brew.clara.net/club/
Mag Frequency: Quarterly
Subscription: £30 (£22 special rate for OAPs) - and request info on current special offer
Single Issue: £7.50
Overseas: Subs $66/single issue £20
Payment terms to contributors: Free copy or sub extension

W
WRITERS' EXPRESS

Short stories, articles, letters page, advice and encouragement for new writers. Regular competitions, open to non-subscribers, SAE for details. Free advice and appraisals for subscribers. A good read! No unsolicited manuscripts, essential to buy a sample copy or send SAE for guidelines.

Address: Linden Cottage, 45 Burton Road, Little Neston, S Wirral L64 4AE
Fax: 0151 353 0967
Email: helicon@globalnet.co.uk
Mag Frequency: Bi-monthly
Subscription: £10 for 4 issues
Single Issue: £2.50
Back Issue: £2
Overseas: Send IRC for price list
Payment in: Sterling cheques/IRCs
Payable to: Cherrybite Publications
Inserts accepted: Yes
Terms: Reciprocal
Circulation approx: 250
Payment terms to contributors: No payment
Accept/rejection approx times: 1 month

WRITERS' FORUM

Britain's most complete 'How to Write' magazine. Dedicated to helping writers develop their skills by publishing teaching-articles. Guidance on how to prepare and submit manuscripts is included, as well as detailed market news and dates of competitions, courses and seminars. Free critique of a poem or short story for subscribers. Sponsors a poetry and short story competition each issue.

Address: 21 Belle Vue Street, Filey, North Yorkshire YO14 9HU
Fax: 01723 513279
Email: wf@btinternet.com
Mag Frequency: Quarterly
Subscription: £14.50
Single Issue: £3.75
Back Issue: £2
Overseas: £20 Europe/£29.50 RoW
Payment in: Cheque/PO
Payable to: Writers' Forum
Inserts accepted: Yes
Circulation approx: 5000
Payment terms to contributors: On publication
Accept/rejection approx times: 1 month

W
WRITING COMPETITIONS MONTHLY

A monthly listings magazine containing all writing competitions currently running in the UK (as near as dammit) and a few interesting overseas competitions. Information includes entry fee, closing date, brief outline of rules, prizes and contact address. Competition organisers are urged to send their details ASAP for free listing. We are also happy to publish results. Only 6 months old and proving to be hugely popular. Circulation is growing each month. An ideal way to give your comp maximum exposure - free!

Editor Name(s): Carole Baldock
Address: Linden Cottage, 45 Burton Road, Little Neston, South Wirral L64 4AE
Telephone: 0151 353 0967 (Shelagh Nugent contact)
Fax: 0151 353 0967
Email: helicon@globalnet.co.uk
Mag Frequency: Monthly
Subscription: £10 for 6 issues
Single Issue: £2
Overseas: Send IRC for price list
Payment in: Sterling cheque/IRCs
Payable to: Cherrybite Publications
Inserts accepted: Yes
Terms: Depending on size of current mag & weight
Advertising Rates: £20 full pg/£10 half/£5 qtr/Lineage free
Circulation approx: 300 and rising
Payment terms to contributors: N/A
Accept/rejection approx times: N/A

WRITING WOMEN

Writing Women publishes poetry and prose by women. The aim is to demonstrate the high quality and the diversity and creative achievement amongst women writers. Our prose contributions are generally less than 3000 words in length. We only accept six poems at a time. An SAE is essential. We do not have a narrow ideological approach - we are interested in innovative work of all kinds.

Address: PO Box 111, Newcastle Upon Tyne NE3 1WF
Mag Frequency: Bi-annually
Subscription: £7.50 for 2 issues
Single Issue: £4/£4.50 overseas
Back Issue: £2.50 (inc postage)/£2 overseas
Overseas: £14 including airmail
Payment in: Cheque/PO
Payable to: Writing Women
Inserts accepted: Yes
Terms: Exchange basis
Circulation approx: 1000
Payment terms to contributors: £10 per 1000 words/£10 per poem/+ free subscription
Accept/rejection approx times: 2-4 Months

χ
XENOS

Established 1990, Xenos is the premier short story magazine for both readers and writers. Submissions welcomed in all genres except blood and gore, gratuitous violence, pornography of the purely romantic. We publish short stories only (ie no poetry, plays, articles reviews etc). Please submit only one story at a time. We give honest, constructive criticisms on nearly all material received, and suggest ideas for revising at no charge. Good, clear presentation and an acceptable knowledge of English spelling and grammar are essential. Suitably stamped sae or sufficient IRCs must be included for reply. Our turnaround time is normally no more than 4 weeks. Word lengths: upper limit 10,000, lower limit 2000. Each issue of Xenos carries 6-7 excellent and varied stories. The evaluation section allows readers to give constructive criticism on the stories in the previous issue. We have been publishing Xenos for over 6 years and every issue has appeared on time. We have a loyal readership of all ages, both nationally and internationally. Our continuing aim is to help and advise writers of all abilities.

Address: 29 Prebend Street, Bedford MK40 1QN
Mag Frequency: Bi-monthly
Subscription: £16.50
Single Issue: £3.45
Overseas: EU as UK/RoW£22.50
Payment in: UK cheque/PO; Overseas Sterling only
Payable to: Xenos
Inserts accepted: No
Circulation approx: Increasing
Payment terms to contributors: Complimentary copy of magazine/Annual competition awards cash and subscription

THE YELLOW CRANE

Interesting new poems from South Wales and beyond . . .

Address: J. Brookes, Flat 6, 23 Richmond Crescent, Roath, Cardiff CF2 3AH
Mag Frequency: Quarterly
Subscription: £7
Single Issue: £1.50
Overseas: £10
Payment in: IMO/Cheque/PO
Payable to: The Yellow Crane
Inserts accepted: No
Circulation approx: Growing
Payment terms to contributors: 2 copies of magazine
Accept/rejection approx times: Goodness knows

⅄ YORKSHIRE JOURNAL

Yorkshire Journal is an entirely new publication based on the quality journals that were popular until the early part of this century. We have re-established this fine tradition with an attractively-designed and well-produced quarterly periodical of 120 pages about Yorkshire, its history, culture, landscape, customs and people, produced in the heart of the county - and all for only £2.95 an issue. From a wide range of writers, photographers and illustrators, many of them experts in their fields, come substantial articles on folklore, art, current events, architecture, short stories and poetry. Topics vary from the informative, the illuminating and the controversial to the not-so-serious and downright light-hearted. Send synopsis in first instance.

Address: Ilkley Road, Otley, West Yorkshire LS21 3JP
Fax: 01943 850057
Email: (edit): mwhitley@smith-settle.co.uk or (sales): sales@smith-settle.co.uk
Mag Frequency: Quarterly
Subscription: £12
Single Issue: £2.95
Overseas: £16
Payment in: Visa/Access
Payable to: Smith Settle
Inserts accepted: Yes
Terms: On application
Circulation approx: 3000
Payment terms to contributors: Poems - complimentary copy/Articles - varies
Accept/rejection approx times: 2-4 weeks

Z

ZENE

Zene is the only British writers' magazine dedicated to the small and independent press (worldwide!). Every issue features detailed contributors' guidelines for markets you will not find elsewhere, and many of these publications pay very well. You'll learn about new magazines, anthologies, comics, novels, etc, which are looking for all kinds of writing including fiction, poetry and non-fiction of all genres. Zene also lists current competitions, news and views of writers, including feedback on how they've been treated, plus changes of address/circumstance/requirements of publishers. Zene is never out of date! We publish regular articles on all aspects of writing but are never patronising. Finally, our comprehensive reviews section covers about 100 further titles - and, often controversially, we tell it like it is! Unsolicited submissions are welcome for all sections as long as they follow standard ms format and are accompanied by SAE and covering letter. Guidelines and review copies are also welcome from all publishers, including those in this book.

Editor Name(s): Team Zene
Address: 5 Martins Lane, Witcham, Ely, Cambs CB6 2LB
Telephone: 01353 777931
Email: ttapress@aol.com
Website: http://purl.oclc.org/net/ttaonline/
Mag Frequency: Bimonthly (6 issues pa)
Subscription: £12 (6 issues)
Single Issue: Subscription only
Back Issue: Sold out
Overseas: Europe £15/USA & Canada US$24/RoW£18
Payment in: Cheque/PO/Eurocheque/Foreign currency cheques at amount equivalent to above (preferably no foreign cash)
Payable to: TTA Press
Inserts accepted: Yes
Terms: Negotiable
Advertising Rates: Ad space available
Circulation approx: Over 6000
Payment terms to contributors: Negotiable
Accept/rejection approx times: 1 month average

Z

THE ZERONAUT SOCIETY NEWSLETTER

The aim of the Zeronaut Society is for its members to generate works of art in the form of poetry, short stories, short plays, drawings, and so on. The aim of the Society is also to allow for members' own style and individuality so that the Zeronaut Newsletter may have a variety of styles both from handwritten and typed contributions. To this end members type or handwrite their own submissions. There is no censorship in The Zeronaut Society which means all subjects will be printed in the Newsletter. However there will be a warning to members regarding certain subjects so that they may exercise their right to read something or not. The Zeronaut Society is dedicated to its art-contributing members and thus it welcomes new contributing members that enjoy the challenge of a weekly newsletter. All Zeronaut Society contributing members are expected to help with the financial running of the Newsletter through the subscription costs given above and thus contributors are not paid and the copyright of all work remains with each contributor.

Address: 101 St Benedicts Close, Tooting, London SW17 9NX
Fax: 0181 767 5089
Mag Frequency: Weekly
Subscription: Weekly first class stamp or £10 per year
Single Issue: £2
Overseas: Weekly SASE
Payment in: PO/cheque/weekly SASE
Payable to: Mirtha Clark
Inserts accepted: No
Circulation approx: 16
Payment terms to contributors: N/A
Accept/rejection approx times: Weekly

Z

ZINC

Zinc accepts work from new and established writers and welcomes submissions from overseas writers. There are no restrictions on the style or subject or length of pieces with the exceptions of racism and sexism. Zinc presents work on single subjects by groups or individuals - the subjects are nominated by the editors, who will also include information relevant to the subject such as contact addresses, essays and articles.

Address: 51 Wollaston Road, Cleethorpes, Lincolnshire DN35 8DY.
Mag Frequency: Twice in each subscription
Subscription: £3 plus 2 A5 SAE
Single Issue: Free
Back Issue: Not available
Overseas: $6 US+2 International reply coupons
Payable to: Ian Brocklebank
Inserts accepted: Yes
Circulation approx: Combined 750
Payment terms to contributors: No payment except in copies
Accept/rejection approx times: 1 month for both titles

Z

ZINE ZONE

Zine Zone is a courant de pensees publication primarily aimed at creative youth. We have developed a production style in keeping with the photocopied 'zine' tradition. This gives the magazine an edge that appeals to visual, print and design makers, as well as writers and musicians. The language and commentary reflect the cream and mud of creativity left out by media moguls. Increase in demand and contribution lead Zine Zone to publish an unpredicable and chaotic mix of illustrative work including poetry, reviews, short stories. We also organise events. Work can be sent in black& white prints. Clear handwritten texts are accepted. We also take work on 3.5 inch Macintosh formatted floppy disks. Save text as 'Text' file. Contact ZZ for further details. Add details to reviews: ie band/artist, titles, formats, venue, contact, issue #, dates, prices, ISBN etc. No slides/CVs necessary. London-based Zine Zone is distributed mainly in the UK (70%) and in a dozen countries including South Africa, China, Greece, Japan and the USA!

Address: 47 Retreat Place, London E9 6RH
Fax: 0181 525 1466
Mag Frequency: Every 41 days
Subscription: £12 (8 issues/1 year) £8 (4 issues/6 mos)
Single Issue: £1.95
Back Issue: Varies, write for details
Overseas: £15 Europe/£18 RoW
Payment in: Cheque/PO/IMO
Payable to: Zine Zone
Inserts accepted: Yes
Circulation approx: 2000
Payment terms to contributors: Negotiable, payment is only made for commissioned work
Accept/rejection approx times: 3 months

THE ZONE

The Zone is the last word in science fiction magazines; with excellent short fiction, big name interviews, insightful criticism and incisive articles - plus complete coverage of SF in the media, with illustrated review columns in every issue . . . The Zone publishes original SF stories alongside genre poetry and experimental or stylist prose of the highest quality. Nonfiction is of vital importance too, and so The Zone features interviews, articles, essays and regular review columns - covering all manner of relevant (and irrelevant) science fictional topics and themes in the media. Unsolicited mss are welcome. We are looking for high quality, speculative fiction, with plenty of ideas and imagination - but it does not have to be 'hard-SF'. We are not interested in 'epic fantasy quest sagas' (with wizards and warriors, etc) or any traditional or contemporary horror (satanism, werewolves/needless gore of serial killers, respectively). However, subtle SF-fantasy may be acceptable. Fiction for The Zone should be of approx 1000 to 5000 words. SF poetry is published in The Zone, by invitation only. The work of one genre poet will be featured in the magazine's poetry showcase. Nonfiction: original articles on any aspect of science fiction (retrospective or topical) will be considered. Please write first, outlining your idea. Several special projects are ongoing and others are in development - send an SAE/IRC if you want details of these. Length of any nonfiction works, by arrangement with the magazine's editors, but articles of 1000 to 5000 words (or longer if serialised), will be considered. Book reviews (approx 250 to 500+ words) by arrangement with editors. Send samples of your published reviews and list of your favourite SF authors. Designed for the discerning readers of SF fandom. The Zone aims to please the lifetime enthusiast and the genre newcomer alike.

Address: Pigasus Press, 13 Hazely Combe, Arreton, Isle of Wight, PO30 3AJ
Mag Frequency: Irregular
Subscription: £12 for 4 issues
Single Issue: £3.20
Back Issue: £2.50
Overseas: Write for details, enclosing IRC
Payable to: Tony Lee
Inserts accepted: No
Advertising Rates: Available on request, send SAE/IRC
Circulation approx: Unknown
Payment terms to contributors: Token payment (currently £5/$10) plus free copy, paid on publication
Accept/rejection approx times: 4-6 weeks

Organisations and resources of interest to Poets and Writers

Association Of Little Presses
32 Downside Road, Sutton, Surrey SM2 5HP

The Society Of Authors
84 Drayton Gardens, London SW10 9SB
Phone 0171 3736642

The Poetry Library
Level 5, Royal Festival Hall, South Bank Centre, London SE1 8XX
Phone 0171 9210943
Huge holdings of little mags and poetry titles. Issues current awareness lists of poetry publishers, organisations, magazines and competitions.

The Little Magazine Collection And Poetry Store
Mss & Rare Books Room, University College of London Library, Gower Street, London WC1E 6BT
Phone 0171 3807796
Geoffrey Soar and David Miller's collection of more than 3500 poetry mags.

The Poetry School
130c Evering Road, London N16 7BD
Phone 0181 9850090
Tuition in reading and writing poetry; courses, workshops, readings and events. Provides a practitioners' forum.

Millennium Edition

Writers' Bookshop invites entries for the Small Press Guide 2000

Entries or enquiries before 1 September 1999 to:
Editor, Small Press Guide
Writers' Bookshop
1-2 Wainman Road
Woodston
Peterborough
PE2 7BU